The New World Dutch Barn

Wortendyke Barn in Park Ridge, Bergen County, New Jersey. Roofline with classic proportions. Lowest side walls of any Dutch barn at 6 ft. Circa 1790. Fitchen talked of visiting this barn. Gregory Huber gave his first talk on Dutch barns here in September 1977.

The New World

DUTCH BARN

SECOND EDITION

*The Evolution, Forms, and Structure
of a Disappearing Icon*

John Fitchen

*Edited and with New Material
by Gregory D. Huber*

SYRACUSE UNIVERSITY PRESS

Second edition copyright © 2001 by Syracuse University Press
Syracuse, New York 13244–5160

First edition 1968

04   05   06   6   5   4   3   2

This book is funded in part by a generous grant from FURTHERMORE . . . the Publication Program of the J. M. Kaplan Fund.

The paper used in this publication meets the minimum requirements of American National Standard for Information Sciences—Permanence of Paper for Printed Library Materials, ANSI Z39.48–1984.∞™

Library of Congress Cataloging-in-Publication Data

Fitchen, John.
    The New World Dutch barn : the evolution, forms, and structure of a disappearing icon
    / John Fitchen ; edited and with new material by Gregory D. Huber.—2nd ed.
      p. cm.
    Includes bibliographical references and index.
    ISBN 0-8156-0690-7 (pbk. : alk. paper)
    1. Barns—New York. 2. Building, Wooden—New York. 3. Vernacular
architecture—New York. I. Huber, Gregory D. II. Title.
TH4930.F52 2001
690'.8922'09747—dc21

00-046379

Manufactured in the United States of America

To John Hardy Fitchen

In homage to his pervasive humanity

Contents

Drawings

Plates

Illustrations New to the Second Edition

All photographs by Gregory D. Huber
All drawings by Glen Guarino

John Fitchen was a professor of fine arts at Colgate University, a registered architect, and president of the Central New York Architectural Historians. He was a contributor to scholarly publications in his field and was author of *Construction of Gothic Cathedrals: A Study of Medieval Vault Erection* and *Building Construction Before Mechanization*.

Gregory D. Huber is an architectural historian and consultant who has studied and documented Dutch American barns since 1975. He edited and published the *Dutch Barn Research Journal* from 1991 to 1994 and has written for periodicals such as *Material Culture, Timber Framing, de Halve Maen,* and *Joiners Quarterly.* In 1997 he received the Alice P. Kenney award for furthering the appreciation of Dutch American culture.

Preface

THIS BOOK is largely a technical account. It deals with a distinctive class of early all-wood New World barns in a combination of three separate but related approaches; namely, (1) a systematic and detailed description of the barns in question, (2) an analysis of their structural system, and (3) a conjectural recreation of the erectional procedures and the progression that was probably followed in their construction.

This kind of comprehensive coverage has not been undertaken heretofore with respect to any American barns. The Europeans, however—particularly those of northern Europe—have for some generations been preserving and publishing accounts of their anonymous rural architecture extensively and in thorough detail. It seems high time that we in this country should begin to emulate our opposite numbers across the ocean in seriously studying and reporting on our heritage of early barns, and in cherishing these durable, long-lived, impressive links with the past.

For a long time poets and novelists, along with painters, illustrators, and now more recently photographers have been aware of barns and have used them from time to time as the setting or locale for some episode or scene of rural action. But no one with architectural training and professional competence has as yet undertaken a comprehensive investigation of all types of early American barns, or a detailed scrutiny of their layout and structural framing.

There are a number of reasons why there has been little if any systematic historical study of the early barns of America up to now.

For one thing, almost all barns—certainly all early barns—in this country are devoid of those details to which the trained observer is able to assign a fairly precise date. Because these barns were built to satisfy exclusively utilitarian needs, they lacked even the fairly simple features and the common amenities and refinements of other classes of buildings:

such characteristics as moldings, panelwork, carved or decorative details, even glazed windows. Thus early barns are without the built-in evidence that could furnish the historian with reliable data for determining their age more or less exactly.

Another reason why early American barns have not been studied in any systematic way is that there is an almost complete absence of written documentation about them. To the older school of architectural historians this lack of literary reference or written documentation condemns such buildings to oblivion. Being generally unreported in manuscript or printed record, they simply do not exist as proper subjects for study on the part of those scholars whose interest, training, and competence are all ruled out because of the absence of the tools they rely on for their research.

Fortunately, we are beginning to see the emergence of a new breed of architectural historians who do not consider the study of whole classes of buildings as not respectable merely because there are no previous writers to quote—that is, no authorities either to substantiate viewpoints or to disagree with them; no bases from which to demonstrate new attitudes, to buttress arguments or prove theories. What we need—and what we are just beginning to see developing in America—is a new phase of scholarly activity that derives from a knowledge of practical matters. This new concern is with the materials and the structure and the erectional techniques of buildings rather than with a continuation of the older scholarship that relied so exclusively on the written word. That scholarship emphasized dates and formal comparisons, decorative origins and aesthetic influences seen in contemporary texts and/or drawings, to the virtual exclusion of any concern for the compelling practical considerations observed in a knowledgeable firsthand investigation of the buildings themselves.

We need in America, too, the kind of organized, professional expertise that has been developed over the years in central and northern Europe, in Holland particularly. There, for example (as in Scandinavia, Germany, Switzerland, and elsewhere on the Continent), agricultural historians are a respected specialized group of highly informed men who are familiar with all phases of farm operation, equipment, and physical plant, in a precise but wide-ranging historical perspective. These men meet periodically in nationwide conferences with other related groups—architects, architectural historians, folklorists, antiquarians, geographers, etc.—to pool knowledge and exchange information to the benefit of all concerned.

The adoption of similar practices and activities in this country would doubtless be beneficial to America as well. For here, the tradition of frame construction, established at the outset by the earliest colonists along the eastern seaboard, and perpetuated by the pioneer settlers clearing the wilderness and ever moving westward, has continued to this day in the predominantly wooden construction of our houses, as well as all sorts of rural buildings including barns.

Yet, for America, very little has been written about the requirements that determined the shape and internal arrangements, the number and kinds and locations of the openings, and other such considerations that made the early barns of this country practical, effective, and convenient. And, so far we do not have detailed monographs whose intent is to analyze the structure of barns. What seem to be lacking entirely, both here and abroad, are any systematic, comprehensive accounts of the actual *erection* of old barns; that is, specific and detailed information on the problems overcome and the techniques followed in barn construction.

Hopefully, the present study will engender further interest in the structure and in the erectional techniques of timber buildings generally, and particularly in those anonymous examples of the carpenter's art, the early timber barns of America.

This writer's first encounter with a New York State Dutch barn occurred on September 29, 1962, in the company of DeVere Card, antique dealer and student of Mohawk Valley lore, Lee Brown Coye, artist, craftsman, and silversmith, and Arthur Meggett, architect, all of Hamilton. The expedition was to the Larger Wemp barn as the result of a suggestion made by Richard N. Wright, president of the Onondaga Historical Association. On that occasion we spent some hours examining this fine barn, measuring it, and speculating about it. This impressive introduction led to many Dutch barn-hunting expeditions during the ensuing years, mainly on the part of three of us: Mr. Card, the late Robert H. Palmiter, estates appraiser and museum consultant, and myself. We have returned more than once to some of the finer barns—for example, the Larger Wemp, East of Sharon, Wemple, Deertz, Van Wie (though in ruins)—to measure, to verify, to photograph, and to be impressed anew.

Although I alone am responsible for the drawings and the text, I none the less acknowledge a prodigious debt of gratitude for the help, the interest, and the encouragement of Messrs. Card of Hamilton and Palmiter of Bouckville. The former's wide-ranging historical knowledge of the area and of the times has been enlightening through many conversations. Mr. Palmiter's discerning eye, his enquiring mind and encyclopedic knowledge have been of the greatest value from the start; for it was he who discovered most of the barns we have come to examine, and it was he whose eye picked up the unusual or the distinctive or the unaccounted for in them.

Scott Phoenix of Hamilton took most of the photographs that appear in this book. The drawings are based on my own pictorial notes, made on the spot at the various sites.

Finally, it is especially satisfying to report that, almost invariably, the present proprietors were found to be proud of their barns, courteous and helpful, and interested in our interest. To them, our thanks.

JOHN FITCHEN

November, 1967
Colgate University
Hamilton, New York

Introduction to the Second Edition

New Dutch American Barn Investigations

Gregory D. Huber

ONE OF THE FORGOTTEN early vernacular farm structures, the American barn, has long been relegated to an almost nonexistent status as a subject of proper historical study. Even the popular *Encyclopedia Britannica* remarkably has only a two-paragraph discussion on the barn, despite the barn's manifest appearance on the American country homestead and its absolute necessity to the farmer in carrying out daily farm activities. Taken in a broad anthropological context, this lack of attention to the barn is all the more startling given the fact that early humans could not have advanced from a nomadic life to a civilized species had they not developed this instrument of storage.

Historians' distinct detachment from studying the character of the barn and its contribution to American life began to take a decided turn in the 1950s with the writings of a few authors. It was not until Eric Sloane, the well known painter of early Americana, wrote his *American Barns and Covered Bridges* in 1954 that anything of note gave credence to the barn as a singularly important farm building.[1] In fact, it appears that his book was the first that was ever published in North America on this subject. It was Sloane who broke the proverbial ice in the realization that barns were more than "mere curiosities." He gave new significance to the manner in which materials and tools were used in constructing and erecting them.

In the mid-1950s, two books were published on a particular barn form. The first book, *The Pennsylvania Barn*, by Alfred Shoemaker et al., was a

---

1. Eric Sloane, *American Barns and Covered Bridges* (New York: Funk and Wagnalls, 1954).

general treatise on the forebay or overshoot style of barn first developed in that state.[2] The second book, *Pennsylvania German Barns*, by Charles Dornbusch and John Heyl, was the first attempt to plot the evolution of the various subtypes of this barn form.[3] These authors, however, ignored much of the structural fine points of the barns.

Beginning in 1965, the famed folklorist Henry Glassie wrote scholarly treatises on several American barn types. The articles include the *The Old Barns of Appalachia*, *The Pennsylvania Barn in the South*, *The Double-Crib Barn in South-Central Pennsylvania* and *The Variation of Concepts Within Tradition: Barn Building in Otsego County, New York*.[4] This last study is a major treatise in which Glassie delineated a number of the major characteristics of the barns, including a diverse and rare view of bent (timber frame) typologies of the barns. The erudition of Glassie's work through a ten-year period gave impetus to other scholars to record barns in an analytical way.

Then, in 1966, came Eric Sloane's classic book, *An Age of Barns*.[5] With one broad sweep of his pen, Sloane provided the first recognition of the multiplicity of barn forms and accessory buildings found across much of the American cultural landscape. With the publication of this book, barns were put on the map. Sloane, however, paid scant attention to the fine structural layout of many of the farm buildings he depicted, including only a two page spread on Dutch American barns. Nevertheless, his book prompted the general reading public to view barns for the first time with discerning and appreciative eyes.

Two years following Sloane's second barn book appeared the first edition of John Fitchen's seminal work, *The New World Dutch Barn*. It was the first time a professionally trained architect had made an in-depth study of an early vernacular barn form. The book was written primarily as a critical account. Significantly, unlike his few predecessors, Fitchen noted the various primary constructional features of Dutch American barns and estab-

2. Alfred Shoemaker, *The Pennsylvania Barn* (Lancaster: Pennsylvania Dutch Folklore Center, Franklin and Marshall College, 1955).

3. Charles Dornbusch and John K. Heyl, "Pennsylvania German Barns," *Pennsylvania German Folklore Society* 21 (1956).

4. Henry Glassie, "The Old Barns of Appalachia," *Mountain Life and Work* 41, no. 2 (summer 1965): 21–30; "The Pennsylvania Barn in the South, Part 1", *Pennsylvania Folklife* 15, no. 2 (1965): 8–19; "The Pennsylvania Barn in the South, Part 2," *Pennsylvania Folklife* 15, no. 4 (1966): 12–25; "The Double-Crib Barn in South-Central Pennsylvania, Part 4," *Pioneer America* 2, no. 2 (July 1970): 23–34; "The Variation of Concepts Within Tradition: Barn Building in Otsego County, New York," in *Man and Cultural Heritage*, vol. 5 of *Geoscience and Man*, ed. H. J. Walker and W. G. Haag (Baton Rouge: Louisiana State Univ., 1974), 177–235.

5. Eric Sloane, *An Age of Barns* (New York: Funk and Wagnalls, 1966).

lished a basic nomenclature that is still in wide use today. Both in 1968, when the book was first published, and in subsequent years, his work was eagerly accepted and received excellent reviews. John Fitchen's labor was trailblazing work.

In 1972 Eric Arthur and Dudley Witney published their widely acclaimed book *The Barn: A Vanishing Landmark in North America*.[6] It was the first half-coffee-table–half-scholarly book, replete with photographs, that dealt with a wide array of farm structures in both the United States and parts of Canada. The authors recognized the Dutch American barn and John Fitchen's contributions. *The Barn* greatly accelerated the general public's awareness of a cultural heritage that was rapidly disappearing.

Barn observers' newfound consciousness was further enhanced by several books that started to appear about 1975. There are now a few dozen books on the subject, many of them emphasizing different aspects of barns in their various geographic locales. Many of them are basically pictorial in nature. None of them, however, approaches the erudition of Fitchen's work, with the single exception of the outstanding work seen in Robert Ensminger's 1992 treatise *The Pennsylvania Barn: Its Origin, Evolution, and Distribution in North America*.[7] He discovered that the rugged topography of eastern Switzerland spawned the form of the two-level forebay barn and noted three major forms and eighteen subtypes in the United States.

Among the numerous barn books that have been published, John Fitchen's discourse on the Dutch American barn still ranks highest in terms of elucidating the actual structure of the various framing components that constitute a particular early (pre–1830) barn style. It was his pioneering effort that made intelligible sense out of the wide array of confusing elements that confronted any early barn viewers. Fitchen's diligence has made it easy for us to discuss the basic constitution and fabric of a Dutch American barn. At first, however, it was necessary to delineate the barn's principal and secondary features such as H-frames, roof and side aisle structures, various connecting members, and disposition of sills and doors. Fitchen's book outlines these attributes for barns in the Mohawk, Schoharie, and Hudson River Valleys in New York State (he examined just one barn in New Jersey).

6. Eric Arthur and Dudley Witney, *The Barn: A Vanishing Landmark in North America* (Toronto: M. F. Feheley Arts Co., 1972).

7. Robert Ensminger, *The Pennsylvania Barn: Its Origin, Evolution, and Distribution in North America* (Baltimore and London: Johns Hopkins Univ. Press, 1992).

Fitchen's Inspections of Barns

Fitchen documented a number of details of thirty to thirty-five barns (see Appendix C) and provided a more general overview of an additional thirty to forty barns. While this process permitted him a good working knowledge of the fundamental structure of Dutch American barns, he did not work from an extensive statistical cross-section. For example, he conducted a brief examination of only two barns in all of Albany County, New York, now known to be home to at least five dozen barns. Consequently, his accounts and descriptions of Dutch American barns are incomplete and sometimes erroneous. Current research indicates that he left gaps in certain types of structural expressions found in several areas of New York and in virtually all of New Jersey, where more than 140 barns have been discovered to date. A great deal of new information has been generated, especially during the late 1980s and the 1990s, based on visits to approximately 650 barns by various observers. I have documented to varying degrees about 570 of these barns. The number of barns discovered has been surprising to everyone. Despite a much expanded information base, it should be emphasized that Fitchen's work still serves as the proper foundation for understanding the fundamental elements of Dutch barns.

It is important to note that throughout most of his original text Fitchen used the terms "New World Dutch barn" or "New York Dutch barn" when referring in general to barns of a Dutch type built in America. He infrequently used the term "Dutch barn." He almost never referred to barns in New Jersey because he only ever examined one barn in that state. When he occasionally discussed barns that appeared in the Netherlands, he used the term "Old World Barn" to distinguish them from New World Dutch barns. Throughout the rest of this introduction and in Appendixes C and D, I will refer to the structures that were built in America simply as Dutch barns, unless noted otherwise.

Recent Findings

Major new areas of investigations have unveiled new insight into the constitutional make up of Dutch barns. Numerous cultural factors, many borrowed from continental Europe, have dictated the form that seventeenth-, eighteenth-, and early-nineteenth-century builders used in fulfilling the needs of Dutch farmers. Several of these influences and some structural and environmental considerations are delineated in this introduction, which, along with Appendixes C and D, the glossary, and the index, is new to the second edition. These sections provide an overview of new findings that have emerged since the publication of Fitchen's first edition. This new material serves to supplement Fitchen's original research.

The Dutch barn, it will be seen, actually assumed several forms that came out of its single defining element, internalized posts. The barns also have a greater geographic distribution than was previously thought, as twenty-nine counties in New York and New Jersey are now represented. It is now possible to know within about fifteen years when a Dutch barn was erected. Dating a structure is perhaps the single most interesting aspect that most people, including historians, are curious about. Dating also provides information for understanding the evolution of the Dutch barn. Regionalisms, or modes of expression in certain geographic areas, are significant conditions in the overall appearance of Dutch barns that came out of perceived localized needs. Major joinery types, reconstruction of original barns, and wood species usage are other focal points that will be addressed.

In addressing these topics, I hope to render a more comprehensive look at a broad array of influences that determined the appearance of the Dutch barn as a complex component in an early cultural milieu. Dutch barns formed part of a larger whole. Their specific utility played a vital role in the overall economy and was successful in its particular agricultural setting. The barn maintained prominence, but only in a specific time frame. Its layout served well, but as the early nineteenth century wore on other competing barn forms in the Industrial Revolution eventually won out, and the original Dutch barn mode was sacrificed. During the last third of the twentieth century, the public's increased awareness of the current mass disappearance of these structures from the landscape has demanded that museums be established to safeguard the survival of at least a token few. Only a handful of barns remain to give us any sense of what existed two hundred to three hundred years ago. As a result, the best written record is ultimately only a partial one.

What I am offering is a broad overview of the most salient parts of my research. Here, the most important information will give the reader a greater in-depth exposure to what these barns are about. Like Fitchen's own text, the supplementation that I provide is largely a technical account. In the text that follows, I refer to specific barns (numbered 1 to 76) that appear in Appendix C and correspond to Fitchen's original barn checklist.

The Essence of a Dutch Barn

A number of the basic characteristics of Dutch barns were delineated by John Fitchen. Of all these features, the most important is the presence of H-frames, which virtually all three-aisle Dutch barns have and which vary in number in any given barn. Each frame has a horizontal anchorbeam and two posts at each end that are reinforced by end braces. These structural elements form a capital letter H. The central nature of a Dutch barn, however, lies in the fact that the posts are positioned internally, with an average distance from the side walls of 10 to 11 ft.[8] The basic form of the Dutch barn, then, is derived from these strategically placed posts. And significantly, it is the range of posts at each side that both dictates the three-aisle nature of these barns—a central aisle or nave, and two side aisles—and permits the main hay wagon entries to be centered on the gable walls.

The H-frame posts are connected at their tops longitudinally by purlin plates. It is here that the roof obtains its major, if not exclusive, support. I have observed several excellent illustrations of the effectiveness of this support system in several barns that have had their roofs essentially remain intact even though one (rarely two) side wall(s) has completely disappeared. In English barns, posts are positioned at the side walls, and when these side walls are no longer standing the roofs are either seriously jeopardized or they collapse.[9] Any vernacular barn in the Northeast that has its main roof support through internally positioned posts is a Dutch barn or most likely a Dutch barn derivative.

The general external appearance of a Dutch barn is that of an unbalanced structure that has wide gable walls with a high peak, relatively low side walls, and often a steep to fairly steep roof line. Except when surrounded by other farm structures and later additions or other changes to the original barn, the Dutch barn is often easily recognizable from fair distances because of the broad proportions that come from the wide space between the side walls—frequently 45 ft. or more. It is the wide separation of the internal posts that actually permits the extended distances between the side walls to occur. Many observers have often quickly identified this ethnic barn style in their travels from the broad sweeping lines just described without ever actually entering the buildings themselves. In contrast, early contemporary English barns (whose side walls are most often about 30 ft. apart) have very different proportions, so confusion (disregarding geographic considerations) between the two barn types rarely occurs.

Some may argue that certain New England barns with both the three-aisle arrangement and gable wall main wagon door entries could be

8. Fitchen referred to the vertical timbers of the H-frames as *columns* when they should be called *posts*, a more accurate architectural term.

9. English barns are variously called *Yankee, three-bay, Connecticut,* and *New England* barns. The main wagon doors are always on the side walls.

Dutch-related because some of these barns have bents with internally positioned posts that reach the roof. They appear, however, not to have been built with any Dutch influence. In addition, their middle aisles were used for wagon drive-through and not for threshing.

It is not, then, strictly speaking the anchorbeam, with its salient, extended tenons, that bespeaks the vital element of a Dutch barn. In fact, one barn in Montgomery County, New York, has no anchorbeams at all, and therefore the inner posts are not connected transversely and there are no H-frames to speak of. With the exception of anchorbeams and their attendant braces, this barn has almost all the basic structural elements of a Dutch barn. It is still standing firm and strong after nearly two hundred years. This example demonstrates that, theoretically, a builder could eliminate anchorbeams in a barn and the form would still remain true. If the builder had eliminated the H-frame posts, however, a very different form would have emerged. It is the internal positioning of the posts that allows the tenon of the anchorbeam to be extended into the free space of the barn, so to speak.[10] It is interesting to note, too, that there is much more information about the fundamental framing and disposition of Dutch barns contained in H-frame posts than in anchorbeams. This information is found in the posts' numerous notches, cut outs, and mortises, which are indicative of attachments of various structural members. Only the anchorbeams' length reflects the width of the nave. Thus, we see a new significance assigned to the H-frame posts that departs from the emphasis Fitchen placed upon the anchorbeams.

This is not to minimize the importance of the anchorbeams. Their large dimensions, regularly 15 to 20 in. in depth, permitted enormous amounts of crops to be stored above on sapling poles that stretch between them. Often, they were over-engineered, and beams only a foot in height (in many cases) were adequate to render the proper support for the temporary placement of farmers' harvests. In the final analysis, however, it is the post that creates the Dutch barn form and underpins the roof, the protective element that secures all within.

Forms of Dutch Barns

I will describe the five fundamental forms of the Dutch barn that have been identified on the Dutch American cultural landscape. One of these

---

10. If this extension were done on the "dropped" tie beam of an English barn, the tenon would be outside the confines of the barn walls and left unprotected and subject to rot.

forms is unique. All of the forms have a series of H-frames and were presumably built under Dutch influence. The last four forms of the Dutch barn were not recognized by John Fitchen. Other forms may appear in the future.

The first barn form is the *classic or true-form barn*, characterized by a three-aisle arrangement, with a central aisle or nave for threshing and wagon drive-through, and two side aisles, most often for the stabling of animals. Original main wagon doors are centered on either one, or mot often two, gable walls. The aisle arrangement basically qualifies these barns as true ground barns, even though the side aisles are 1 to 2 ft. below the threshing floor level. This description most closely resembles the barn form Fitchen portrayed.

A few classic barns have original condition basements under their threshing floors ostensibly for general storage, including two barns in New Jersey, one of which is dated 1788. Several barns may have been built that did not include original provisions for stabling; that is, both side aisles were presumably entirely for crop storage.

Most Schoharie County, New York, barns have only one gable wall wagon entrance. This condition is also seen in the several U-barns of Ulster County, New York, where the last bay is fully dirt and thus not part of the threshing floor. Other barns, including U-barns, have their last inner bent with low positioned anchorbeams that prevent wagons from exiting out the far gable wall.

Cantilevered gable walls appeared in five or six barns, and this configuration may have been utilized occasionally in pre-Revolutionary times (see Illus. 1).[11] Cantilevers assumed two forms. One was five-sided, as is the case with the Verplanck–Van Wyck barn (Appendix C, barn no. 2) and the other form is a simple triangle, like the barn I found in Ho-Ho-Kus, New Jersey, in 1996.

The second barn form, known as the *true hybrid barn* or *original Dutch-Anglo barn*, is subject to the same basic definition as the classic barn except that the central aisle is often not used for threshing, and wagon entries always appear on the side walls as in English-style barns. All true hybrid barns were originally built in this manner, although many existing barns with a basic Dutch-Anglo form were not originally built as such. The true hybrid barn may or may not have either a gable wall wagon entry or an original basement. Often these barns have low positioned anchor-

---

11. See Greg Huber, "Cantilevered Dutch-American Barns," *Timber Framing*, no. 43 (Mar. 1997): 8–9. Another cantilevered barn was the Dirck Dey Barn in Wayne, New Jersey, which was dismantled about 1930.

Illus. 1. Verplanck–Van Wyck barn. Relocated to Mount Gulian historic site in Beacon, Dutchess County, New York. Upper gable wall is cantilevered 18 in. over main wagon doors. Five-sided cantilever duplicates five-sided form of entire gable wall.

beams that prevent wagon traffic through the full length of the barn (gable to gable wall). Barns in this category are quite often of three-bay construction.

It is important to note that many classic Dutch barns became out-moded and then underwent changes in the mid-nineteenth century due to new economic environments that resulted in the main wagon entrance being positioned on the side wall in English style. Thus, these barns were not originally built as true hybrid barns. True hybrid barns were originally built with two ethnic expressions integrally incorporated into the structure: the Dutch trait, a series of H-frames; and the English trait, a side wall entrance.

In true hybrid Dutch-Anglo barns, the H-frames are positioned differently relative to the ridgeline. Some are oriented parallel to the ridgeline, in which case the purlin plates that connect all H-frame posts run transversely in the barns. English-type queen posts spring from these transverse plates, which in turn support longitudinal purlins above them that actually hold up the roofs. This timber configuration appears to be the only exception to the rule that states the H-frame posts support the roof

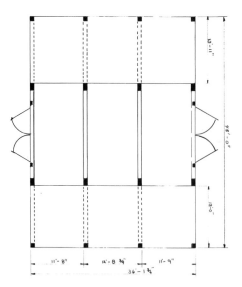

Illus. 2. Barn in Marlboro, Monmouth County, New Jersey. True hybrid barn of three bays with H-frames parallel to ridgeline. Original side-wall wagon entrances. Dimensions 48 ft. (side wall) by 36 ft. (gable wall). Circa 1810.

Illus. 3. Barn west of Pluckemin in Somerset County, New Jersey. Original side-wall entrance, three-bay barn with bents perpendicular to ridgeline with double anchor-beams per bent that flank the widened middle bay. Dated 1837.

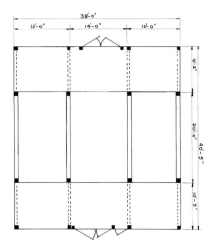

Illus. 4. Barn in Branchburg, Somerset County, New Jersey. True hybrid barn of three bays with H-frames perpendicular to ridgeline. Original side-wall wagon entrances. Dimensions 38 ft. (side wall) by 40 ft. (gable wall). Circa 1810.

Illus 5. Barn north of Poughkeepsie in Dutchess County, New York. Side-wall view of partial and original fourth aisle that is 9¹/₂ ft. wide and 22 ft. long. Square rule era built with round pole rafters with original side-wall entrance opposite wall with partial aisle. Side-wall height (exclusive of partial fourth aisle) is 13 ft. Circa 1825.

(see Illus. 2). Other true hybrid barns have H-frames perpendicular to the ridgeline, where the posts assume their normal function in supporting the roof. In both cases wagon entry is through the side walls. (See Illus. 3 and Illus. 4.)

There are two original three-bay Dutch-Anglo barns in Montgomery County, built 1800–1810, with side-wall entrances and H-frames parallel to side walls. The H-frame posts adjacent to the side walls extend to the roof, as do both inner H-frame posts, making posts of distinctly dissimilar heights. There is also a barn in Rockland County (circa 1840), and one in Columbia County, that has this trait. There may be others.

A few true hybrid barns east of the Hudson River in New York have side-wall entries in line with ramps in the side aisles that lead up to a plank floor between the two adjacent anchorbeams, most often in the middle bay, that allowed for hay wagons to be unloaded. One was the unique, nonextant, seven-bay barn near Troy, New York.

An original condition barn (circa 1820) in Dutchess County, New York, is unique in that it has a partial fourth aisle that is adjacent to the side of one of the regular side aisles (see Illus. 5). This barn has both original gable and side-wall entrances.

Some variations of the true hybrid form are often seen in barns built after 1815 (known as square rule era barns) with small timbers and anchorbeam tenons that normally extend little or not at all. A number of these barns have basements. Most of them have posts with raising holes.

The builders or farmers, or both, associated with true hybrid barns may have been influenced by true English-style side-entrance barns in surrounding non-Dutch areas, as they saw certain advantages in the non-Dutch form. The two greatest benefits were (1) access that allowed for unloading of hay wagons in or near the middle of the barn at the side wall, which provided greater efficiency, and (2) much increased storage capacities. This increased storage was possible because of high side walls and because the bays (except for the drive-through bay) could often be completely filled with crops.

It is probable that most of the true hybrid barns were built after about 1800 or even 1820. This was mostly in response to the fundamental changes in the agricultural economy owing mainly to the Industrial Revolution, with a result that fewer and fewer classic barns were being built.

The third Dutch barn form is the *one-aisle barn*. There are a number of barns in both New York and New Jersey that were built without side aisles. These barns were probably fashioned and erected by the same builders, ostensibly of Dutch extraction, who built the classic and true hybrid barn types. (See Illus. 6 and 7.) H-frame posts appear at the side walls. In one-aisle barns, queen posts that normally support purlin plates in many English barns do not emanate from the bents. They should be considered accessory buildings and are often adjacent to the main classic or true hybrid barns at particular homesteads. They can have either gable-wall or side-wall entrances, or both. One-aisle barns were fairly often built during the period prior to 1815 (known as the scribe rule era). Barns built during this period often have 2-foot scribe marks on the anchorbeams. A few barns have collar ties uniting rafters in alternating pairs. It is difficult to know what function these barns performed, but crop storage was probably the major use, and there was possibly some stabling of farm animals.

The fourth form of Dutch barn is the *double-decker barn*. One unique barn, built circa 1845 in Marbletown, Ulster County, New York, is quite similar to double-decker barns that were built in Chester County and some other counties in Pennsylvania. There are entrances on three different levels. The top deck or high-drive level (with an entrance at one side wall) is the main floor, where the H-frames are seen. The posts have raising holes. The second deck, or level, opens at the front gable wall that leads into the granary floor section, which has many bin-like compartments constructed for extensive grain storage. The third level is located

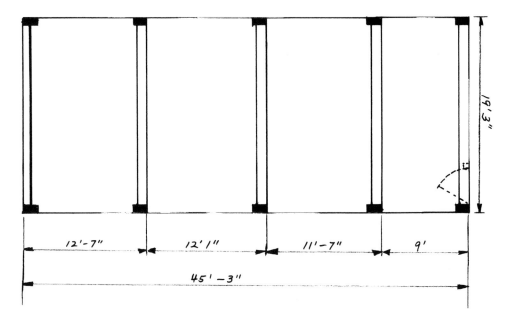

Illus. 6. Barn in Millstone, Somerset County, New Jersey. One-aisle barn of four bays. Dimensions 45 ft. 3 in. (side wall) by 19 ft. 3 in. (gable wall). Circa 1800.

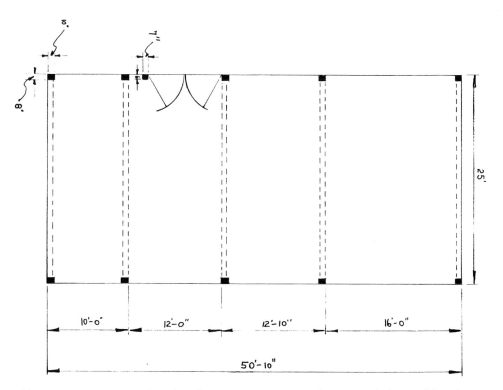

Illus. 7. Barn near Woodstock, Ulster County, New York. One-aisle barn of four bays. Dimensions 50 ft. 10 in. (side wall) by 25 ft. (gable wall). Circa 1820. Possible entrance(s) at gable wall(s).

Illus. 8. Barn in Marbletown, Ulster County, New York. Unique double decker barn similar to a number of barns in Chester County, Pennsylvania, with the same name. Entrance in gable wall leading into second floor with grain bin compartments. Top level on side wall on right (out of view) has ramp leading up to level with H-frames. Bottom or basement level on opposite wall (out of view) with entrance that leads into stabling area. Circa 1845.

on the ground. It has a main entrance on the side wall opposite the top level that leads into the stabling area (see Illus. 8). This barn has an enormous total volume in which tremendous amounts of crops could be stored, as it is about 65 ft. long by 48 ft. wide with very high side walls.

The final Dutch barn form is the *derivative barn*. There are a number of barns that retain the feature of H-frames with relatively small-sized anchorbeams without extended tenons and almost always have original sidewall entrances and basements. These barns were built quite late, from 1840 to 1880, and often have both hewn and milled timbers. Rafters are almost always milled. These much later barns often have raising holes and very high side walls. They appear to have been built under a Dutch influence. They should not, however, be considered as part of the traditional Dutch barn building era that ended about 1840. Again, the barns were for high-volume crop storage and stabling.

New York and New Jersey comprise the primary domain where Dutch barns were built and erected.[12] The Dutch settled in areas that predominantly followed water courses which paralleled the conditions found in their homeland. Fitchen, in his travels, saw barns in nine counties in New York and one county (one barn) in New Jersey. To date, barns in New York have been reported in an additional eleven counties, including Fulton, Otsego, Saratoga, Nassau, Kings, Queens, Richmond, Putnam, Orange, Rockland, and Rensselaer. Other counties may be added to this list in the future. The three counties in present-day New York City have no extant barns.[13] More than five hundred barns have been sighted in New York State, with the heaviest concentrations (more than fifty barns each) in Montgomery, Albany, Schoharie, Ulster, and Dutchess Counties (Ulster County has the most, with nearly one hundred barns). This high concentration is followed by more than twenty-five barns in Columbia County, eleven barns in Rockland County, and a half dozen barns in Fulton, Nassau, Greene, and Rensselaer Counties. The remaining counties have one to five barns each.

The most barns Fitchen encountered in one county was twenty-seven in Schoharie County, with the heaviest concentration along the Middleburgh Flats near Fultonham. Next was Montgomery County, with fourteen barns, then Ulster County with nine, Dutchess County with six, Columbia County with five, Greene County with three, Albany County with two, and Schenectady and Herkimer Counties with one each. He examined only one barn in all of New Jersey, located in Somerset County.

New Jersey barns now identified number close to 140 and are found in nine counties. The central part of the state reports the greatest number by far, with Somerset County having close to sixty. Next is Monmouth and Hunterdon Counties, each with close to twenty barns, and then Mercer and Middlesex Counties with about three each. In the northwest part of the state, Warren and Sussex Counties each has one or two barns. In

12. Greg Huber, "Where Are Dutch Barns?" *Dutch Barn Research Journal* 1 and 2 (1991 and 1992): 69–77.

13. For Brooklyn (Kings County), see Rosalie F. Bailey, *Pre-Revolutionary Dutch Houses and Families in Northern New Jersey and Southern New York* (New York: Dover, 1968), 63, 67, 69, 73, 76, 78, and 90. Because these barns appear at Dutch homesteads and the dimensions that are provided reflect Dutch barn proportions, I assume they are indeed Dutch barns. For Staten Island (Richmond County), see the painting at Richmondtown Restoration by Jasper Cropsey of the Cortelyou Farm, which includes a Dutch barn. For Queens (Queens County), see *History of Queens County, New York* (New York: Munsell, 1882), 250B, 343. Two Dutch barns are depicted.

northern New Jersey, Bergen County has twenty-five barns and Passaic County has one barn. More barns, especially Dutch-Anglo ones, will be found, particularly in Hunterdon County.

I suspect that another 150 barns, including remnant ones, are still to be discovered in the various counties of both states. The final count could approach about eight hundred barns.

Beyond the primary domain, very little has been reported on the appearance of the traditional Dutch barn. One exception concerns a migration of Dutch settlers around 1780 to Mercer County, Kentucky, where six to eight Dutch-Anglo-style barns[14] with side-wall entries have been observed, all with the diagnostic H-frames.[15] Other states, particularly Michigan,[16] have barns of post-1840 vintage resembling the Dutch style, but it is not known if these barns have direct ties to traditions established in the east. In addition, one or two Dutch barns have been seen in Vermont.[17] Finally, a few forebay or overshoot style barns in Bucks County in extreme eastern Pennsylvania have a single-arched anchorbeam with extended and wedged tenons that stretch between adjacent bents on the middle of the upper floor and may represent a Dutch influence from adjacent New Jersey.

EUROPEAN ORIGIN AND USE OF FRAMING TECHNOLOGY

Tie Beams in the Netherlands

It should be recognized that John Fitchen coined the term *anchorbeam*. It was derived directly from the Dutch word *ankerbalk (ankerbalkgebint)*, a term of traditional construction that is still in use in the Netherlands. Three other traditional methods were used there to join large horizontal tie beams to posts in barns of three-aisle arrangement: (1) *tussenbalk (tussenbalkgebint)*, which is the same construction as *ankerbalk* except there is no extended tenon; (2) *kopbalk (kopbalkgebint)*, in which both ends of a tie

14. A Dutch-Anglo barn (as described on pp. xxvi–xxvii) is a barn that contains H-frames in the Dutch tradition somewhere in its structural timbering and has wagon entry doors on at least one or two side walls (eave walls), which is normally seen in English barns. Barns in this category may or may not be originally built as such and may or may not have original basements. Some original condition Dutch-Anglo barns have both gable and side wall entries.

15. Conversation with Howard Gregory of Harrodsburg, Kentucky, on September 15, 1991.

16. John Fitchen told me in September 1978 that barns that resemble the Dutch form appear in the Grand Rapids, Michigan, area. See also Peter Sinclair, "Dutch Barn Influence Alive in Michigan Barns" *Joiners Quarterly*, no. 18 (summer 1991) 18-20.

17. Jan Lewandoski, a timberframer, gave me this information in January 1994.

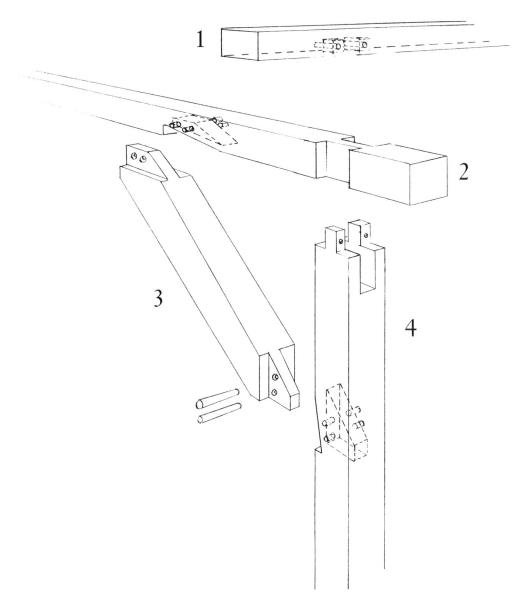

Illus. 9. *Kopbalkgebint* tie beam construction, exploded view. Slotted post receives widely grooved, double-side-faced tie beam. No post extension above tie. Designation of four beams: (1) purlin plate, (2) *kopbalk*, (3) brace, and (4) post.

beam are trenched at both sides to fit onto the top of a widely slotted post (see Illus. 9); and (3) *dekbalk (dekbalkgebint)*, in which a tie beam at both ends is mortised on its soffit to receive a tenoned post that the tie oversails by several inches or more (see Illus. 10).[18]

18. For a well-illustrated book with many drawings and photographs of the numerous types of Dutch framing styles and variations in the Netherlands, see G. Berends, *Historische Houtconstructies in Nederland* (Arnhem, Netherlands: Stichting Historisch Boerderij-Onderzoek, 1996).

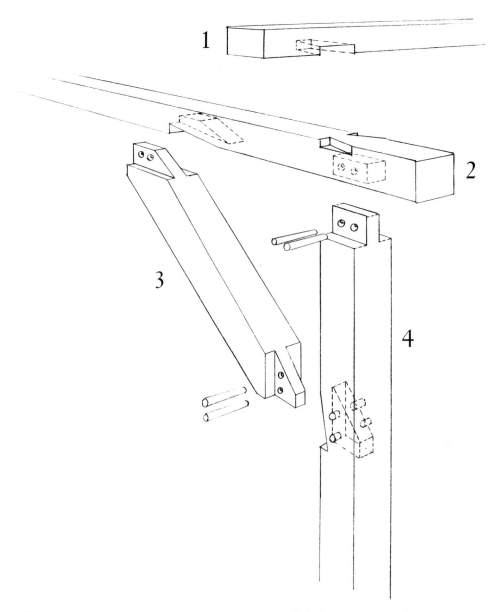

Illus. 10. *Dekbalkgebint* tie beam construction, exploded view. Tenoned post receives mortised tie beam. No post extension above tie. Designation of four beams: (1) purlin plate, (2) *dekbalk*, (3) brace, and (4) post. Drawings courtesy of Stichting Historisch Boerderij-Onderzoek.

When the Dutch came to settle in the New World in the seventeenth century, they could have utilized any or all four of the tie beam types found in their fatherland that were seen in agricultural structures that had varying sizes and proportions. Which of the types they did use is a matter of conjecture. Three of the four types of tie (main horizontal beam) construction have been identified in examples of extant barns in Dutch-

American-settled areas.[19] They include the ubiquitous *ankerbalk* (anchor-beam), which was referred to as *loft beam* in early Dutch American seventeenth-century contracts.[20] Various specimens, mostly of later vintage, of the *tussenbalk* type have been found. I identified and documented (in part) one unique specimen of the *dekbalk* type in Bergen County. The beams were of tuliptree and 15 in. deep, and its braces were lapped with half-dovetailed tenons. Other barns with the *dekbalk* form could have been used.

It is certain that the anchorbeam type (or possibly *tussenbalk*) appeared very early because a house-barn contract from 1641 at Achter Col (present-day Bogota, Bergen County) indicates construction that included posts with extensions (*verdiepingh*) above the tie or crossbeam.[21] Both *dekbalk* and *kopbalk* include no provisions for extensions above the tie beam. Neither type has ever been identified in building contracts from the seventeenth century or beyond.

Competitive Processes and Verdiepinghs

In the beginning there may have been experimentation by builders, farmers, and others (of Dutch extraction and other ethnic stock) among the four types of tie construction as to which one or ones would best suit the needs of a people in a new environment that was decidedly different from continental Europe. All four types initially could have been utilized. There may have been a competitive selection process, however, that ultimately resulted in the anchorbeam (and its very close relation, the *tussenbalk*) predominating because this form afforded a particular advantage over the other types. This advantage may well have concerned the *verdiepingh* or extension of the H-frame post above the ties. Apparently, from the beginning, Dutch barns were constructed for the stabling of animals and, more important, for the storage of crops. Because the fertility of

19. A variation of the *kopbalkgebint*, a fourth method, is found only at the top of gunstocked gable wall H-frame posts that join to upper tie beams in a barn just south of Schoharie Village in Schoharie County. The regular anchorbeams appear in all bents. The posts are slotted at their very tops, which receive long, thin tenons that are received into the undersurfaces of rafters adjacent to the gable walls. The two tie beams are not true examples of the *kopbalk* form and probably do not have a direct connection to continental Europe. Other variations of *kopbalk*s may appear in some Montgomery County barns.

20. Henk Zantkuyl, "The Netherlands Town House: How and Why It Works," *New World Dutch Studies: Dutch Arts and Culture in Colonial America, 1609–1776*, (Albany, N.Y.: Albany Institute of History and Art, 1987), 143–60.

21. Reginald McMahon, "The Achter Col Colony on the Hackensack," *New Jersey History* (The New Jersey Historical Society) (winter 1971): 227.

the soil was very high in most Dutch settled areas, the yields farmers could obtain from their plantings were similarly high. Therefore, the need for extensive storage capacities was also high. If barns were built with *dekbalk* or *kopbalk* construction, with their attendant lack of post extension, there would seem to be a severe limitation to the amount of storage afforded above the tie beams. With anchorbeam construction a builder could extend the upper post length to any desired height (a seven-bay barn in Rensselaer County, New York, had a *verdiepingh* of 18 ft.) and tremendous storage volumes could have been effected, although very early barns probably had relatively short *verdiepingh*s. The use of the *ankerbalk* form still would have allowed for greater storage capabilities than either the *dekbalk* or *kopbalk* form could have provided.

By choosing to construct *dekbalk* and *kopbalk* forms, early builders could have extended the oversailing part of the tie beams beyond the posts by perhaps a few feet and thereby expanded storage capacities a great deal. But apparently this was not done. The much harsher climate in the New World may not have lent itself well to a construction form that relied on horizontal extensions of tie beams. The vertical post extension seen in anchorbeam construction may well have withstood severe snow loads and other environmental and structural stresses much better. Another consideration for the choice of *ankerbalk* form may have been the abundant availability of long, straight timbers that was not easily obtained in the Netherlands. The large timber sizes would have permitted the more substantial H-frames that were needed to have been built and erected.

Others considerations may further explain the wide use of the anchorbeam form in America. A possible structural reason for the use of the form was the post extension, which allowed the H-frame to give the loft a much greater load-bearing capacity than either the *dekbalk* or *kopbalk* forms would have rendered. It was this load-bearing ability that made possible the great storage dimensions of these barns. One example of how the barn form may have been influenced by cultural factors was seen in the widening of the central nave, which filled the need for large threshing areas in the barns in the rich, wheat-growing settlement areas of the Dutch in New York and New Jersey.

First Effective Settlement and Simplification

Immigrants from Holland and other nearby lowland regions may have come from areas where specific joinery methods along with their attendant building styles predominated. These regional traits may have influenced builders in America to use particular tie construction forms.

Once specific constructional techniques took hold, the concept of "first effective settlement," proposed by cultural geographer Wilbur Zelinsky in 1973, would have dictated builders resolve to build in certain ways. Zelinsky theorized that the first group able to establish a viable self-perpetuating society (including certain forms of its material culture) in an empty land is of crucial significance for the later social and cultural geography of the area, regardless of how small the initial group of settlers may have been.[22] This concept of first effective settlement may well explain the proliferation of the use of the anchorbeam and the absence of other potentially competitive forms that could have been used but apparently were not.

A further illustration of the wide use of the *ankerbalk* form in America may be seen in the process of "simplification," by which Europeans overseas (in America) established drastically simplified versions of European culture. While considerable Old World diversity was brought into colonial regions, strong selective frontier pressures acted to reduce this complexity. Agricultural structures had differing sizes and proportions in the Netherlands, where all four of the main tie construction types that could have given rise to the barn form that proliferated in America were utilized. This simplification process, described by Dell Upton as a process of "social winnowing," left only the *ankerbalk* form dominant in the Dutch American agricultural landscape. The *dekbalk* and *kopbalk* forms, if used at all, most likely vanished from the architectural scene very early.[23]

European Prototype

The form of the Dutch American barn that did emerge raises the question of what its direct European prototype may have actually been and its location. No one has completely explained this origin of the barn, although one of the five major barn forms in the Netherlands, the *hallehuis*, most closely resembles the classic Dutch American barn.[24] This form presently has the widest geographic distribution from northern Drente south to Brabant. However, it is not known how widespread the form was when

22. The author has seen several poignant examples of this amazing phenomenon in several areas of the Northeast, including areas adjacent to the Dutch culture. See Wilbur Zelinsky, *The Cultural Geography of the United States* (Englewood Cliffs, N.J.: Prentice Hall, 1973), 13.

23. See R. H. Harris, "The Simplification of Europe Overseas," *Annals of the Association of American Geographers* 67 (1977): 467–83. Also see Dell Upton, "Vernacular Domestic Architecture in Eighteenth Century Virginia," *Winterthur Portfolio* 17 (1982): 95–119.

24. Van Wijk, Piet, "Form and Function in the Netherlands' Agricultural Architecture," *New World Dutch Studies: Dutch Arts and Culture in Colonial America, 1609–1776* (Albany, N.Y.: Albany Institute of History and Art, 1987), 161–69.

America was initially settled by the Dutch in the middle third of the seventeenth century. The *hallehuis* has many variations, but its three major characteristics include: (1) an aisle structure with H-frames typified by anchorbeams with extended and wedged tenons; (2) a central nave for threshing whose floor is made of a composition of clay, sand, and thin manure for hardness (no wooden floors are known to exist); and (3) cattle stalled in the side aisles with noses to the nave. These traits in general bear a striking likeness to the Dutch American barn.

The Frisian barn form has features that contrast markedly from the *hallehuis*. Characteristics include an aisled form that has a high central nave used for crop storage from the floor to the roof peak, the result of the exclusive use of *dekbalk* construction. Cattle were kept in the side aisle with noses to the side wall. Unloading of hay wagons was done on the other side aisle. Clearly, this barn form was not the prototype of the Dutch American form. Other barn forms are the *Dwarhuis* or "compartment house" group, the Zeeland barn with three adjacent threshing floors, and the Flemish barn or double-aisled structure. All three building types have a distinctive form that could not have given rise to the American barn.

The European barn form most similar to the Dutch American barn may actually be found along the northwest boundary of Germany (the Niederrhein), adjacent to the Netherlands.[25] The structural framing system of these barns is more consistent with the American barn than with barns in any area of Holland. This raises the issue of the proper use of the word "Dutch" in Dutch barn. The term "Dutch barn" was nevertheless used in newspaper advertisements in New Jersey as early as the 1760s.

One of the best treatises on the possible origin of the so-called Dutch American barn appears in an obscure booklet by George Ellis Burcaw.[26] He discusses the origin, development, and distribution of the aisled form dating back more than two thousand years. It is this form of construction that may have ultimately given rise to the Dutch barn in America. The known development of the Saxon House (of three-aisle form) started with excavations in the northern Netherlands and in northwest Germany. Digs at Jengum near the River Ems and at Ezinge northwest of Groningen re-

25. Conversation with Jaap Schipper of Amsterdam, Netherlands, June 16, 1998. A curious coincidence of another major icon of Dutch material culture in America is seen in the Kas. Several forms of this furniture type (cupboard for placing linens and other valuables) occurred in Holland, but another form that closely resembles the post-1720 Dutch American Kas again came from northwest Germany. See Peter Keney et al., *American Kasten* (New York: Metropolitan Museum of Art, 1991), 8.

26. George Ellis Burcaw, *The Saxon House: A Cultural Index in European Ethnography* (Moscow: Univ. Press of Idaho, 1979), 1–126.

vealed prototypes (dating from 300 B.C. and earlier) of the Saxon House. The form developed and had a continuous sequence of construction that utilized certain techniques and had particular interior space arrangements from old Roman times to the late Middle Ages. Burcaw believes this building form eventually found expression in the Dutch barn in Europe and then in the Dutch American barn.

The Saxon House format should not be confused with the Basilica construction style found in Britain, which is Roman or a Roman-native hybrid type. Burcaw argues that scholars confuse Roman and Saxon architecture, and he maintains that there is no actual connection between the two.

The Palatine German Contribution

It was apparently not only the Dutch who built Dutch barns. Palatine Germans are known to have settled sporadically among the Dutch on both sides of the Hudson River in Ulster, Dutchess, Columbia, and Rensselaer Counties and in the Schoharie and Mohawk River valleys. Their early migrations to America came in two major waves, the first starting in 1709 and the other in the 1720s.[27] No documentary information has come to light as to any Palatine settler building any particular barn style in New York or New Jersey. Almost no early (pre-1810) barn type other than Dutch has ever been identified in the areas these Palatines came to, so it would appear that the doctrine of first effective settlement would again dictate the choice of the Dutch barn mode in the case of Germans carrying out their agricultural practices.

In considering the principle of "first effective settlement," it is important to know that other ethnic groups in Europe also came to America and they apparently adopted the Dutch barn mode in "Dutch" settled areas. They accepted Dutch standards in various cultural ways and were thus also subject to the principle. The total ethnic landscape was of a polyglot nature, and the Dutch barn served the needs of a diverse group.[28]

Joinery

Joinery, or the method of uniting timbers, was executed in specific ways that are found in all traditional timber frame buildings, regardless of eth-

---

27. Walter Allen Knittle, *Early Eighteenth Century Palatine Emigration* (Philadelphia: Dorrance, 1937).

28. David Cohen, "How Dutch Were the Dutch in New Netherland?" *New York History* 62 (1980): 43–60.

nic origin. The four major types of joinery found in Dutch barns are regular mortise and tenon joinery, half-dovetail lapped joinery, scarf joinery, and wedged half-dovetail joinery.[29]

In regular mortise and tenon joinery, the tenon or tongue of wood (which is not visible when the joint is fully assembled) is housed within a chiseled-out area or mortise (see Dwg. 7A and 7B). This is by far the most common method used.

Half-dovetail lapped joinery occurs where the tenon is lapped over the timber to which it is joined in the form of a half dovetail and is plainly visible. This method has ancient traditional roots seen at least as early as the eleventh century in England. It is not normally seen in Dutch barns, except possibly in the construction of the sills and in the infrequent use of collar ties. It is, however, commonly seen in the pre-Revolutionary barns in Ulster County (which had major and minor rafter systems) and in some barns in Bergen and Rockland County barns.

Scarf joinery is seen where plates and sills are spliced with various angles and cuts. This joint is seen between two timbers that meet end to end. This method, too, is rather rare.

Wedged half-dovetail joinery occurs in a tie or tie beam where the bottom surface of a tenon is cut at an angle to effect a half dovetail. A mortise in a post is then cut with a corresponding angle on its bottom edge to receive the dovetail edge tightly. On top of the tenon, a wedge is driven from the outer side of the post toward its opposite side to secure the joint (see Dwg. 7C). One barn originally in Rensselaer County (moved to Connecticut) has its anchorbeams uniquely joined to their posts in this manner. This last joinery technique is known in only five other Dutch barns, one of which is the larger Wemp barn (Appendix C, barn no. 31). Another is in a unique bent in southern Dutchess County.

Tenons are offset in most cases because of common framing practices of builders. Builders used framer's squares with arms (blades) that had particular widths, and when timbers were cut they often used these widths to position both tenons and mortises.[30]

Most anchorbeams are secured to their posts with two pegs, although many of the earlier ones (pre-1790) are secured with three pegs. One barn in Somerset County amazingly has no pegs. Three barns in Monmouth County each have only one peg at each union. Normally, either one or two pegs secure the H-frame braces at either end, although many of the earlier barns have three pegs at each end of the braces, as seen in the Van Bergen

29. Greg Huber, "Joinery in Dutch-American Barns", *Joiners Quarterly*, no. 32 (Aug./Sept./Oct. 1996): 19–22.
30. Conversation with Jan Lewandoski of Greenboro Bend, Vermont, August 1998. Jan Lewandoski is a longtime traditional timber framer.

barn (Appendix C, barn no. 37). One nonextant barn, located in Monmouth County, New Jersey, had these braces secured with three pegs but only at their lower end.

DATING AND THE EVOLUTION OF THE DUTCH BARN

Seventeenth-Century Barns

It is possible to get a general sense of what Dutch barns looked like from almost the earliest days of European settlement in the New World. The two areas initially occupied in the 1620s were Manhattan and Fort Orange, which later became Albany. The earliest barns were built on or near these sites. A lengthy but not exhaustive review of seventeenth-century Dutch American manuscripts revealed a number of building contracts that include various dimensions for five barns and six house-barns (structures for accommodating humans as well as animals and crop storage).[31] Only two documents included side-aisle dimensions. Other contracts mention barns fairly often but do not provide any dimensions.

Each barn and house-barn is numbered, with dates of erection and with dimensions given in feet:

Barns

No.	Erection Date	Length (side wall)	Nave Width
1	1638	40	18
2	1642	50	20
3	1647	60	28
4	1675	50	26
5	1679	30	28

House-Barns

No.	Erection Date	Length (side wall)	Nave Width
6	1634	80	25
7	1642	100	24
8	1642	90	24
9	1643	80	25
10	1643	120	28
11	1648	60	24

31. Various seventeenth-century contracts are taken from these sources: New York Historical Manuscripts, Dutch, Vols. 1, 2 and 3, trans. Van Laer (Baltimore, Md.); Early Records of Albany, Notarial Papers 1 and 2, 1600–1696; Van Rensselaer-Bowier Manuscripts; Dutch Settlers Society of Albany, Yearbook 3.

Three of the house-barns are divided into house lengths and barn lengths:

No.	House Length	Barn Length
7	50	50
10	40	80
11	24	36

The dates of erection are significant for two reasons. First, both building types were being constructed at the same time—during the 1630s and 1640s. Second, the dates of the six house-barns suggest that they may have been built only during that fairly narrow time frame. One should keep in mind, however, that statistically six buildings (house-barns) offer only a very small cross-section of data.

It is interesting and curious that all length dimensions of all barns and house-barns—a total of eleven buildings—were in multiples of 10 ft. In addition, even the individual house and barn part lengths in two cases measure in multiples of 10 ft. This is unlike most extant barns, whose lengths can measure anywhere between 30 and 65 ft. The widths of naves seen in the contracts, however, are often found in extant barns. Ten-foot length increments may have been the standard unit utilized in very early barn construction, but this standard probably was not always used. This trait may have been carried over to the eighteenth century, as 10-ft.-wide side aisles are often seen in Dutch barns that are still standing. A word of caution is important here, as the measurement or length of the early Dutch foot is not precisely the same length as the later (after about 1800?) English foot.

There are numerous other individual traits included in the eleven contracts. Barn no. 1, located at Achtervelt on Long Island, had a 24-ft.-high roof. Barn no. 4, located at Kinderhook, with ten-foot side aisles, had both gable walls with sloping or truncated peaks (jerkin-head) with five bents, but only three of the bents had brackets, which can be interpreted as three inner bents having end braces, and bents adjacent to gable walls that had no braces. This trait was also recorded in a number of house contracts. The height of loft beams (from the floor) in three house-barns (nos. 6, 8, and 9) were 12, 12, and 12$\frac{1}{2}$ ft., respectively. House-barn no. 8 had ten bents of nine-bay construction, and loft beams (anchorbeams) were 9 x 14 in. House-barns no. 8 and 11 each had a perpendicular gable wall and a truncated gable wall (wolf roof?) at the other end.

Factors Influencing Dating

After the initial period of Dutch settlement, there is some difficulty dating barns. Fitchen, however, made an insightful prediction when he stated that future historians trying to assign precise dates of erection to Dutch barns would use data "on the basis of a combination of many factors—[drawn from] on-the-spot interpretation of information presented by the fabric and constitution of the building itself." This prediction has indeed been found to be the case. Unfortunately, however, Fitchen thought it was impossible in his day to assign a precise date or even an accurate idea of the chronology of barns. It is now possible to assign general dates of construction within about fifteen to twenty years, as there are certain design features in particular structural elements that are indicative of particular time frames of erection. In other words, modes or expressions of building layout and design form evolved over time because of innovations related to new types of tools used in the trade, different manners of timber cutting and joining, new materials available, new client (farmer) demands owing to altering agricultural economies in different areas, and possibly even cultural pressures to build in particular ways.

All of these alterations are indicative of the evolution the Dutch barn underwent throughout its two hundred years of existence (1630 to about 1830). The dating of these barns provides the raw information for an understanding of how the development of these barns took place. It was a dynamic process, and the various decisions the many builders and farmers made is now fixed into the structure and fabric of each barn. Comparing the various elements in the barns gives us a sense of the growth of the Dutch barn style.

The Scribe Rule Method—Pre-1815

One of the most significant findings in dating barns involves two methods of fashioning joints in timber framing in different building eras. The first of the methods was known as the scribe rule, which was used prior to about 1815 (the later method, known as the square rule, is discussed in the following section). This scribe rule system involved cutting joints, for example, with the result that all corresponding members in a series of H-frames in a given Dutch barn (all anchorbeams, posts, and braces) were not interchangeable among all the bents. That is, each particular anchorbeam, because their tenons were cut in a specific manner, could only be received into two particular posts. They were "meant for each other." They would not fit into or be joined to another set of posts. Therefore, a framer would have to keep close track of all structural members to prevent confusion when all the barn timbers were assembled. To do this, he would often use some means such as a chisel or other tool to cut marks called "marriage marks" into corresponding bent parts, usually in the form of Roman numerals. It should be understood that all timbers in the barns, including H-frames, were joined with the scribe rule method. Other ethnic buildings, such as English barns and Pennsylvania Swiss-German barns, also employed the scribe rule method.

One sure way of determining whether a barn is of the scribe rule era is to check for the presence of the so-called "2-foot scribe marks." These are vertical lines scribed or marked on the vertical lay-out faces of anchorbeams that are found 2 ft. from the outside or lateral face of H-frame posts with circles or half-circles often intersecting them. Barns built from about 1780 to 1810 often have them. Curiously, though, before this time they fairly often lack them (e.g., Appendix C, barns no. 10, 32, and 42).

Anchorbeams are joined to H-frame posts in two specific ways. The earlier method occurs where the joint was formed by a tapered cut on both beams for a tight fit (refer to Plates 32 to 35). This joint formation is often referred to as diminished haunch. Often the pegs that unite these timbers are 1 in. or less in diameter (see Illus. 11.). It is interesting to note that timber framers virtually always united anchorbeams to posts with these tapered cuts in Dutch brick and frame houses built prior to about 1770. This earlier method is used a majority of the time in barns built to about 1790. After this period, anchorbeams were increasingly joined to posts with the so-called square shouldering seen with square cuts at both the top and bottom (refer to Fitchen Plate 22) until the end of the scribe rule era.

An early trait seen in other barns is long hewn purlin braces that attach just above or below the anchorbeams. Most post-1790 barns have these braces attached above the half-way point on the H-frame post extension (*verdiepingh*) above the anchorbeam. Many barns built from 1800 to 1820 and all those built later have milled purlin braces. Most pre-1810 Dutch barns have hewn rafters and hewn H-frame braces. It appears in general that Fitchen may be correct when he states that barns made of hard pine were from a date earlier than about 1790. Fitchen believed that barns made predominately of oak could indicate an early date of construction. Oak barns, however, were made both in the eighteenth and the first few decades of the nineteenth century.

Other early traits (pre-1790) in general include wider naves (26 to 30 ft.), wider H-frame braces (especially in pine barns that approach or equal the width of the posts), longer anchorbeam tenons (greater than 12 in.), steeper roofs, lower side walls (9 to 13 ft.), shorter *verdiepingh*s (3 to 8 ft.),

Illus. 11. Barn near Altamont in Albany County, New York. Standard format of early or probable pre–Revolutionary War–era barn with massive H-frame brace, 13¹/₄ in. wide, that spans full width of post and is attached at both ends with three pegs. Hard-pine anchorbeam of 17-in. depth received into post with diminished haunch and joint secured with three pegs (each of 1-in. diameter or less) and double wedges. Tenons extend 14 in. with round contour typical of most soft pine anchorbeams. Most hard pine anchorbeams have squarish tenons. Note empty post mortise, which indicates former existence of purlin brace that attached below anchorbeam.

and better quality craftsmanship. Certain later barns in this era have some of these attributes to lesser degrees. In general, barns built between 1790 to 1815 have somewhat more narrow naves and H-frame braces, shorter extended anchorbeam tenons, more moderately pitched roofs, side walls that are 12–18 ft. high, and *verdiepingh*s that are 8–12 ft. or more; in addition, the quality of craftsmanship is increasingly sacrificed. In summary, the more one observes these various conditions the more one becomes conscious of the total fabric in which barns were fashioned, which affords a better sense of the time frame in which a particular barn may have been built.

There are a number of barns from the pre-Revolutionary War era that are very good examples of the use of the scribe rule method. The earliest extant New World Dutch barn appears to be the Bull barn in Orange County, New York, and its characteristics can give us a sense of how H-frames and certain dimensions appeared in a specific barn in the early eighteenth century. Only the Bull barn's H-frames and purlin plates are original, as its side aisles and roof were replaced about 1790. The original part was dated 1725 by means of dendrochronology.[32] It is of three-bay construction, and the nave is (a surprisingly narrow) 22 ft. wide. The barn length is 40 ft. This length is curious in that it is consistent with the 10-ft. length increments noted in seventeenth-century barns and house barns. All timbering is oak. Inner anchorbeams are 10 by 16 in. with 12-in. tenon extensions. Their union with posts are triple-pegged and double-wedged with diminished haunched shoulders. The *verdiepingh* is a low 54 in. All posts have offset raising holes and the purlin braces were originally joined with lapped half-dovetail tenons that attached several inches above the anchorbeams.

The Teller-Schermerhorn barn (depicted in Fitchen Plate 15) was a possible pre-1725 barn that had an exceptionally steep roof with a very high peak and quite low side walls. Its traits are described in Appendix C after barn no. 37. The Van Bergen barn was another early barn, built about 1730[33] (see Appendix C, barn no. 37). Five other pre-Revolutionary barns include the Verplanck–Van Wyck barn (Appendix C, barn no. 2), the Skinkle barn (no. 10), the Van Alstyne barn (no. 11), the Wemple barn (no. 32), and the Nieuwkerk barn (no. 42).

I wrote an article that delineated the traits that appeared to establish some twenty-six barns (several were remnant barns) in the pre-Revolutionary War era in Ulster County, New York (nineteen barns), and Bergen County, New Jersey, and adjacent Rockland County, New York (seven barns).[34] These characteristics were seen to varying degrees, and included the unique major and minor rafter system, where large (major) hewn rafters alternate with round pole (minor) rafters and a four-sided ridge beam; upper purlin plates and collar ties also appear (see Illus. 12).

32. This method of dating and its present state of development is largely attributed to A. E. Douglas, who first worked in this field in 1905. For an excellent review of his work and a general history and the methodology employed, see M. G. L. Baille, *Tree-Ring Dating and Archaeology* (Chicago: Univ. of Chicago Press, 1982).

33. See Greg Huber, "The Van Bergen Barn at Old Catskill," *Greene County Historical Journal* 20, no. 3 (fall 1996): 23–27.

34. Gregory D. Huber, "Framing Techniques as Clues to Dating in Certain Pre-Revolutionary Dutch Barns: Major and Minor Rafter Systems, Lapped Dovetail Joinery, Verdiepinghs, and Other Traits," *Material Culture* 29, no. 2 (summer 1997): 1–42. A unique and important pre-Revolutionary Dutch barn in Ulster County, New York, southwest of Marble-town that does not fit precisely in this category has a variant major and minor rafter system that has large hewn rafters above the single purlin plate (per side) and noticeably smaller, fully hewn rafters below the plate. All H-frame and purlin braces and nongable wall collar ties (now gone) have lapped half-dovetail joinery, but there is no ridgebeam nor any cup marks (marriage marks), and there is a 72-in. *verdiepingh*. The roof was never changed and the circa 1760 barn has classic proportions. This barn was built by timber framers who were probably closely associated with builders who built and erected the pre-Revolutionary barns with major and minor rafter systems.

Illus. 12. Barn south of Saugerties, New York. Major and minor rafter system that includes ridgebeam at roof peak and collar ties that support upper purlin plate. Three-bay construction with 26-ft.-wide nave and low side-wall height of $9^1/_2$ ft. Dimensions include $45^1/_2$-ft. gable wall and $35^1/_2$-ft. side wall. Circa 1765.

Also seen in all the barns is the rare lapped half-dovetail joinery in differing degrees in H-frame and purlin braces (Illus. 13), cup (oval-shaped) marriage marks (in eleven barns), short *verdiepingh*s (in all barns)[35] (Illus. 14). Long purlin braces attach 20 to 40 in. below the anchorbeam soffits in Ulster County barns and 13 to 17 in. below in Bergen and Rockland County barns. This general scheme is seen in barn no. 42 (Appendix C) and was probably present in barn no. 39, dated 1758. Three Ulster County study barns were dated 1750 and 1766 twice, which initially helped to substantiate this group as pre-Revolutionary. These traits, taken as a whole, were only seen during the scribe rule era and are found nowhere else in the entire Dutch barn realm, the only exception being a Greene County, New York, barn (circa 1745).

Exterior dimensions of seven nonextant barns at Dutch homesteads in Brooklyn, New York, are cited in a 1796 tax list presented in Rosalie

35. A few instances of this term can be found in contracts cited in Zantkuyl, "Netherlands Townhouse," pp. 143–60. This is an early-seventeenth-century Dutch term to denote the extension of H-frame post between the top of the anchorbeam and the bottom of the purlin plate. I reintroduced this term to architectural historians in the fall of 1991 to emphasize its importance in dating. *Verdiepingh* is also a modern Dutch word for story or floor.

Illus. 13. Barn north of Saugerties in Ulster County, New York. This rare two-bay barn (later changed to a Dutch-Anglo form) was built in the Ulster County pre–Revolutionary War–era tradition, with lapped half-dovetail joinery. Purlin braces uniquely attach both just above and just below the anchorbeam on same H-frame post. Lapped joinery also seen in H-frame braces. Circa 1760.

Bailey's book *Pre-Revolutionary Dutch Houses and Families in Northern New Jersey and Southern New York*.[36] The dimensions of these barns (all of which are from the scribe rule era) in feet are as follows: 48 x 52, 44 x 42, 40 x 56 and 36 x 46 (two at the same homestead), 36 x 48, 44 x 36, and 44 x 30. It cannot be stated with certainty what dimensions refer to either lengths or widths, but the barns with numbers in the thirties most likely indicate a three-bay barn. There is nothing remarkable about these dimensions, as many later square rule barns assume these general proportions.

The Square Rule Method—Post-1815.

The Northeast was experiencing tremendous cultural and economic changes starting about 1810 to 1820.[37] Mechanization was beginning to

---

36. Rosalie F. Bailey, *Pre-Revolutionary Dutch Houses*.

37. Andrew Hill Clark, "Suggestions for the Geographical Study of Agricultural Change in the United States, 1790–1840," *Agricultural History* 46, no. 1 (Jan. 1972). See also John H. Liehard, "The Rate of Technological Improvement Before and After the 1830s," *Technology and Culture* 20, no. 3 (July 1979).

Illus. 14. Barn near Hurley in Ulster County, New York. Short (54 in.) *verdiepingh* or extension of H-frame post above anchorbeam. Long purlin braces attach below anchorbeam (out of view). View of minor round pole rafters with major rafters in extreme upper corners. One anchorbeam has initials and is dated, "AHM 1766." This barn is described in Appendix C (barn 42). AHM (Dutch): stands for "in the year of our Lord made."

alter the lives of most people. In response to these changes, barn technology saw fundamental modifications both in a micro sense, such as how timbers were cut and joined, and in a macro sense, such as changes in sidewall height, roof pitch, bent framing, and access mode.

Dutch barn framers started to cut timbers and unite them so that, for example, all corresponding H-frame elements were interchangeable among all the bents, and as a result marriage marks were often unnecessary and therefore frequently absent. This new method greatly accelerated the production of barns and reflected the speed with which life was proceeding in the first third of the nineteenth century. Braces were let into joined timbers with wide shoulders. Anchorbeams were always joined to posts with the square shoulder method.

In the transitional phase between the scribe rule and square rule eras, apparently certain timbers in individual barns were joined by the scribe method while other timbers were joined by the square method. The scribe method was much more labor intensive. Some scribe rule barns were probably built as late as the 1820s and perhaps beyond. It is important to understand that particular areas may have seen certain barns built with the square rule method as early as 1800 to 1810.

Many of the pure hybrid barns were of this era. The use of round pole and milled rafters was more common in the 1820s and 1830s. Milled or sawn braces became the rule in post-1820 barns.

Compared to the late part of the scribe rule era, and possibly depending on the area, anchorbeams were increasingly made with smaller dimensions (2 to 4 in. shorter). Tenons often extended less or occasionally not at all. Naves and H-frame braces were smaller. Side-wall heights were taller on average. *Verdiepingh*s were 10 to 18 ft. high. In Dutch-Anglo barns certain bents often had low positioned tie beams (anchorbeams) that prevented wagons moving from gable to gable wall. However, certain fairly exceptional post-1815 barns could assume at least some dimensions normally seen in pre-1790 barns.

During the scribe and square rule eras, New York barns were, on average, larger than barns in New Jersey, especially in Bergen County. In addition, barns in Bergen and adjacent Rockland Counties from any era had short side walls (6 to $10^1/_2$ ft. high); *verdiepingh*s were 2 to $4^1/_2$ ft. long, and purlin braces attached just above or below the anchor beams.

The Dutch barn building tradition lasted approximately two hundred years, ending about 1840. The barn form, based primarily on medieval farming practices, became outmoded because of forces brought on mostly by the Industrial Revolution. Dutch barns consequently started to assume certain traits of the English barn (with its side entry), while still maintaining their primary diagnostic feature—internalized posts.

REGIONALISMS

One of the most important aspects of understanding why Dutch barns were built in particular ways involves the concept of regionalisms.[38] A regionalism is generally defined as a particular barn characteristic that is seen to a certain degree within a certain geographic area. This characteristic may infrequently, rarely, or never be seen in other areas. Regionalisms developed out of certain perceived localized needs, and initially ideas spread and certain builders or farmers used them. However, these ideas spread only so far. Regionalisms can be found in a quite narrow range, as little as two to four miles in the case of Albany County, New York, where four barns have distinctive and identical anchorbeam tenon

---

38. Greg Huber, "Regionalisms in Dutch Barns: A Possibility for Future Subtyping," *Dutch Barn Research Journal* 1 and 2 (1991 and 1992): 78–87.

contours that were probably fashioned by the same builder. Or they can be found in an area as broad as an entire state, as in New Jersey, where only three—or four-bay barns are seen. The following subsections present examples of regionalisms.

New York

In Montgomery County, many barns have gable wall H-frame posts, whose wider dimension is parallel to the same wall that allows for a wider surface at its top for the joining of an upper tie beam and a purlin plate. A variation of the *kopbalk* form may be used in some of these joints. Normally, the post's wider dimension is parallel to the side walls.

In Schoharie County, almost all barns have only one gable-wall wagon entry. Several barns have 25-ft. naves and 45-ft. gable walls with 10-ft. side aisles.

Barns in the Mohawk and Schoharie valleys, and to some extent in the upper Hudson River valley, have mortises in gable wall anchorbeams (at either one or two gable walls) for insertion of pentice arms. In these barns, built-in ladders are joined to H-frame posts. Wooden pintles for wooden threshing floor door hinges are recessed into door posts. Double raising holes are fairly often seen in each H-frame post. Anchorbeams' extended tenons quite often have no wedges. A median floor sill receives threshing floor planks that are half the width of the nave. Two or three transverse side-aisle ties join to longitudinal ties between adjacent H-frame posts. Wall plates are grooved to receive tenons of rafter ends (see Dwg. 10A, B, and F).

In Ulster County barns, pentice arms appear as sapling poles extending from the first inner anchorbeam over the top of the gable wall anchorbeam and then to the exterior by about 4 ft. Wooden pintles for wooden threshing floor door hinges appear on the top surface (not recessed) of door posts. In this county, there are U-barns in which the last bay is in dirt, as are the side aisles that combine to form the letter U. This arrangement is ostensibly for the stabling of animals. In these barns, the last inner-bent often has double tie beams and single height doors that closely resemble the lower half of the threshing floor doors. As noted earlier, a number of barns have several identifying traits such as lapped half-dovetail joinery and major and minor rafter systems that indicate a pre-Revolutionary War-era date of erection.

Several barns in Rensselaer County have anchorbeams with recessed upper corners that flank the middle bay for positioning of a plank floor for hay wagons to traverse from an original side-wall opening. One barn in

Greene County also has this trait. Two barns have the unique original feature of an elevated area (like house shed dormers) on one roof slope for accommodating loaded hay wagons to enter through the original side wall.

New Jersey

In Bergen County, barns tend to have narrow naves that are 18 to 22 ft. wide (rarely more than this). *Verdiepingh*s are consistently short, in the 22- to 55-in. range. Purlin braces consistently attach just above or, more often, below the anchorbeams. Longitudinal ties are uniquely half lapped to H-frame posts. Side-wall heights are from 6 to 10 ft. Raising holes are not often seen. (These traits are nearly identical to barns found in adjacent Rockland County, New York.)

In central New Jersey, a number of barns have notches that are normally angled at the bottom of the inner face of H-frame posts to receive manger boards. This trait is widely seen in Monmouth County and occasionally in Somerset County. Threshing floor door posts have flared sections at approximately their bottom 3 ft. that are slotted, ostensibly for insertion of boards either to keep out some farm animals or perhaps to contain threshed grain or both. These posts appear in several Monmouth County barns. Upper tie beams (about 12 to 18 in. below the H-frame post tops) appear at every bent in several barns.

The most interesting aspect of New Jersey barns is that only three- and four-bay ones were constructed, and only one two-bay nonextant barn is known. This may be because there was less agricultural acreage under cultivation at certain farms, necessitating smaller barns that stored smaller amounts of crops. A specific trait of New Jersey barns is that they were never constructed of softwood timbers, with the single exception of a Monmouth County barn with purlin plates of probable hard pine.

There are dozens of classic barns in both the northeastern and central parts of the state that underwent transformations in the mid-nineteenth century that resulted in a Dutch-Anglo form. Original roofs and side aisles were removed and then new side bays were erected. New roofs were then reoriented 90 degrees so that the main wagon entries were then on the side walls in English style. There are several variations of this Dutch-Anglo form. Except in Ulster County (rarely) and in Rockland County, these barn roof changes almost never occurred in New York, possibly because barns were bigger there on average and their storage capacities were adequate.[39]

39. Gregory D. Huber, "Ninety-Degree Roof Rotations in New Jersey Dutch Barns," *Material Culture* 31, no. 1 (spring 1999): 1–20.

About a dozen barns in the central and western central part of the state have gunstock posts or flared sections at their tops that receive both purlin plates and upper tie beams. What influence this was derived from is difficult to determine. Only one or two New York barns have posts with slight flares.

There are a number of true hybrid barns without basements. Most were built in the early nineteenth century. Four three-bay barns in Monmouth County are of the scribe rule era, built 1800 to 1810, with original side entrances. The H-frames are oriented parallel to the side walls. Almost uniquely, the end bent posts rise above the purlin plates by about one foot, allowing framing of the side walls to occur. Curiously, all inner anchorbeams are uniquely joined to their posts with only one peg, which suggests the same builder may have erected them. Two other three-bay barns in Somerset County have side entrances and bents that flank the widened middle bays, each with double anchorbeams that are oriented parallel to the gable walls. One is dated 1837, and both barns have hewn rafters.

Anchorbeams and Geographic Distribution of Wood Species

Anchorbeams are the structural members with the greatest cross-sectional dimensions, and they render the best glimpse into the size of original trees in the primordial forest from which Dutch barn timbers came. They also reflect in general a major species of tree in the local original forest cover.

Anchorbeams can vary in depth from barn to barn from about 10 or 12 in. to 25 in. Gable wall ones are consistently smaller in a given barn by 2 to 4 in. Occasionally, inner anchorbeams can vary from a few to several inches in height in particular barns. The greatest average-sized inner anchorbeams probably appear in the Schoharie and Mohawk River valleys and average about 18 in. in depth. The majority are of white pine (*Pinus strobus*), which reflects the lush primeval forest cover. Most have rounded tenons. In Albany County pitch pine (*Pinus rigida*) is more often found, and anchorbeams are perhaps one to 3 in. shorter and often have squarish tenons. Tenon contours seem to be related to annual growth rings of wood and to the transition from fast growing spring cells to slower growing summer cells.[40] In hard pines the transition is abrupt, leaving wood splintery and therefore difficult to cut, and tenons are often left squarish. In soft or white pines the transition is gradual, leaving wood smooth and

40. See Greg Huber, "Dutch Barn Wood Species" *Timber Framing*, no. 46 (Dec. 1997): 8–11.

therefore easy to cut, and tenons are most often left round. Basswood *(Tilia americana-?)* was used infrequently, which is fortunate because this wood is almost always extensively worm eaten with powder post beetle.

There was a transition in the primeval forest cover in the mid-Hudson River valley in Greene and northern Ulster Counties on the west and Rensselaer and Columbia Counties on the east. Going south, pine started to give way to oak *(Quercus spp.)*.[41] Many barns in this region have the stronger oak for H-frame posts and bigger pine for anchorbeams. This mixture of timber species can be seen in the upcountry (defined as the Mohawk and Schoharie River Valleys and the west side of the upper Hudson River Valley) but is less frequent.

In most of Dutchess County and the southern two-thirds of Ulster County, oak is almost always found and anchorbeams average 14 to 17 in. in depth. Tenon contours are often squarish, and this is reflected in the abrupt transition from early to late wood, leaving wood splintery and thus making it generally difficult to cut on the round.

In New Jersey, oak comprises 80 to 90 percent of barns; anchorbeam depth in the central part of the state is from 15 to 18 in., and tenons are often squarish with clipped corners. (See Illus. 15). Several barns with oak anchorbeams have tenons that are rounded. Perhaps ten to twelve barns have anchorbeams over 20 in. in depth, and one barn has one beam with a $24^{1}/_{2}$-in. depth.

Tuliptree *(Liriodendron tulipifera)* anchorbeams appear in a dozen or more barns in New Jersey, averaging 16 to 18 in. in depth. One barn in Monmouth County has an anchorbeam depth of 25 in., the greatest depth of any barn in either state. A barn in Bergen County had a tulipwood anchorbeam that was 18 in. in depth. Wood transition is gradual, but most tenons are squarish perhaps reflecting a cultural copying of neighboring oak barns. Chestnut *(Castanea americana)* and a few other timber types are occasionally found in some barns.

Wood species used in rafters, floors, and sills have not been closely examined but reflect in general the species used in the H-frames, connecting ties and wall framing.

It should be noted that occasionally double anchorbeams with fully extended tenons appear on one bent in particular barns. The anchorbeams are not generally large and are used in special situations such as in U-barns or side wall entrance Dutch-Anglo barns.

41. For an excellent treatise on primeval forest types in New York and New Jersey, see E. Lucy Braun, *Deciduous Forests of Eastern North America* (New York: Hafner Press, Div. of Macmillan, 1950).

Illus. 15. Barn near Hillsborough, New Jersey. Anchorbeam tenon extends with square contour as is typical in oak construction.

Two Important Functional Features of the Barns

Two major aspects of Dutch barns that Fitchen did not address involved conspicuous constructional traits that were associated with obtaining and storing seed from the grains Dutch farmers harvested from their fields. The first aspect was the threshing floor, on which the seed was separated from the chaff of the grain, and the second was granary rooms, which were used to store the seed.

Threshing Floors

The threshing floor occupied the entire width and length of the center aisle, the full area of which varied considerably from barn to barn. The floor was composed of planks that averaged between 2 and 3 in. in thickness and could be up to 6 in. thick, as was the case in the Wemple barn. These great thicknesses were necessary because of the heavy loaded hay wagons that traversed the floor. A fully original threshing floor is quite rare. The disposition of the planks assumed three basic types: the first involved planks that spanned the entire width of the floor; the second involved the use of an exposed median floor sill that ran the entire length of the barn and had undersquinted recesses or angles that allowed for tight fits with the angled ends of planks that stretched half the width of the nave; the last type saw planks simply butt up against each other in various positions at or near the axial midpoint of the floor. The planks were normally from 8 or 10 in., to up to nearly 2 ft. wide. Most barns had planks secured to the sill system with pegs. Nails were also used.

Threshing itself was performed on the floor. Probably in early times, and then even up to the mid-nineteenth century, this process was accomplished with a flail or two-part wooden stick-like tool that beat the grain, causing the separation of the seed and the chaff to occur. Another method involved a horizontally placed conical block studded with dozens of pegs that was connected to a wooden vertical pole attached to an anchorbeam. Horses were tethered to the whole contrivance. The horse trod a circular path on the floor and the pegs crushed the grain, thus effecting the separation. Later, the mass of seed and chaff was separated by a winnower or tray-like device on windy days, ostensibly on the floor. The whole was thrown into the air, the heavier seed fell back into the tray, and the lighter chaff was blown away to the side.

Granary Rooms

Several Dutch barns have their original granary rooms intact. These rooms occupy the full side aisle of a bay adjacent to a gable wall and have a ceiling height of about 7 ft. All four walls are sheathed with horizontal boards up to 16 in. wide, and the ceiling is similarly formed with boards. An entry door was constructed of vertical boards in front and horizontal battens on the reverse side, which swung on wrought Dutch hinges with typical round nail pads (pancake disks). These rooms are partitioned into several grain bins. Two outstanding examples exist, one in a Dutchess County barn and the other in a Montgomery County barn. It is not known if granary rooms were always part of the barns' original fabric.

Rebuilding and Later Reconstruction

Very few barns retain most of their original timbering and original unbroken walls. Changes to the original core structure have been going on since almost the very beginning of Dutch building practices. For example, there is a contract from April 1661 for the repair and lengthening of the barn of Jan Barentsen Wemp in the colony of Rensselaerswyck. The contractor was to lay new sills on one side and replace "old" rafters as needed.

The barn was to be lengthened 15 ft. by making two or three bents at the option of the employer.[42]

Fundamental changes in agricultural economies, especially during the Industrial Revolution, dictated structural modifications in timber layout that allowed for new and better access. As mentioned above, many original New Jersey barns had new roofs reoriented 90 degrees. Moreover, two barns retained their basic true form layout but their roofs were raised by means of either short beams that suspended the rafters by perhaps 3 to 4 ft. from the purlin plates or by superimposing newer and higher purlin plates over the original plates.

Certain barns in both Somerset and Bergen Counties apparently proved inadequate in size or proportions and were completely disassembled. In these cases, the original anchorbeams were reincorporated into new H-frames in new bigger barns.

Ulster County saw an extensive tradition of modification of roofs of pre-Revolutionary barns after about 1830. This modification was effected by splicing new lengths of timber onto the original H-frame posts or in one case by reorienting a new roof 90 degrees. As in the manner of many New Jersey barns, the disassembling of the entire barn structure occasionally occurred, and timbers were recycled into new barns that reflected the objectives of owners in new agricultural climates in the 1830s to 1860s.

These methods are only a few of the procedures that were used. Many more barns were modified in other ways at the whims of their owners.

Hay Barracks

One of the most interesting aspects of rebuilding involves the recycling of parts of previously used hay barracks. These barracks were small accessory farm structures with four, five, or six posts that had as many sides, respectively. Most often four posts were used. They measured about 15 to 20 ft. on each side and anywhere from about 20 ft. to more than 40 ft. high. They had adjustable roofs and were used for the storage of surplus crops. Some farms had two or more barracks. Contracts from the seventeenth century indicate their use then.[43] The posts were often made of strong and durable oak, and the roof plates were of lighter pine. A number of barns have these barrack parts incorporated into their structure; this practice seemed to have occurred particularly in Albany and Ulster Counties. The

42. Early Records of the City of Albany and the Colony of Rensselaerswyck, 1660–1696 (Albany, 1918), vol. 3, p. 63.

43. Early Records of the City of Albany and the Colony of Rensselaerswyck, 1660–1696 (Albany, 1918), vol. 3, pp. 346, 508, 509.

single most outstanding example of this recycling habit involved four pine roof plates and five oak poles found in an Albany County barn, circa 1815, that were all reused as side-wall posts. The use of hay barracks continued, particularly late into the mid-twentieth century, in central and western New Jersey.[44]

Character and Future

Dutch barns are indeed of noble proportions, as John Fitchen so convincingly conveyed to his readers. This must have been especially true of the very early barns such as the Teller-Schermerhorn barn (discussed after barn no. 37 in Appendix C), which had the single most outstanding roofline. This barn's very low side walls and very high peak evoke an awareness of the spirit in which these barns were constructed and erected. It is noteworthy that although these barns have no pretense whatsoever at ornamentation, their proportions elicit such strong reactions from so many people. One gets a genuine feeling of the protection that these roofs afforded.

As if the Dutch barn roof were not impressive enough, the anchor-beams inside, up to 2 feet thick—the showpieces of these barns—reveal the industry of the early builders and reflect the luxuriant growth of the primeval forest. The message is clear and forthright: these people, the wood artificers and farmers alike, meant business. It was their business to provide for themselves, their families, and a new nation. The nation's barn builders played a pivotal role in permitting a wild, untamed land to be transformed into a workable environment that provided the basic requirements of a newly settled people. Dutch barns were a testimonial to those ends. These barns bespeak a quiet dignity, and their structure reflects the individuality of the people who built and used them. It is to John Fitchen's lasting credit that he was the first to speak of them in the scholarly and eloquent way he did.

It was inevitable that at the close of the twentieth century, because of neglect and progress, the disappearance of the Dutch barn would be in full swing. Out of the fifty to one hundred thousand Dutch barns that originally existed, perhaps only one percent are still standing. There are several museum barns that the general public can freely visit, and which are well worth visiting. With diligent effort, the interested and dedicated student can find many more barns that still dot the Dutch American landscape.

44. Greg Huber, "Remnant Hay Barracks in New York and New Jersey and Conversations about Their Use," *Dutch Barn Research Journal* 3 and 4 (1993 and 1994): 76–80.

Time is of the essence, however, because the Dutch barn will probably be decimated in the next twenty-five years. It is my hope that this new edition of Fitchen's original work will stimulate people to do what Eric Sloane once so aptly advised: "To see where others only look." The forms and timbers of these barns contain messages that come from a forgotten past and can be read by anyone who takes the time.

Dutch Barn Museums

Many new Dutch barn museums have been opened since Fitchen's book appeared in 1968. Following is a partial listing. Visitors can record certain features and begin to make comparisons among the barns they see.

New York State

Montgomery County. This county is home to two Dutch barn museums. The first, the Windfall barn in Saltspringville (circa 1800) has four bays, pine anchorbeams more than 20 in. deep, exterior dimensions of 46 x 41 ft., and *verdiepingh* about 15 ft. The second, Fort Klock in Saint Johnsville (circa 1795), has four bays, unusual side-by-side purlin braces, unusual marriage marks, and H-frame posts at gable walls standing 90 degrees from normal orientation. This barn is relocated from another site in Montgomery County.

Albany County. A barn (circa 1795) located at the Old Songs Association at Altamont Fairgrounds, Altamont, has four bays, anchorbeams close to 20 in. deep, pine timbers, and gable wall H-frame posts oriented 90 degrees from the norm. This barn was relocated in 1994 from Minden in Montgomery County.

Schoharie County. The Old Stone Fort Museum in Schoharie houses the Schaeffer Ingold barn (circa 1790). This barn has four bays, 16-in.-high pine anchorbeams, oak H-frame posts, and dimensions of $45^1/_2$ x $45^1/_2$ ft. There is a 25-ft. nave, a *verdiepingh* of 8 ft., a 13-ft. 3-in.-high side wall, anchorbeams $12^1/_2$-ft. from top to floor, ten pairs of hewn rafters, and a median floor sill. It has double raising holes per H-frame post. It has been relocated $1^1/_2$ miles north of its original location and now stands above the Village of Schoharie. There are recycled timbers from a previous barn in its sill system.

Greene County. The Bronck Museum is located at the Greene County Historical Association in Coxsackie. For a description of this barn, see Appendix C, barn no. 38.

Washington County. The Slate Museum barn, in Granville off Route

22, contains distinctive anchorbeam tenons. This barn was relocated from Albany County off Route 9W near Ravena.

Orange County. The Bull barn (circa 1725 original part; circa 1790 later part), located at the Old Stone House Association in Campbell Hall, is open by appointment only. This barn has three bays, dimensions of 44 x 40 ft., a 22 foot nave, and oak timbering, of which only the H-frames and purlin plates are original. The kingposts, ridgebeam, and both side aisles were introduced later. The barn also contains offset raising holes.

Rockland County. The Post/Sterbenz barn (circa 1810) in Clarkstown was relocated from Chestnut Ridge in 1998. The only surviving true-form barn in the county, the Post/Sterbenz barn has three bays, dimensions of 36 x 30 ft., oak timbers, and side walls that are only $9^{1}/_{2}$ ft. high. Its anchorbeam tenons extend and are wedged, with 2-foot scribe marks. There are lapped dovetail braces in the side walls, and the nave is 18 ft. wide. There are no raising holes in this barn.

Westchester County. The longest three-bay barn known (50 ft.) is located at Philipsburg Manor north of Tarrytown. In 1982 this possible pre-Revolutionary War barn replaced the original museum barn, which burned. The new barn was relocated from near Guilderland in Albany County. It is characterized by very large anchorbeams.

Long Island. At Bethpage Historic Village in Bethpage, there is a Dutch barn (Appendix C, barn no. 33.) that at the time of publication was not officially open to the public.

New Jersey

Bergen County. The Wortendyke barn (circa 1790 and possibly earlier), located at the county's Department of Parks in Park Ridge, is a three-bay barn that became a museum in 1977. It has classic proportions, with the lowest side walls of any Dutch barn (6 ft.). The barn is characterized by much tulipwood timbering, dimensions of $45^{1}/_{2}$ x $37^{1}/_{3}$ ft., inner anchorbeams of 14 x 11 in., no raising holes, and a *verdiepingh* of $21^{1}/_{2}$ in., the shortest in any Dutch barn. Bergen County is also home to the Tice/Hopper barn (circa 1800), located at the Hopper Goetschius House Museum in Upper Saddle River. This barn has three bays and oak timbering, and was relocated in 1989 from a site less than one mile away, where it was in nonoriginal Dutch-Anglo form (thus, it is probable that only the H-frames are original in the newly constructed barn).

Monmouth County. The Longstreet Museum in Holmdel houses a four-bay barn with original woodshakes with wrought nails on one wall, and notches at the bottom of H-frame posts for attachment of manger boards. The barn contains a number of recycled timbers, but the rafters were dendrodated to 1792. A nearby corn crib has tie beams with extended tenons, a condition that is seen at one or two other homesteads in this county.

INQUIRIES

Some readers may have questions, thoughts, and opinions about the history, construction, and preservation of Dutch barns or ideas presented in this book. Others may have thoughts about other ethnic barn styles, such as Pennsylvania forebay, English, and swing-beam types, or about Dutch houses (or other house types) and details of their diverse constructional modes in both New York and New Jersey. Please address correspondence to Gregory D. Huber in care of the Huguenot Historical Society, 18 Broadhead Ave., New Paltz, New York 12561–1403.

The New World Dutch Barn

Historical Introduction

THE DUTCH BARNS of New York were built generally in the era before the Revolutionary War changed the status of the region from that of a colony to that of a state. The eastern part of this region (particularly certain locations at intervals along the chief rivers—the Hudson, the Mohawk, and Schoharie Creek) was the locale for a generation or two of earliest settlement, and it was here that the Dutch established themselves. As these areas became more populous, the forests and the wilderness away from the navigable streams saw the gradual arrival of more Dutch, as well as other hardy pioneers. From New England, and particularly from Connecticut, came ever-increasing numbers of English settlers. Throughout the seventeenth century there was a scattering of Danes and Scots and Scotch-Irish, along with various categories of Frenchmen, but very few Norwegians and Swedes. The Germans generally avoided settlement in what was to become the colony of New York, except for the special case of the Palatines. These persecuted Europeans, driven out of their Rhenish homelands, had been given asylum first in Holland, then in England. Here they were offered tenant lands and essential food allowances to get them started in the New World, first in 1709.

Notwithstanding all this polyglot immigration, it was the Dutch who were first on the scene, and in the largest numbers. It was their culture that took root and that imposed an influence on the area that was not only substantial at the time but continued to be pervasive for many generations to come. Particularly, this was true with respect to trade and commerce, to landholdings, and to agricultural practices. Above all, Dutch husbandry was the model and standard throughout the countryside, and Dutch barns came to be proverbial.

In view of this preeminence it is strange that so little is known about these barns.[1] But perhaps this is not so remarkable after all. Barns have always had a poor press, so to speak; they have not been regarded

1

as fit subjects for historical investigation and publication.[2] It is only in recent times, and only in northern Europe, that barns have been systematically studied and recorded.[3] Outside of that area, although agricultural pursuits may have been of concern for a long time to many, including experimenters, innovators, and the developers of improved methods and practices of farming, the structure and the erectional procedures of the barns themselves have remained almost completely without articulate recorders or qualified commentators.[4]

This perennial lack of recognition is the more unaccountable in light of the fact that throughout history barns have been perhaps the most essential buildings to serve man wherever he has tilled the soil and harvested crops. In the Temperate Zone, at least, his very existence has depended on the shelter that barns have afforded to his grain and to his animals during the inclement nongrowing season. An agricultural economy is absolutely dependent on barns. Without means of storage, civilization would surely never have progressed from the stage of nomadic hunting to that of permanently established communities.

In view of the indispensability of barns it is astonishing that they have been the subject of so little public interest, so little professional writing. This is not to say that the entire field of agricultural pursuits and practices has been neglected. Quite the contrary. Even in the distant past, for example, Roman writers produced a considerable body of literature dealing with agriculture, husbandry, and the layout and management of farms and farm estates. But even the most comprehensive and systematic of these Latin treatises—Columela's twelve-volume *Re Rustica*[5]—says nothing about the structure of barns or how they were erected, though it does describe farm buildings in terms of their various uses and accommodations.

Again, we have plans of ancient Egyptian barns and storage buildings, and lists of what they contained, but no description of their actual appearance and certainly no structural or erectional information about them. For Europe, the early ninth-century Plan of St. Gall shows an extensive layout of farm buildings of many sorts clustered around a large monastery, but only in schematic plan view.

Even in modern times, general descriptions of barns are not numerous. Unaccountably, there is no article on barns in the eleventh edition of the *Encyclopædia Britannica*, the edition that is widely regarded as the most scholarly. In architectural literature, too, the subject has received very abbreviated treatment, even though the importance of barns is readily acknowledged. Fairly typical is this nineteenth-century definition: "*Barn:* A building constructed for the reception of certain descriptions of agricultural produce, with the view of protecting them from injury by the weather. A barn, of greater or lesser dimensions, has been considered an indispensable part of all farm buildings [in England] from the earliest times."[6]

One specific reason why the subject of barns as such has not been covered in any systematic, comprehensive way is that, from remote times, barn and farmhouse as often as not have been one and the same building. S. O. Addy, for example, cites many examples, beginning with ancient Greek megarons through Roman to Viking, Frisian, Saxon, Norwegian, Danish, Irish, and Scottish cultures, in which men, animals, and produce were all housed together in one building. Writing in 1898, this author describes and illustrates a number of surviving structures, built in late medieval times, in which a family together with its servants and its farm hands (if any) still lived, ate, and slept under the same roof with oxen and cows, pigs and horses, along with the stored hay and grain and other produce that sustained them all. To this day in certain tradition-bound and isolated rural areas of Scotland and Ireland, of Germany, of eastern Europe, Russia, and elsewhere, this situation still obtains. Use of a single structure had numerous and evident advantages, as Addy points out, although the comfort and privacy of the human household could not be included among those advantages.[7]

In the less-developed rural parts of Scotland and north England (especially Yorkshire) there were still in Addy's day modest buildings in use that housed both people and farm animals, the animals being given twice the amount of space allotted to the people. The buildings themselves were very old, but the activities they housed and the kinds of inhabitants they accommodated had changed not at all over the span of some centuries. This sheltering of people, animals, and provender all under the same roof is still the common practice throughout rural Holland for new farm buildings as well as old.

In the extensive monastic establishments of the medieval period, of course, and later on, on the great manorial estates of Europe where the land was rich and productive, there was considerable differentiation made between structures assigned to human residence, to the housing of cattle and other farm animals, and to the storage of produce. In the case of farms owned and operated by single families, however, the separation of animals and humans did not come about in England and on the Continent—if indeed it ever did—until long after the American colonies became states. Yet this separation was the established pattern on this side of the

Atlantic in the Dutch-inhabited areas from the time of the very first colonial settlers.

It is worth speculating, therefore, on the possible reasons for a development that ran counter to such a firmly rooted and well-nigh universal practice in the settlers' mother country.

At first, along the Mohawk and the Hudson rivers, huge grants of land were made as an incentive to colonization. It started with the Dutch and their patroon system. The Dutch West India Company offered sixteen miles of frontage along a navigable river to the man who would bring and settle thereon fifty souls above the age of fifteen. Later, under the English Governor Dongan, somewhat similar manors of vast extent were granted in these areas, whereon the settler as a tenant farmer was bound to the land and subject to the law of the aristocratic proprietor.

However much they may have been looking for a new life in America, the seventeenth-century settlers inevitably brought with them many of the feudal conditions and relationships of their countries of origin. Most of those who came to settle the northern colonies had been either peasants or village dwellers, and it was natural for them and their proprietors alike, at first, to repeat the familiar pattern of small settlements made up of closely clustered dwellings. This tradition was strongly reinforced in the New World by the necessity for protecting the larger communities within a stockade.

At first glance, then, it would seem that one of the reasons for the New World separation of human living quarters from the barn structure may have resulted from a carry-over of the familiar tradition of Old World village life as it came to be transformed and adjusted, of necessity, to the New World's stringent need for group safety and protection. The early settlers' stockaded villages were the principal collective safeguard against sudden attack from Indians and other hostile raiders. Yet there was no room within the confinement of the palisades for the big barns on whose stored provender the little community depended. The stockade area at Schenectady on the Mohawk River, and at Kingston high on the west bank of the Hudson, recall the early times when safety and survival itself dictated the separation of houses from barns. Even on the less compact, sparsely inhabited manorial estates in the early days of settlement, no tenant colonists were allowed to establish their farms far from the village church, whose bell could warn them of Indian attack.

Attractive though this explanation would seem to be, it is unlikely to have been the primary or even a determining reason for the separation of human habitation from barns. In America, in those early years, there were too few stockaded communities for them to have brought about such a universally accepted practice. Most of the early settlers lived very much alone and isolated from each other. Under these circumstances their only recourse against Indian attack, if time permitted, was to flee and to hide in the forest, from which they crept back later to find the remains of their farmstead in smoldering ruins. Such burnings were all too common for a number of generations.

A more universal cause needs to be sought, therefore, to account for the fact that in colonial New York the farmer and his family never had their living quarters in the barn. It seems likely that this separation resulted from the imperatives of climate and the exigencies of an unfamiliar environment. To meet the challenge of establishing a foothold in the wilderness, the pioneer in New Netherland had too much to do throughout the first few years to bother with the construction of a decent and comfortable dwelling. From many contemporary records it appears that it was the custom not to build any but a temporary hut before seven years had elapsed. Until he had gathered in at least seven harvests the pioneer farmer had his hands and energies fully occupied in combating the wilderness, wresting a few acres of farmland from the forest, and coming to terms with the inhospitable but potentially productive environment. Until he had in fact gained a precarious foothold in this new environment, he could spare no time for the building of a proper house; instead, a temporary hovel of the rudest and most primitive sort had to suffice. Its small cramped dimensions, which permitted rapid construction in the first place, allowed it to be heated in the wintertime without the expenditure of much time and effort on the settler's part in constantly providing its fireplace with great quantities of wood.

So it was that the earliest New World barns took on, from the very beginning, the proper and specific functions of their purpose as independent utilitarian buildings. Employing many of the framing details recalled or copied from those of the mother country, the New World barns none the less conformed to the conditions and circumstances of the new environment. Wood was one resource the early settler had in abundant supply; it was therefore used in more generous dimensions than it had been in the Old World. Specialized craftsmanship on the other hand was in short supply, and its execution took time away from more pressing demands; so the framing was kept as simple as possible, and decoration was omitted altogether. A barn had to be built in part by the farmer's own labor,[8] and certainly from the materials available on his own land; hence bricks, for example (which would have had to be imported from abroad during the early years of settlement) could not be used. The barn had to be built exclusively of timber, for this was the only material that was immediately available and whose cost was in labor alone. The barn had to accommodate and shelter crops that were in some cases (such as corn) different from those raised in Europe. It had to be able to store a vast quantity of hay, and this was invariably done in the way the Dutch had so often done it in Holland; that is, in the great loft where it was supported on scaffolds of poles, so that it was thoroughly ventilated against mildew and rot, and could be dried out without fear of spontaneous combustion. Built by the pioneer colonists in the most convenient location with respect to each man's acreage, the design of these earliest American barns must have been arrived at during the first generation or so of colonization to meet the particular needs and conditions of life in America. Such barns were undoubtedly erected at first by the combined labor of all the able-bodied men of a given settlement. But this kind of corporate labor, so familiar in the Old World and so immediately at hand at the start in the New World, soon disappeared as a normal and customary procedure. The reason is not hard to find.

Even on the vast estates of the seventeenth century, the tenants came to be dispersed as the settlements along the riverbanks increased in numbers and the Indian menace consequently abated. Such dispersal came about from the desire of individual tenants to work the better farmlands, some of which were not immediately adjacent to the main rivers. Moreover, it is highly significant that, right from the start, there had been some settlers who were independent of these feudal conditions: freemen who were owners of their own small holdings and worked for themselves alone. It was the independent freeholder, in fact, with his family-size farm rather than the landed aristocrat with his many thousands of acres, who more and more set the pattern of northern colonial life and established the beginnings of an agricultural economy in New Netherland. By the end of the seventeenth century it was these small independently-owned farms, scattered throughout the eastern region of the colony, that had begun to determine the character—and the destiny—of American life there. The sites of these holdings were no longer compact settlements, and their dispersal consequently deprived the barn-builder of next-door neighbors on whom he could call for a raising. Now he had to summon help from afar.

It is clear, however, that the earliest settlers were the ones who underwent the roughest and most hazardous experiences in facing and overcoming an alien environment. All kinds of unexpected conditions, unforeseen circumstances, and unprecedented dangers confronted them. With a background of only the static, tradition-bound practices of European husbandry, they had to adapt to the new environment quickly, realistically, and unerringly if they were to survive at all. Those who did survive at the start—not without the severest hardships and suffering, it should be said—passed along their painfully learned experience to those who later settled near them. In this manner, after a generation or two, a body of practical knowledge had developed on how to meet the hard conditions of the new environment: what was needed in order to establish a foothold in the wilderness, how to clear the forest, how to protect and sustain life throughout the long and bitter winters, above all how to accomplish with few hands and limited time the much that had to be done. As more and more pioneers set out to establish themselves in the primeval land, these lessons were of the utmost necessity for success, and often for survival itself.

At the start, the land was all wilderness, and none of it came into agricultural production without a prodigious amount of the most time-consuming and strenuous manual labor. Consequently pioneer farms of the late seventeenth and early eighteenth century in colonial New York were small. They might cover a hundred acres; rarely did they achieve two hundred. Only a portion of this acreage ever got into production as tilled land, for among the early independent settlers farming was a one-family operation with the primary aim of achieving self-sufficiency rather than of supplying distant markets.

As though there were not enough to do to establish a pioneer foothold in the wilderness, to develop productive valley and upland farms, to settle early communities along the rivers, the original settlers were constantly faced with the recurring and at times widespread destruction caused by hostile skirmishes, retaliatory raids, and even open warfare. Whether these hostilities were instigated by Indians, by the French, by the English, or by more locally contending parties, the devastation they caused included the burning of some thousands of barns in the eastern Mohawk Valley alone, up to and during the Revolutionary War.

Nevertheless, the energetic work of the early settlers went on. Houses and barns were rebuilt; others were established on the site of newly cleared land. Innumerable sawmills and gristmills were constructed wherever streams provided waterpower. Churches were erected by the cooperative labor of neighbors who were to benefit from them. Sailing ships were built and operated on the rivers; wagons of various sorts were constructed in large numbers when early roads came to re-place Indian trails and drovers' tracks; and all the expedients essential to trade, commerce, and early industry were established in the larger com-munities, invariably fashioned from the inexhaustible supplies of forest timbers.

We are less concerned here with these larger communities. For it was the farm and farm production that were at the center of colonial life dur-ing the generations of pioneering and early settlement. It was here that the strength of early America lay. It was here that hardihood and self-reliance and industry were tested. It was here that a deep-rooted sense of freedom and independence was fostered.

Because farming by its very nature was an individual family enter-prise, much of it entailed isolation except on the Sabbath. This isolation was particularly evident at the start, whenever some hardy pioneer first undertook to settle in the wilderness and went about establishing a homestead there. A clearing had to be discovered or made in the forest, and a rude temporary shelter erected. Because trees did not largely en-cumber them, swamps and periodically inundated bottomlands were usually first to be requisitioned in the production of crops. Indeed, some swampy lowlands even in their wild state produced grasses that could be used as fodder.

In contrast, much of the virgin forest was festooned with vines and creepers that made passage at times almost impossible. From the Indians, however, the early settlers learned to girdle the trees and then to burn the whole tangled mass of vines and undergrowth and brush along with the trees' dying branches. A meager planting of native corn or of Euro-pean seeds was made between the blackened trunks of the erstwhile forest, and this first small crop had to suffice to tide the pioneer and his few domesticated animals over the first winter. Sometimes during that first winter the tall charred trunks themselves were felled, to be rolled or snaked into giant pyres at the edge of the deforested portion of land. Even so there must still come the uprooting and removal, one by one, of innumerable stumps. This was a most time-consuming and onerous pre-requisite to proper plowing, and was only indirectly productive of crops. But it was part of the early settler's battle with the forest, a necessary step in putting the land into effective production.

Along with all this field preparation, the pioneer farmer had to make adequate provision for himself and his animals for the nongrowing season. For in contrast to the European winters those in colonial New York could be bitterly harsh. Ice invariably froze the lakes and clogged the watercourses. Heavy falls of snow burdened roofs and built up on the ground so that sleighs were a necessary means of transport during almost half the year. Wolves and other marauding predators of the forest threatened both the pioneer and his livestock.

Necessarily, the early settler was far from idle during the winter. There were massive amounts of firewood to cut and haul; there were daily chores to carry out, feeding and tending the livestock; there was farm equipment to fashion and repair. He learned, again from the Indians, how to derive food from the forest even in the winter. Year round, in fact, he supplemented his own food supply of smoked beef and salt pork and flour, along with the dried vegetables and nuts and preserved fruits of the summer season, with venison and wild fowl and fish. The inhospitable winters, though, forced both the farmer and his livestock to stay indoors much of the time, and both had to depend largely on the produce of the previous growing season during the months of early twilight.

So it is that the barn was the most essential and indispensable building of the rural homestead, counted on to accommodate and preserve and shelter both animals and crops against freezing cold and deep-drifting snow and howling blizzard.

Obviously then the barn had to be built first, even before a proper dwelling for the farm family came to be erected. At the start the farmer and his servant or sometimes the farmer and his wife were the only ones to take up residence on the farm-to-be. Here they lived at first in the rudest of shelters. Sometimes it was a cellar-like pit lined and floored with timber and roofed with bark and sod laid across stout poles. Sometimes it was a log cabin whose trunks were set vertically like a palisade instead of in the later fashion of squared, horizontally laid logs. In some cases the pioneer lived for awhile at the nearest neighboring farm until the minimum essentials of his future independent existence could be established.

Later, adjunct structures would be added—sheds and pens and hay barracks—to complete the requirements of an established and well-appointed husbandry. But long before a substantial farmhouse made life more comfortable and convenient for the farmer and his family, there had to be a barn.

The first requisite of the pioneer's barn was protection and shelter for the season's crops of hay and corn and flax and other grains. Since there were no silos at that time, these bulky products were stored largely in the cavernous loft, rather than piled up from the floor as in early

English and many continental examples, including certain types of Dutch barns. Here the valuable hay, in particular, was preserved from sun and wind and rain, from mildew and rot at night as well as from the burning heat of the day.

Obviously the barn had to be big, for there was no feedstore near by, no farmers' supply depot in those early days. The pioneer homesteader and his stock had to subsist on what he himself could produce. So at harvest time the barn bulged with provender, to be drawn upon throughout the ensuing months and hopefully to last until a new growing season could replenish the supply. (Even to this day barn interiors are best observed in late April or May because, in the autumn, there is little to see there—certainly none of the barn's structure—but hay.)

Along with this accommodation for the season's full harvest, a second major requirement of the early settler's barn was that it provide protection and shelter for the livestock. During the summer, to be sure, the cows and pigs were allowed to roam the adjacent forest, foraging for their food there, with the farmer going to them once a week with salt and moving among them so that they would know him and not become wild. But the New York winters were cold, and the wolves bold and ravenous when the harsh season set in, so the farmer had to bring his animals indoors to the shelter of their pens and stalls.

These storage requirements, then—for produce of various sorts and for animals—were the primary and essential functions of the early settler's barn. But there were other significant and useful purposes the barn was put to, especially in the summertime and fall. These additional uses related to the performance of active undertakings rather than the provision and maintenance of passive storage.

For example, the large central area of the barn, invariably floored with heavy planking, was used at the appropriate times as a threshing floor. With hand flails during the early generations, much later with horses drawing a heavy wooden roller round and round a central arbor, the grain was threshed in this central space within the barn. Here, too, the grain was winnowed, the process aided by the through draft between the big wagon doors at either end of the barn. Cleaning flax and cornhusking took place here also.

At times during fair days when they were not otherwise occupied, the women used this large free area to spin long threads, to card wool and flax, and to carry on other activities that required a spacious, airy, but sheltered area for their performance.

Tasks that required fire, however, such as dipping candles (a long slow process) or soapmaking did not take place in the barn. The early barns appear to have been without any provision for fireplaces, whether for heating or cooking or the fashioning of iron farm utensils and equipment. It was too dangerous to have a boiling cauldron or a smith's forge in an all-wood building filled with animals and combustible crops.

At festival times the threshing floor served as a general hall that could accommodate many people, young and old, for a husking bee or a barn dance or a frolic.

Outside the barn, fences were important to the early farmer from the start. Fences did not keep out deer or fox or other wild animals, but they did confine the farmer's own cattle and keep them from overrunning his vegetable garden and his orchard. Some early fences were stump fences, the uprooted remains of the forest. Unfortunately these huge ungainly octopuses of exhumed roots, though effective when ranged in a close-set row, cost a prodigious expenditure of the most difficult labor, and so the area they enclosed was kept to an absolute minimum. Snake fences of split rails, traversing the ground in zigzagging lines, were much easier to build and therefore could encompass orchards and some of the farmer's open fields where his horses (and later his sheep) could graze without straying, as his farm prospered and expanded.

At the start, water had to be fetched from a spring. Later, a well was usually dug to serve household and barnyard alike, convenient to both. In many cases rain water was collected from the broad slopes of the barn roof and channeled via eaves-troughs to a barrel at the corner of the barn.

So the barn served in many essential ways throughout the year. To the pioneer farmer himself his barn was the great repository and storehouse of his livelihood; to his farmer neighbors it was the index of his husbandry, the criterion by which they judged his caliber and worth.

A barn that is both spacious and substantially built—and such attributes are pre-eminently those of New York Dutch barns—is able to withstand the winds of change for generations. The early Dutch barns of New York met the conditions of their own time admirably. With surprisingly little need for adjustment those that survive to our time have come to adapt themselves to various shifts in farm economy and to the largely mechanized practices of modern husbandry. This is no small tribute to the superiority of their structure, their layout, and their craftsmanship.

Description

THE OLD DUTCH BARNS of the New World are enduring manifestations of highly accomplished but anonymous craftsmanship. Their characteristics are specific, and many of their features are quite unlike those of any other barns. Their provenance is limited to certain well-defined areas. And the period when they flourished is early, circumscribed, and without revival or repetition.

CHARACTERISTICS

There are many aspects and attributes that distinguish the Dutch barns of America. Some of the more noteworthy of these are the following. First, the exterior.

One. The barns are simple rectangles in plan, roughly square but almost always wider than they are long.

Two. Wagon entrances, at least originally, occurred only at the center of each gable-end. Consequently, there is only one main floor; and in this respect all these barns are unlike subsequent bank barns that have wagon entrances at two different levels.

Three. The original cladding was almost invariably of horizontal weather boarding, which is still extant on a number of barns. A few were shingled on side walls as well as roof; but to date none has been discovered with either vertical siding or board-and-batten.

Four. The height of the side walls is between thirteen and one-half and sixteen feet, with one or two exceptional instances as low as nine feet.

Five. Roofs are invariably of two slopes, always symmetrical, one on each side of the ridge. The average roof pitch is about ten in twelve, though some are flatter, and a few make an angle of about ninety degrees or even less at the peak. Whether up the rake at the gable-ends or along the unbroken horizontal range of the sides, the eaves were built with minimum projection.

Six. These barns are all wood. The only stones employed are the one or two flat blocks set at intervals as support for the sills, to hold them up off the ground. Metal was used most sparingly, since all the timbers were united with all-wood joints, without exception. Even the great wagon doors usually had wooden hinges, and some of these are still operational.

Many of these old barns have been made to look up-to-date with modern clapboarding. So it is the interior that displays their distinctive features most clearly and unequivocally.

Seven. Inside, the barns are invariably three-aisled, with two rows of widely spaced columns separating the middle space or "nave," so to speak, from the "side aisles."

Eight. This central area is about twice the width of each side aisle, and originally it was always floored with thick wooden planking to serve as the threshing floor.

Nine. The most conspicuous features of the interior, and the ones that most readily identify the building as a Dutch barn, are the anchor-beams. These are deep, heavy, transverse timbers that may be as much as twelve by twenty-four inches in section and up to thirty feet or more in length. They stretch from column to column across the threshing floor at roughly half the height of the columns, and they support poles on which a vast amount of hay can be stored. In most cases the big anchor-beams' tenons protrude well beyond the outer face of the columns they penetrate.

Ten. Each anchorbeam is also linked to its columns, right and left, by a diagonal brace, and all these members together form H-frames that divide the interior longitudinally into bays.

Eleven. The usual number of bays is either three or four. Only six or seven examples of five-bay barns, and two of six-bay barns, have been discovered to date.

Twelve. Shoulder- or head-height struts link the columns longitudinally, and other horizontal struts connect the columns to the side walls. There are normally two tiers of the latter, the upper struts meeting the columns at a level above the anchorbeams.

Thirteen. Both rows of columns are capped by a purlin-plate that is stayed by diagonal braces connecting it with the columns.

Fourteen. And finally, widely spaced pairs of rafters make up the simple roof structure that covers a cavernous interior without the aid of any tie-beams or collars.

Contrast with Old World Examples

The characteristics designated above offer sufficient preliminary identification of New World Dutch barns to warrant comparison with their contemporary European examples, particularly those of Holland which might be expected to be the prototypes of the American barns we are discussing.[1] Some of the differences are as follows (NW stands for New World, and OW for Old World):

One. NW Dutch barns are always simple, nearly square rectangles in plan. OW Dutch barns are often of composite shapes.

Two. NW barns are all wood. OW barns make use of varying amounts of visible masonry. At the very least, this is in the form of plastered brick nogging or wattle-and-daub paneling between the studs or wall posts.

Three. NW barns have a complete horizontal framework of sills, not only for the outside walls but also under the columns and the plank flooring. Contemporary OW barns have their columns supported directly on stone plinths, normally without any sill connections; and they have earthen or clay or pebbled floors instead of wooden planking.

Four. Surviving NW Dutch barns have relatively high side walls with straight unbroken eaves. OW Dutch barns often have side walls less than a man's height, with eaves that break up over wagon doors. These low side walls reflect the fact that OW Dutch barns never have an upper tier of transverse struts linking columns to side walls.

Five. NW Dutch barns are roofed exclusively in two symmetrical planes. On the other hand, one or both of the sides of an OW Dutch barn may have roofs that rise in two different slopes. In addition, the ends of OW barns usually terminate with sloping roofs instead of vertical gables.

Six. NW barns never have collars or other rafter-ties. OW barns always do.

Seven. The rafters of NW barns are always pinned together in pairs at the peak: there is never a ridgepole. OW barns almost invariably have a horizontal pole or beam at the ridge.

Eight. NW rafters are always in one piece from ridge to eaves. OW rafters are usually of two or more lengths.

Nine. In NW barns there is always only one purlin for each roof slope. This is the purlin-plate over which the rafters are balanced and from which they receive their major, if not their exclusive vertical support. OW barns frequently have more than one purlin on each slope; and in any case their rafters are supported at a number of points.

Ten. NW barns never have diagonal bracing in the plane of each roof slope. OW barns invariably have this so-called windbracing to a greater or lesser extent.

Eleven. Except for some degree of natural taper in the rafters, all the timbers of NW barns are uniform in cross-sectional dimensions throughout their length, whatever their size may be. OW barns sometimes employ the hewn trunks of trees in an upside-down position, for example, in order to take advantage of an expanding cross section that will furnish additional bearing surface at a column's top.[2]

Twelve. According to the surviving evidence in the buildings themselves, the roofs of NW barns seem not to have been thatched.[3] Thatching was the almost universal covering employed in contemporary OW Dutch barns.

Thirteen. All NW Dutch barns are three-aisled. Those of the OW have one, two, three, four, or five aisles.

Fourteen. Originally, NW Dutch barns had wagon doors exclusively at the gable-ends, and centered. OW Dutch barns often had one or two wagon doors along the side. When they were located at the end of the barn, they were most often placed off-center.

Fifteen. Both the large size and the straightness of the timbers are noteworthy characteristics of NW barns. OW timbers are much smaller and are often somewhat irregular in shape, following the bends of the tree from which they were hewn.

Sixteen. Finally, a major and unique distinction between NW and OW barns, with respect to occupancy, is that OW barns invariably included living quarters for a farm family; surprisingly, the NW barns appear never to have served in this capacity.

So much for a brief look at the distinctive characteristics of New World Dutch barns. Now, some commentary on the probable dates of their erection.

Dating

With the present state of knowledge about early timber construction in America, it is impossible to assign a precise date to the old Dutch barns of this country. It is even difficult to arrive at an accurate notion of their chronology; that is, which surviving barns are earlier, which later. Considerations of the size or length of a barn do not appear to be trustworthy indices of date. On the other hand, geographical location may sometimes be a general clue to dating, in the sense that barns occurring in upland sites, removed from the major river valleys, wagon trails, and drovers' tracks, are likely to have been built later rather than earlier. In this connection it should be noted that, during most of the period when these barns were being built, a western limit to their occurrence was the boundary beyond which the land was reserved to the Indians.

Apparently these early barns were almost invariably built before the farmer's dwelling was erected. The barn had to be there as soon as the land was cleared, as soon as crops were cultivated. A farmer with extensive holdings would often have to have more than one storage barn in this climate of long harsh winters. (Note the two closely adjacent Wemp barns, only about two hundred feet apart, Plate 6.) In the meantime, the farmer and his family would inhabit some form of crude and simple dwelling, either a cellar-like excavation roofed with bark and sod, or a log cabin of squared and chinked timbers.[4] Often, too, in these early years, there were legal difficulties and interminable delays with respect to the establishment of land titles; sometimes these were not settled for a generation or more. During this period of unresolved tenure, the farmer would not risk the expense of building a proper house. But the business of farming had to go on: it was his livelihood. So the barn on which he and his livestock depended had to be built.

The deeds to the land do not record the numbers, size, or disposition of any buildings thereon. It is rarely, if ever, that deeds to real-estate property describe or even mention any buildings on them.[5] Nor do the earliest newspapers mention the erection of any barns. At most, the building of a fort or a courthouse, or perhaps a church or a large mill, was recorded, but never a barn. Contemporary circumstantial accounts of any building's *erection* are simply nonexistent.[6] Even contemporary descriptions of early barns are scarce.

Dates have been found on only four of the New World Dutch barns so far identified. In these few cases where they do exist, the dates are incised on a vertical face of one of the inner anchorbeams, near the center of the span. The earliest date so far discovered is 1758. Another, much later date (1796) is in an adjacent barn on the same farm (Suydam), only one hundred feet or so from the 1758 barn. This second date—chiseled with elegant skill in letters and numerals about five inches high (Dwg. 19)—is in a very large barn that is obviously a rearrangement and reconstruction that made use of timbers from other structures —in fact, from parts of three previous barns on the same property, according to the long-time tenant. Hence the date may well be that of the rebuilding. Apparently it was no more the usual custom to carve the date of construction in an early barn than it was to record its erection in either a legal deed or the popular press. In any event, there are too few carved dates—assuming they are both authentic and contemporaneous— to rely on them for barn-dating generally.

As any architectural historian knows, one of the surest indices of date in the case of medieval churches, whether of wood or of stone, is the character and make-up of their moldings. New World Dutch barns, however, have no moldings whatsoever. The craftsmanship of these structures, though often of very high quality, is completely utilitarian, without any trace of carving or decorative detail.[7]

Where they have survived the covetousness of antique collectors, a few wrought-iron hinges are still extant and in use on the smaller doors of certain barns; and the style and character of these attest to an early date (Plate 49). Furthermore, the all-wood hinges of the big wagon doors—some cut off but still retaining their jamb morticings—are equally indicative of very early date (Plates 47 and 48). So, too, with respect to the hand-forged rose-headed nails that secure the clapboarding in these barns wherever the original siding survives.

Very rarely, one or two of the short diagonal braces connecting anchorbeam to column have been found with curving soffits; but they occur as isolated examples without any apparent motive or comprehensible intention. Only a single barn (South of Germantown, Plate 29) has been discovered where these braces are shaped consistently as short curving members. These unique members are much lighter than most anchorbeam braces, perhaps because the central span here is relatively narrow. This particular barn is probably later than most, judging by other more general characteristics. Except for this one example, however, it is clear that there are too few instances of curves of any sort, in the timber framing of these early barns, to derive from them a clue to the date of the building.

The above considerations reveal some of the difficulties encountered in trying to assign a precise date to any New World Dutch barn. Accurate determination of the date of individual barns, if such ever comes to be made, must be on the basis of a combination of many factors. Probably the surest data will prove to be not from written records that may yet come to light but from internal evidence; that is, on-the-spot interpretation of information presented by the fabric and constitution of the building itself. Useful factors that can assist in the sequential or chronological dating of barns are the various changes that came to be made to them: alterations, repairs and partial rebuildings, obvious re-uses and relocations of some of the timbers, and outright additions. However, previous to any changes that were made after the original completion of the barn, there are various intrinsic features that help to determine relative earliness or lateness of construction. In general, for example, the smaller, shorter, and more numerous the diagonal members that make up the sway-bracing, the later the barn appears to be. Apparently, earlier barns have fewer, longer sway-braces connecting columns and purlin plate (Dwg. 5). Again, the widespread use of hard pine, and probably that of oak, for most of the structural members, may indicate an earlier date than those barns in which timbers of white pine predominate. So, too, the wide spacing of the column bays, as well as the large size and regular spacing of the wall studs, are other characteristics which apparently indicate earlier rather than later construction. In fact, among the most valuable and trustworthy manifestations with respect to dating are certainly the major timbers and their connections. For it seems to be undeniable that those barns are the earliest that utilized the largest beams, displayed the most careful, finished craftsmanship, and incorporated the greatest degree of uniformity in similar members.[8]

In any event, it is probably safe to assert that, in general, the still-surviving Dutch barns of the New World were built during a period of some one hundred years, ending roughly about the time of the Revolutionary War. Supposedly, there are a few barns of this type that still remain from the seventeenth century. The earliest of these is thought to have been built in the 1680's near Leeds. Whether such a remote date can ever be convincingly verified or not, it appears to be certain that all the Dutch barns we are here concerned with were constructed well before 1800. The old barns that were built subsequently followed an entirely different layout and employed a totally different framing system.

PROVENANCE

New World Dutch barns are unique to those areas that were settled by the Holland Dutch (and probably the Palatines); they are utterly different from the so-called Pennsylvania-Dutch barns. Mr. Robert H. Palmiter, Mr. DeVere Card, and the writer have identified some seventy-five New York Dutch barns (mostly still in continuous and active use, though in many cases more or less altered, mutilated, and/or added to) in three principal areas of the eastern part of New York State. These areas are: the Hudson Valley between Poughkeepsie and Albany, the eastern Mohawk Valley, and the Schoharie Valley (see map, facing p. 95). Professor François Bucher has called our attention to some examples in the Princeton area of New Jersey, not unexpected in view of Peter Kalm's description.[9] Undoubtedly there are others yet to be identified in areas settled by the Dutch that we have not yet explored. These areas would include parts of New Jersey, Long Island, and the lower Hudson Valley. Certain concentrations of these barns are to be found to this day in such areas as Middleburg in the Schoharie Valley, the Amsterdam-Fort Plain stretch of the Mohawk Valley, west of Hurley on the west side of the Hudson Valley, and elsewhere.

A few rather late Dutch barns can be found across the St. Lawrence River, north of New York State, in Canada. They are known locally as "Schoharie Barns," and their presence north of the border is to be accounted for by the emigration of Loyalists at the time of the Revolutionary War. Since the principal localities where New World Dutch barns occur are in New York State, however, the present account refers to all examples indiscriminately as either New World or New York Dutch barns, to distinguish them from the Pennsylvania-Dutch, the New England, and other early types of barns.

In spite of their wide geographical distribution (the wider, in effect, because of the difficulty of intercommunication and the isolation of so many of their sites at the time the barns were built), it is astonishing to note how similar these early Dutch barns are, how identical their layout and structural system are in areas as distant from each other as the Mohawk Valley and central New Jersey. All the examples so far identified are far more alike in every respect than any one of them is like a single example of any Old World barn.

What regional variations do occur are both slight and fairly inconsequential. The longest and the most consistently rounded anchorbeam tongues are to be found in the Mohawk Valley (Plates 21 and 22), where white pine is perhaps more frequently employed than elsewhere. Square tongues are somewhat more common in the Schoharie Valley. Only in the Princeton area have barns been found whose original wall cladding is of shingles. There is perhaps greater variation in the width of the central nave or threshing floor throughout the Hudson Valley than elsewhere. However, these are only generalizations that are neither absolute nor particularly significant. The basic similarities, even in the case of details, are remarkably consistent and uniform among all New World Dutch barns, whatever their locale.

Each year, nowadays, a few more of these early barns disappear. There is evidence that as late as a generation ago there may have been three or four times as many Dutch barns in existence as there are now. Disappearance is due to many causes: lightning,[10] arson, perhaps spontaneous combustion, as well as collapse owing to the cutting away of essential timbers or continuing neglect in maintaining the roof surface. But the chief cause that has accelerated their disappearance in recent years is the inexorable march of "progress": notably, the encroachment of suburbs in many formerly rural areas, the creation of new or much wider highways everywhere, and changes in the nature and the practices of farm economy generally. What is remarkable is that so many early Dutch barns have survived at all. It is certainly not any weakness or deficiency in their structural make-up that has brought about their collapse. On the contrary. Granted a reasonable amount of roof maintenance, the surviving examples of these barns have far outlived a great many younger, even quite recently built barns.

A careful and comprehensive investigation of their layout and structure will demonstrate the reasons for their longevity. We will pass at once, therefore, to a description of their ordering, their disposition, and their common attributes.

Specific Description

All New York Dutch barns were laid out as simple rectangles at the start, and were covered by a ROOF *in two symmetrical slopes* (Plates 1, 4, 7, 10, 11, 16, etc.). They were much wider than other contemporary barns[11]—and than most subsequently built barns, in fact—because they were invariably three-aisled within. Where they remain free-standing without any later accretion of attached additions, most of these Dutch barns are recognizable from a distance by their proportions generally, and particularly by the fact that their *width almost always exceeds their length*, and their *height to the ridge is always more than twice the height of their side walls*.

There seems to have been no predetermined standard of ORIENTATION in the case of New York Dutch barns. About as many examples are set with east-west axes as with north-south axes; and there are barns that align with a N.E.-S.W. direction, others with a N.W.-S.E. direction. Apparently, what determined the orientation of each barn were local considerations such as the lay of the land in the immediate vicinity, or the protection afforded by stands of trees, or convenience with respect to access roads.

A small number of early Dutch barns retain considerable portions of their original CLAPBOARDING (e.g., Plates 2, 4, 7, and 10). Apparently this clapboarding was never painted. The wood employed (either white pine or yellow pine) stood up sufficiently well without the need for the coating of red lead that came to be almost universal on barns throughout the state in later times. Over the years, however, this original siding has taken on a darkly weathered patina of age.

Neither the vertical siding nor the board-and-batten cladding of more recent times was used on early Dutch barns in America. With the exception of a few that were originally shingled, the walls of New World Dutch barns were invariably clapboarded. The timber framing of the side walls would have permitted attachment for vertical boarding (with or without batten strips covering the joints) only at the sill and the plate—a distance of about fourteen or fifteen feet in most cases. But with horizontal weatherboarding, *attachment was at every stud*, and these were usually spaced not more than five feet apart.

The clapboards of early Dutch barns in this country were often wide, although they varied considerably and were not of uniform width throughout a given barn. Two barns (the Larger Wemp, and one about a mile southwest of Middleburg's traffic light) retain some of their original clapboarding in a quite unweathered state. This came about owing to the fact that these barns were lengthened by the addition of two bays at an early date, and thus retain, as interior panels, some portions of a former outside gable wall. The Middleburg clapboards average about eleven or twelve inches wide; those of the Larger Wemp barn are a little wider (up to fourteen inches). The original clapboards of all New York Dutch barns *were not tapered in section*; they were true boards, of the same thickness throughout. No standard thickness was adopted, however, some boards being ⅞ inches, some as much as 1¼ inches thick. This weatherboarding was never mitred at the exterior corners. Instead, it abutted a narrow vertical strip that was not much thicker than the clapboards themselves; hence the corner strips merely blocked the triangular voids created by the staggered overlap of the clapboards.

Rose-headed handwrought NAILS were used to attach the clapboards, with one nail at each stud. The boards were lapped 1½ to 1¾ inches (Plate 44); and the nail was driven through each clapboard about this same distance above the *lower* edge so that it usually just missed going through the top of the under clapboard. This scheme not only maintained a close contact against the wind, along the horizontal joint of the overlap; it also allowed the wide boards to expand and contract with changes of temperature, without causing them to split.

Cut through the weatherboarding high in the gable-ends are one or more characteristically shaped openings (Dwg. 17). Mrs. Grant refers to these as "martin holes."[12] Because they were always open to the weather, without flap or glazing, they were available at all seasons of the year for the passage of birds. But they were also—and most importantly —useful as VENTILATING PORTS. Sometimes there are as many as six of these ports in one gable, in a one-over-two-over-three arrangement, where all the openings are of the same shape and size (Plate 7). There are even gables with as many as eight martin holes, the openings themselves of three different shapes. More often there are but two or three ports in a gable (Plates 4 and 10). Shapes C and D, in Dwg. 17, would seem to be the oldest; and two identical ports in one gable would seem to indicate an earlier barn than those that have more numerous and different openings.

Many, but not all barns, had WOODEN EAVES-TROUGHS supported on horizontal brackets that projected through the wall posts opposite the interior columns. Although the round holes for these supporting brackets have been noted in a number of barns, only one eaves-trough, apparently an original one, has so far been discovered (at the barn one mile south of Hurley). When found, it had fallen and broken into two portions; it had obviously been a single piece originally, however, that stretched the full length of the barn (about thirty-eight feet). It measures 3½ inches by 6½ inches in section (Plate 50). The number of supports for it, as for the eaves-troughs of many other barns, was the same as the number of columns in one of the interior ranges: thus, four supports for a three-bay barn, five for a four-bay barn. In the Wemple barn, however, the eaves-trough holes occur in every other wall stud instead of opposite the main columns; consequently their spacing is somewhat closer here, being about 9'-5" on centers, longitudinally.

The HOLES FOR THE EAVES-TROUGH SUPPORTS range in a slightly pitched sequence from one end of a barn to the other. Their high point, at one corner of the barn, is down only 1¾ inches below the soffit of the wall plate in the Larger Bradt barn; this would indicate both the minimum of eaves projection here, and the impossibility of this roof ever having been thatched. The Wemple barn's holes are 1½ inches in diameter, and the drop is ¾ of an inch in a two-stud run. The drop is about ¾ of an inch between brackets, in fact, whatever their spacing happens to be. The diameter of the bracket holes measures two inches in the Larger Wemp barn. Here the stub of an oak bracket has been found *in situ;* but the projection and conformation of its salient portion has long since disintegrated, and the way the eaves-trough was attached to it is no longer recoverable (Dwg. 18).

PENTICES over each of the wagon doors were regular features of New York Dutch barns. Although they continue to be used in many cases, none of the existing ones is original (e.g., Plates 4, 7, 9, 11, and 16). So neither their slope nor their projection, as originally built, is known. One thing is certain, however: they were never strutted by diagonal braces from below, as in the case of those Dutch and other European structures that employed pentices over doorways. Instead, their main support was in the form of wooden cantilevers. Rectangular mortice-holes for these cantilevers—usually three of them, cut horizontally through the gable-end anchorbeams—occur in many barns; and two of them (Larger Wemp and East of Sharon) still retain the non-exterior portions of the wooden members they housed (Dwg. 16 at A).

The pentices were not installed to make the top of the wagon doors especially weather- or windproof. Nor were they needed to protect those metal tracks on which more modern barn doors are hung (for sliding them sideways); needless to say, there were no such tracks, of course, in the early days when these barns flourished. But the presence of pentices on practically all New World Dutch barns was nonetheless due to a valid practical reason. This reason was *the protection they afforded to the gable-end sill*—the wagon-door threshold—by the projection of their roof canopies. Since the wagons entered and departed here at the ground level, the sills too had to be practically at grade, with just a slight ramp of earth in front of them. It was therefore important to keep the earth that was in contact with these mud-sills as dry as possible to preserve them from dampness and rot.

At first, the WAGON DOORS were invariably located at the center of each gable-end. They were in two leaves that always swung inward, usually on *all-wood hinges* (Plates 47 and 48). At least one of these leaves was always fashioned as a "Dutch door"; that is, it was divided at about half its height, and the upper and lower halves swung separately. Hence the upper half, for example, could remain open while the lower half was closed. In many instances a removable post was provided that could be set into sinkages, above and below, at the crack where the right and left door leaves came together, to secure the big doors in a closed position from within when they needed to be made fast. Alternatively, a horizontal bar of timber was set across the closed doors from jamb post to jamb post from within, when they were shut.

A few SMALL DOORS for humans—and sometimes for animals, too— occurred at various positions in the periphery of the barn. More often than in the case of the big wagon doors, these small doors usually turned on handwrought iron hinges. The commonest location for the secondary doors was next to one or both of the corners on the gable-end (e.g., Plates 1, 2, 4, 10, 11, 13, 15, and 16). The Larger Wemp barn has a small door immediately adjacent to the wagon door of the north gable, to the right; and the latter's pentice originally extended to one side sufficiently to shelter this door along with the big wagon doors (Plate 4). Similar situations occur in the East of Sharon barn (see Dwg. 2). Sometimes, as in the Larger Wemp barn, again, there was a small door along one of the flanks; here it was on the east side, centered about thirteen feet from the north corner (Plate 28). These small doors, and the big wagon doors whenever good weather permitted them to remain open, seem to have provided sufficient daylight within the barn for whatever tasks took place there during the daytime. Apparently there were no glazed windows, originally, in any New York Dutch barns.

The clear height of the wagon-door openings is usually between 10½ feet and 11 feet, high enough to accommodate a loaded hay wain. Different examples vary a few inches, plus or minus, from these dimensions. The gable-end anchorbeams are customarily somewhat shallower than those within, although the tops of all anchorbeams are at the same height in order to provide a level platform of poles for the vast hayloft.

In this connection it should be noted that the height of the wagon-door opening has a close relationship to the height of the eaves of the barn. This is demonstrated in the drawings of transverse sections for a representative number of barns (Dwg. 4). Except in a few examples (as at K, L, and M, where they were not included as part of the framing system), the upper-level struts across the side-aisles always linked the columns and wall posts from above the former to below the plate of the latter. This is why the great majority of New World Dutch barns have side walls that are about fifteen feet to the eaves. Such a height was arrived at by the sum of the following: an eleven-foot door opening, plus a sixteen- to twenty-two-inch anchorbeam, plus a few inches to the soffit of the upper transverse link, whose six- to eight-inch depth meets the wall post a few inches below the wall plate of the side-aisle.

Inside, New World Dutch barns are invariably *three-aisled*, with a row of columns on either side of a wide central space, and much narrower areas flanking it to right and left. Originally, the central area served as the THRESHING FLOOR, and was *paved with heavy planking* supported on big timber sills (Plate 41). One or both of the side areas were either left un-floored or were furnished with removable planking. The latter condition may still be observed in the Deertz barn, for example (Plate 42). On one side, at least, and sometimes on both, the alcoved side-aisles accommodated animals: stables for the oxen, quarters for the young stock, and a horse stall or two. The animals always faced inward; and the evidence of their slatted mangers is still extant in a few barns (Plate 40). In those examples—usually the smaller and less exemplary barns—where the side areas are not floored with planking, the ground there is anywhere from a foot and a half to four feet or so below the level of the threshing floor (Plates 24 and 43). This in itself, along with the convenience in removing manure and facilitating the passage of the stock in and out, would account for the small doors located tight against the corners of the building on one or both of the gable-ends.

The most striking features of the interior, however, are the great ANCHORBEAMS. It is they that afford the quickest and surest means of identifying the building as an early New World Dutch barn. These anchorbeams stretch transversely from column to column across the central threshing floor, spanning as much as twenty-eight and one half feet in the clear (Plate 18). Their tenons pass through the columns and usually protrude as *salient tongues* beyond the outer face of the columns, sometimes as much as fourteen or sixteen inches—even twenty-one inches in the Indian Castle barn (Plate 22).

The anchorbeams are the only timbers in New World Dutch barns whose *depth greatly exceeds their thickness*, as a consistent and obviously intentional practice. In a number of cases the former dimension is as much as twice the latter. This is most unusual—one might assert that it is practically unique—with respect to old timber construction anywhere. Nowadays we are familiar enough with thin joists and rafters in the form of 2x10's or 2x12's set on edge for a favorable stiffness-to-weight ratio. But it was quite different in the days before power saws, when timbers were hewn by hand. In the past, including medieval times, heavy wooden members were hewn directly from the felled logs. At least in the New World, the tools that were utilized for shaping the timbers from logs were the broadax more often than the adze, plus the slick, and the plane.[13] Hence, all other big timbers had formerly followed the squared-up dimensions of the original tree. Alternatively, logs had been split longitudinally with wedges. It was even customary for rafters to be broadaxed only along their top surfaces (in order to provide a more even and wider seating there for the slats or boards of the roof). In Europe, when the rafters of former times were split—whether or not their sides were squared to form a rectangular cross section—they were invariably set flat-wise instead of with their larger dimension upright. Even major beams and girders were customarily framed, in the past, so that their width was somewhat greater than their depth. Consequently, the unprecedented depth-to-thickness ratio of the anchorbeams, along with their massive size, make them the most unusual and conspicuous visual features of New York Dutch barns. Only in these barns are timbers encountered of such huge and deep proportions, and only in these barns are tongues of such great size and projection to be found.

In connection with the hewing of logs and the shaping of timbers, it should be noted that the commonest SPECIES OF WOOD encountered in New World Dutch barns are oak, white pine, and a hard, rather dense variety of yellow pine that is long since extinct in this region. Taking all Dutch barns together, it appears that oak was utilized about as much as pine, for the structural members. In individual barns, however, sometimes pine—either white or the hard variety—is the principal wood, and few members are of oak (Larger Wemp, Van Bergen, and East of Sharon, for example). In others, oak is the predominant wood employed throughout (Ripking, and Cure; even the long slender rafters of the latter are of oak!). In a number of barns the anchorbeams are of yellow pine, the columns of oak (e.g., South of Stuyvesant Falls, Kaufman, and Verplanck-Van Wyck). Exceptional instances include the unusually tall columns of oak in the five-bay barn south of Germantown, and the oak anchorbeams in both the Numrich and the Acker barns; those of the latter measure as much as 11¾ inches by 20 inches in section. The Deertz barn has anchorbeams of white pine, columns of yellow pine, and braces of oak. One barn, northwest of Cobleskill, has basswood anchorbeams, but they are now worm-eaten and ruinous. Sometimes, not all the columns of a given barn are of the same species of wood; sometimes the anchorbeams, too, have been hewn from unsimilar species (e.g., Andreas de Witt). But pine was invariably used for the weatherboarding, and for the vertical boards that make up the barn doors. All pins and wedges are of oak. Oak, too, was invariably used for the planking of the threshing floor, for the door posts, and (when they were of wood) for the hinges.

In most cases all this wood has remained remarkably sound.[14] In addition, except for the flooring within and the exposed clapboarding outside, it continues to look remarkably fresh and unaged. In the Larger Bradt barn, for example, the condition and appearance of the big anchorbeams is so clean and undulled with age as to belie the facts of their real age and length of service.

The great anchorbeams are well named, for in most cases they are the sole structural links above the floor level (except at the gable-ends) between the two sides of the barn. Hence they are indispensable in maintaining structural unity and continuity between the two halves of the building. A few barns do incorporate a high tie linking a pair of columns, transversely, at a level eight or ten inches below their tops. Where such ties span between every pair of columns, however, they seem to be an indication of relatively late date. One or two earlier barns (East of Sharon, for example, which is a four-bay barn) have a single high tie linking the column-tops of the middle frame. But, in general, it is only the anchorbeams that unite the two sides of these early, New World Dutch barns in a rigid framework between the two gable-ends.

There are two features of the anchorbeams that contribute to the transverse stability of this rigid framework. One is the noteworthy depth of the anchorbeams themselves, in conjunction with their multiple-pinned and often wedged connection with the columns. The other feature is the pair of DIAGONAL BRACES—one brace at either side of the threshing floor—that strut the anchorbeam to its columns (Plates 23 and 27).

As essential elements in preventing lateral racking of the H-frames (the columns and their anchorbeam links), the braces are always present in these New World Dutch barns. Morticed and pinned into both column and anchorbeam on either hand, they stretch between them as thick sturdy struts at an angle that is usually slightly steeper than forty-five degrees. Sometimes they are centered on both column and anchorbeam (e.g., Larger Wemp); more often, one of their side faces is flush with the surface of both the column's and the anchorbeam's lateral face on that side (e.g., East of Sharon). In any case, they are always morticed rather than rebated or half-lapped into the face of the two members they connect.

HORIZONTAL STRUTS at head height link the columns longitudinally, and it is into these members (at least, on one side of the threshing floor) that the oak slats for confining the manger's hay allotment were fixed, set slant-wise down to a timber outrigger supported on horizontal brackets projecting from the sides of adjacent columns (Plate 40).

Each of the columns is also linked to a post in the side wall by a horizontal beam that is set at or near this same head-height level. In addition, the column is usually linked to the outside wall by another tie, higher up; this is morticed into the column just above the anchorbeam, and into the wall post just below its plate. Thus the side walls are secured laterally by these *upper and lower transverse struts*. In a few instances the framing was designed so as to dispense with the upper strut, and the omission of this feature, as we have seen, resulted in barns that had fairly low side-wall eaves. (Kinderhook, Verplanck-Van Wyck, and Ripking are examples. See Dwg. 4.)

The side walls themselves are framed in STOUT STUDS, and incorporate at least one pair of diagonal braces that are morticed into the wall plate, often from the corner posts. Usually, but not always (the Larger Wemp barn is an exception; see Plate 28), the studs are more or less evenly spaced about five feet on centers, and identical in cross section. Whatever the spacing, it must obviously be such that a stud—sometimes in the form of a heavier wall post—may occur directly opposite a column, in order to accommodate the transverse links between these two vertical members.

Ranging across the tops of the columns on either side of the central area are the PURLIN-PLATES: they form the high-level link connecting the column-tops longitudinally. They are always in one piece from gable-end to gable-end, morticed to receive the column-top tenons that are pegged to them with one or two oak pins (Plates 18, 30, and 37).

Longitudinal stability throughout the barn is primarily handled at this high level. It is in the form of a conspicuous SERIES OF DIAGONAL BRACES from the columns to the purlin-plate. These braces—collectively known as sway-bracing—are found in a number of different patterns (Dwg. 5). The commonest, though surely not the earliest pattern, is the most regular and consists of rather short diagonals that branch upward to the purlin-plate from the lateral faces of each column. What appear to be earlier examples have fewer and much longer braces, sometimes (as in the Wemple barn, for example) slanting upward from a point on the column that is actually below the level of the anchorbeams. The Deertz barn is unique in having its sway-bracing inverted; that is, instead of being secured to the purlin-plate, the braces slope *downward* from each column to horizontal struts that link the columns longitudinally at an exceptional above-head-height level. In all other examples, however, the diagonal struts of the sway-bracing are tenoned into mortices on the underside of the purlin plate. It is at this high level, therefore, that the structural framework of the barn's timberwork core is secured against any racking in the longitudinal direction.

The ROOF STRUCTURE is surprisingly light, and its framing system is uniquely simple. Slender rafters, usually spaced about five feet apart, stretch from ridge to outer wall plate in one piece. Pairs of these rafters are joined at the ridge in a pinned tongue-and-fork attachment (Dwg. 8). Customarily, wherever superior craftsmanship prevailed, rafters were neatly squared, following the natural taper of the young tree from which they had been cut. One of the reasons for the wide spacing of these rafters was to obviate the need for shimming up any discrepancies in their straightness that were due to natural waviness or irregularity in the shape of the tree log.

New York Dutch barns never had projecting eaves. Instead, the upper surface of the rafters came down to terminate in a sharp edge exactly in line with the top outer edge of the wall plate (Dwg. 10). Beyond this point, the topmost clapboard tucked up under the lowest of the wide roofers; and the lowest, outermost course of shingles undoubtedly projected only slightly beyond, in order to drip rain water into the WOODEN EAVES-TROUGH, set close in against the weatherboarding (Dwg. 18).

There is never either a ridgepole or any transverse tie linking the rafters. Their feet rest on the outer wall plate without positive attachment there.[15] The only positive attachment of the rafters is midway in their length, where they are notched in order to rest on the purlin-plate (Dwg. 9). Here, alone, a single oak pin secures them. No other attachment is needed, thanks to their being balanced on their points of bearing, the purlin-plates. Consequently, the entire space-volume of the hayloft is unencumbered with structural members: from below, where sapling poles are laid across the anchorbeams, to the very peak of the roof, above. Wide roofing boards—or, in rare cases, narrow wooden strips spaced three or four times as far apart as their own width—form a surface for the shingles of the roof.

Contemporary Modifications

Previous to any significant alterations in completed barns, a very few of the larger and/or longer barns had adopted modifications of the basic design that gained more storage space of two sorts. This was the expedient of setting the ANCHORBEAMS *at a lower level* in those bays that were farthest from the main gable entrance. (Examples are the East of Sharon Springs, and the Deertz barns [Plate 39].) Thus the floor level of the innermost bays—those that were opposite the most convenient and most often used wagon entrance—no longer had to serve as a corridor for wagons but could accommodate produce, equipment, or pens of various sorts. At the same time, additional loft space of considerable volume was provided, above, by the drop in the level of its platform of poles (down thirty-six inches in the Deertz barn). This greater storage capacity was gained at the expense of considerable inconvenience, however. For either the wagons had to be backed out of the door through which they had entered, after unloading, or, if the central area of the barn floor was wide enough to permit it, they had to be turned and backed and turned about in order to be driven forward, out through the door of entrance.

It was to correct this time-consuming inconvenience that a more efficient arrangement for wagon circulation came to be adopted. This was apparently the first major change in the layout and accommodations of New York Dutch barns, after they were first built: namely, the elimination of one of the gable-end wagon doors and the substitution for it of a wagon door more or less midway along one side of the barn (Plates 6 and 37). Such a reorganization produced more storage space by removing the necessity for maintaining an axial thoroughfare for wagons throughout the length of the building: that is, *in* at one gable-end, *out* at the far end.

Probably none of the New World Dutch barns was built originally with a WAGON ENTRANCE *at one side.* But considerable numbers of them were subsequently altered, apparently at an early date, to provide this convenience. The evidence for this is that a number of wagon entrances —both side and end ones—have doors that swing, to this day, on allwood hinges.

There was more than one way that structural changes were made so as to implement the more efficient pattern of wagon traffic, within the barn, that has just been described. The most common alteration, and the one that involved the least trouble to effect, was simply to saw away the head-height longitudinal strut, on the side where the door was to be located, that linked the two columns bounding its bay on that side. Occasionally, a much more basic change—a major structural alteration, in fact—was resorted to (as in the barn south of Stuyvesant Falls, for example). This consisted of shifting the position of one entire H-frame—columns and anchorbeam together—so that the bay lengths were uneven, with a short bay adjacent to the newly widened one that accommodated the relocated side entranceway for wagons. The evidence for this alteration survives in the soffit of the purlin-plate, where the old mortices mark the former location of column and sway-braces. Later (apparently much later), wagon entrances were established at opposite sides of some barns, replacing the blocked-up ones at either of the gable-ends. (The Smaller Wemp barn is a very clear example.)

Another way in which New York Dutch barns were changed from their original state at an early date was to lengthen them by *adding one or more bays*. Such extension could have taken place either sooner or later in the life of the barn, of course. But there is clear evidence, from the similarity of construction generally, that a number of barns were lengthened only a generation or two after they were originally built. (For example: Larger Wemp, Glen Road, and N.W. of Middleburg barns.) In all but a very few instances, the additional length consisted of a single bay that was added to one end of a three-bay barn. Where such an extension was made, the barn's total length was almost invariably increased by considerably more than a third, owing to the fact that the added bay was an abnormally long one—sometimes up to twice the size of a normal bay. In any case, the addition is always recognizable from the fact that the purlin-plate is spliced at the point where the addition joins the original structure.

Structural Considerations

SOME PROPERTIES OF WOOD

WHEREVER the Dutch settled in the New World, the land abounded in excellent timber trees of many varieties. Inevitably, their wood was utilized both as a finish material and in a structural capacity. It is the latter use—whether of hardwoods or softwoods—that is of particular concern in the study of barns.

In recognition of the extraordinary versatility and effectiveness of wood as a structural material, it is illuminating to recall some of the conditions that have to be met by the living tree itself before its timber is cut and utilized for building purposes. First, the trunk of the tree *acts as a column*. It has to be strong and resistant enough to support the weight of the superstructure: the main branches, crown, leaves in season, and perhaps ice and snow at times. Thus the trunk acts structurally in compression, withstanding gravitational axial loads.

But the trunk also *acts as a vertical cantilever* whenever the wind blows. Unstayed by guys or any other external props, its only anchorage against swaying and overturning is the ground. It must rely exclusively on its own internal structure to check and forestall any tilting downfall. Consequently, when a tree bends to the force of the wind, the fibers on the windward side undergo tension, and those on the lee side are in compression. However, the wind may come from *any* direction. Hence, all the fibers around the circumference of the trunk are subject, at one time or another, to both tensile and compressive stresses.

There are other structurally desirable properties of timber, including its resistance to racking or twisting, its high degree of dimensional stability longitudinally, and its resistance to shear across the grain.[1] But it is important to note that some of the structural properties of wood are of variable and disparate usefulness, being advantageous in some circumstances and undesirable in others. For example, there is the case of RESISTANCE TO LONGITUDINAL SHEAR. Most species of timber are highly resistant to shear *across* the grain, but are notably less able to withstand this kind of stress in the longitudinal direction. Consequently, the connections that are subject to tension, in a framework of timbers, constitute areas of critical weakness and have to be supplemented or taken care of in some equivalent fashion elsewhere. Yet this property of vulnerability along the grain bestows a welcome advantage at the time the timbers are first fashioned from logs, by allowing the trunk of the felled tree to be split with wedges, longitudinally. Such a method of fashioning big timbers from ponderous logs obviously requires far less expenditure of effort than would the process of sawing them by hand; and therefore weakness in resistance to longitudinal shear is a distinct advantage in the reduction of big logs to squared timbers.

However, this particular weakness is the source of the most critical deficiency in timber *framing*. The defect stems from the fact that, although wood in its natural state (that is, in the living tree) is almost equally effective in its resistance to both compression and tension, it is impossible to utilize its full tension-resisting potential in man-made joints. An instance of this is demonstrated at C and D in Dwg. 12. Here the tensional stress is transmitted from the tenon (which is only about one-third of the timber's area in cross section) via a wooden pin (which bears against perhaps one-quarter of the tenon's cross section). Thus only about one-twelfth of the timber's substance, in section, is actively engaged in RESISTANCE TO TENSION. In contrast to this deficiency under tension, it should be noted that the *entire* cross-sectional area can be involved in RESISTANCE TO COMPRESSION, as in the bearing of a column's base.

PROVISION FOR MEETING TENSILE STRESSES

When a wood joint fails under tension, it does so by ripping out along the grain, as shown at D in Dwg. 12. This action, as we have seen, follows the line of least resistance in the wood; namely, its weakness in resistance to longitudinal shear. This weakness can be ameliorated, however, by *lengthening the tenon*. Such an expedient provides a very much increased area of resistance to longitudinal shear, making it unlikely that the pin or wedge will rip its way out through the end of the tenon. A small but conspicuous example of lengthening the tenon is seen in the upper transverse tie shown at F. The same purpose was achieved, of course, by the far-protruding tongues of the great anchorbeams. As shown in the examples at F, E, and B, each of these tongues has pairs of wedges bearing against the outer face of the column, as well as oak pins that pass through the column. One or two isolated instances have been discovered where the wedges have indeed ripped out along the grain of the tongue, leaving long slots from column-face to tenon-end. But these are very exceptional, and must be attributed to some special, extraordinary period of stress. Occasionally, the anchorbeam tongues were not secured with wedges, although that was certainly the normal practice. In any case, the far-protruding tongues prevented the oak pins from shearing out along the grain of these tongues.

Function of Diagonal Braces

In situations of potentially serious stress, the problem posed by the inadequate resistance of wood to tension in man-made joints was met much more effectively by resorting to a completely different scheme of framing. This scheme involved the use of PAIRS OF DIAGONAL BRACES, in which sometimes one sometimes the other strut functioned in compression.

We have already noted that all of the surface of a wooden member that is in bearing can be counted on to provide resistance to compression, particularly where the stress acts in an axial direction. Hence, by bringing into play this counteracting capability of wood—that is, by substituting its greater compressive resistance for its less-effective tensile resistance—a more efficient and trustworthy stability is secured in the timber framework.

Dwg. 12 at A illustrates this scheme in the case of one of the main H-frames of a New York Dutch barn. Although the pins and wedges impart considerable rigidity to the connection between anchorbeam and column, to right and left, these are not sufficient, even with deep anchorbeams, to resist the swaying action imposed by strong winds driving against the entire building—against one whole side wall and the roof slope on that side. So, diagonal braces were employed to secure rigidity in the framing, thereby preventing lateral displacement and maintaining verticality in the columns.

This action of the diagonal braces is indicated by the impossibly exaggerated diagram at A in Dwg. 12. Here the left-hand brace, being subject to tension (T), has pulled away at its lower end, rupturing the joint there. (It might equally well have pulled apart at the upper joint—whichever was the weaker—but not both at once.) In the present instance, however, it is the right-hand brace that is fully operative in resisting the tendency of the columns to tilt out of the vertical.

Compressive resistance via this diagonal brace is transmitted to only a limited degree by a pin at both joints. Primarily, the compressive resistance is achieved (1) by the butt-end of each tenon bearing against the snug confinement of its mortice, within, and, much more, (2) by the brace's shoulders that are in bearing against a transverse notch in the anchorbeam's soffit, at one end, and in the column's face, at the other end. Hence, the amount of the timber brace's substance that is engaged in *resistance to compression* is many times as great as that where resistance to tension is involved. Of the two diagonal braces, it is primarily the one that acts in compression, then, that performs the task of maintaining rigidity in the structural frame. The other brace is there in readiness to serve a similar function whenever a corresponding swaying to the left causes that brace, in turn, to act in compression.

Obviously, to be effective, the joints must be accurately cut and fitted in order to secure the required rigidity in the framework. There must be a snug fit, with practically *no play in any of the joints*. This integrity of workmanship in the joiner's art was particularly essential in the framing of diagonal braces, both in the longitudinal and in the transverse direction. For it is in the precise framing of these not-too-numerous diagonal members that the stability of the entire structure is secured and maintained. The skill with which this precision was accomplished is apparent to this day, from the fact that there is still no creaking or groaning of the timber framework during a high wind, even after a barn has withstood the storms of many generations.

Test Assembling

Such accuracy in the lengths and jointings of the timber framework could not possibly have been achieved without previous *test assembling*, on the ground, not only of individual pieces but for major ensembles of the structure, as well. And because specific mortices, tenons, and peg holes were involved for each and every joint of these ensembles, it was absolutely essential to number all the pre-assembled members so that there could be no mistaken substitution or confusion in their subsequent installation. The NUMBERING OF THE TIMBERS consisted of chisel marks in Roman numerals, cut near the point where each member was to be joined to another. (Plate 38). The numerals were executed, of course, on that surface of the timbers that faced *up* at the time of the test assembling.

The identification of members by the use of Roman numerals was complicated by the need for two different test-assemblages, one for the transverse framing, the other for the longitudinal framing. On the one hand, an H-frame (consisting of anchorbeam, diagonal braces, and a pair of columns) had to be test assembled along with the upper and lower side-aisle links to the outer wall posts on each side. But the main columns were also integral units in the longitudinal framing. So, on the other hand, a row of these columns had to be separately test assembled with their head-height links, below, and the purlin-plate, above, together with the latter's complement of sway-bracing diagonals. Thus the columns, laid out flat on the ground, were test assembled in one direction, then *dismantled and test assembled in another direction,* before they came to be raised into their final vertical position. This meant that the columns had to be numbered on two adjacent sides: (1) on their outer faces, wherever the timbers that ranged longitudinally were framed into them (Dwg. 12 at E), and (2) on one of their side faces, wherever anchorbeam and diagonal braces, along with transverse side-aisle ties, all converged on the column at their respective heights (Dwg. 6 at A; Dwg. 7 at A).

Along the side walls, it was customary not to number all the studs but only the wall posts—those studs, often heavier than the others, that aligned with the main columns and therefore received the transverse side-aisle ties, upper and lower. The rafters were apparently never numbered. They did not have to be because they were not morticed and tenoned into other timbers such as the wall plate or the purlin-plate.

It should be noted that, in spite of the snug fitting of all joints, there was some degree of tapering or reduction at the extremity of every tenon. Even a slight tapering here allowed the tenon to be inserted into its mortice without undue difficulty. This feature is most noticeable, of course, at the ends of the anchorbeams, for, unlike most tenons, the anchorbeam tongues pass through their mortices and protrude a considerable distance beyond them. Sometimes the *tapering of the tenons* is so slight and brief as to be hardly apparent, hence serving only as an easement at the time of insertion. Sometimes, as at B and F in Dwg. 6, there is a neat and craftsman-like chamfering, which could almost be considered a decorative feature. Sometimes the tapering is very marked, crude, and irregular, as at E in Dwg. 12, where it is obviously solely utilitarian.

Other than the anchorbeams, all joints are usually *pinned with a single oak peg* or "tree nail." At times there are instances of joints that are secured with two pins (for example, Dwg. 7 at A and B, Dwg. 10 at G and H, and Dwg. 12 at F). But this is not the most common practice. In most cases the pins are made long enough to go all the way through their holes, whatever may be the thickness of the timber, and then project an inch or two beyond. These wooden pins are usually driven in flush with the surface, so that they normally project only at their pointed end. (An exception is shown in Dwg. 10 at H.)

Regarding these pins, one's first thought would be that their projecting ends designate that the framing was assembled with that side down—that the pins *were driven from above* when the timbers were grouped together on the ground and joined there in their original test assemblage. This was undoubtedly the case when they were first framed together. But after they had thus been assembled, they had to be subsequently disassembled, as we have seen, for regrouping and reassembling in another direction. Hence the final framing—that of the permanent erection in a vertical plane—would not necessarily have duplicated the practices and procedures of the original test assemblage. In other words, it is not at all certain whether, for the final pin-driving, the timber frames would have come up heads or tails, so to speak. Obviously, for example, the pins utilized in the framing of gable-ends and side walls would have had to be driven inward rather than outward, in their final permanent assemblage, so that their projecting points would not interfere with the smooth and regular attachment of the clapboards. Yet the four outside sections of framing—one for each of the enclosing walls of the barn—would not necessarily have been test assembled with their outside surfaces facing upward. Evidence for this is the fact that the numbering of the transverse timbers of the frame at each gable-end reads from the interior of the barn. The reassembling of the timbers of the gable-ends would seem to have involved a redirecting of the oak pins there, when they were inserted for the permanent framing.

Although the augur-produced holes were always round, the oak pins that were driven into these holes were not invariably cylindrical. In the first place, the pins were pointed—sometimes with rather short conical ends (as at E in Dwg. 12), sometimes with long, gradually tapering points (as at F in Dwg. 10 and at B in Dwg. 9). Furthermore, many of the oak pins were fashioned so as to be *octagonal in section*—really chamfered squares, in section. This was undoubtedly intentional rather than a case of hasty workmanship. For it utilized the blunt arrises along the sides of the pin to effect a surer grip when the pins were driven into the hole, without causing the timber to split. Incidentally, the oak plank-ing of the threshing floor was often attached to the sills with *square* pegs in round holes, doubtless for the same reason.

It should be clearly understood that the bearing ends of the tenons, in every diagonal brace, were cut in an orthogonic fashion; that is, verti-cally and horizontally rather than at right angles to the axis of the brace. The chief and overriding reason for this is that such a shaping of the tenon was absolutely essential *to permit assemblage;* for it would have been impossible to join the timbers together and to pin them in their proper alignment if it were not for this detail of stereotomy. The situa-tion is most clearly evident in the case of the diagonal sway-bracing (Dwg. 14). Here, during the course of erection, the long purlin-plate had to be eased down over a considerable number of tenons: those of the column-tops and those of the diagonal braces. The characteristic shape of the tenons provided snug and proper bearing in compression, with sufficient substance for each of the oak pins to pass through its tenon without the likelihood of shearing through it, under a moderate degree of tensional stress. But the overriding purpose in shaping these tenon-ends with vertical and horizontal rectangularity was to accommodate their assemblage with the purlin-plate.

It is clear, too, from the details in Dwg. 14, that the oak pins at either end of the diagonal braces are there primarily to assure a constant and close connection at all times. As we have already seen in the case of the anchorbeam braces, it is their action under compression—now from one direction, now from the other—rather than their action under ten-sion that makes their presence in the timberwork assemblage indispensa-ble. Here, too, in the diagonal members of the sway-bracing, the pins are highly useful in tacking these struts in place and seeing to it that they remain there. But it is the strutting function of the diagonals *when they are subject to compression* that fulfils their major reason for being. This is when these braces are most efficient; this is when their resistance is depended on. Their effective performance in *tension* is neither expected nor required as long as they are certain to *operate unfailingly under compression.* The pins are there, then, to make sure that these braces will remain securely in position at all times, in order that they can be counted on to withstand the compressional forces they are subject to from time to time.

There are three situations in which diagonal braces are encountered in New York Dutch barns; and it is to be noted that they are always to be found in pairs, for the reasons cited above. One situation involves braces at either end of each anchorbeam. These braces assure the stability of each of the central H-frames, and prevent the barn from leaning transversely. The other main system of diagonals is the sway-bracing from columns to purlin plate on either side of the central area. These higher braces maintain the verticality of the columns in the longitudinal direction, and withstand any tendency of the barn to tilt toward one of the gable-ends. The third situation occurs in the outer side walls. Here there is a pair or two of diagonal braces (for example, at F in Dwg. 10) from stud to wall plate that prevent any racking deformation, longitudinally, in the plane of the wall. What is conspicuously lacking, in comparison with the universal practice throughout England and the Continent, is any diagonal bracing in the plane of the roof slopes. None of the New World Dutch barns was ever supplied with any of this so-called windbracing.

This omission is the more remarkable because of the unusual size of the roof, because of the wide spacing and relative lightness of its timbers, and because of the simplicity of its framing. Most foreign roofs—even those of considerably less span—were customarily built of massive and at times redundant timberwork.[2] In this country, however, the roof structure consisted of nothing more than slender, widely spaced rafters without any of the ties, collars, transverse frames, windbracing, king posts, diagonal braces, and other struts that make so many of the foreign examples look heavy and highly complicated. The security of the roofs, in the case of New World Dutch barns, must be attributed largely to the assured rigidity imparted to them by the internal structure of the barns; that is, by the UNYIELDING TIMBER SKELETON of H-frames and diagonally stiffened purlin-plates on which the integrity of the envelope, whether side-wall clapboarding or roof surfacing, depended (Dwg. 13).

RESISTANCE TO WIND LOADS

The wind-imposed pressures against one of the roof slopes were equalized because of the location of the roof's support. Thus, with the rafters balanced on the purlin-plate at approximately the middle of their length, any wind load pressed more or less equally against the upper and the lower half of the roof slope, and was transmitted to the rigid skeleton of timberwork, below, primarily via the purlin-plate on that side. There was some degree of resistance, too, of course, at either end of the rafters: in their alignment with the wall plate, below, and in the pinned connection each made with an abutting rafter of the lee slope, at the ridge. But stabilization from these two sources was relatively secondary and minor compared to the rigid, primary support received from the purlin-plate.

Similarly, the WIND LOAD against the gable-end did not create a critically dangerous situation. Thanks again to the balancing of the rafters, the upper triangle of the gable wall, above, worked along with the trapezoid of this same wall, lower down, in bringing their combined wind loads to bear against the ends of the purlin-plates. Altogether, there was a great deal of vertical surface for the wind to press against here. For it will be remembered that most New York Dutch barns are wider than they are long, and of considerable height from threshold to peak. But this gable-end wall is prevented from leaning with the force of the wind by the rigidity of the structure behind it, within the barn's interior. There, it is the sway-bracing that maintains strict verticality by means of its system of diagonal braces.

In many of these old barns, moreover, there was a further precaution that was taken against the sliding or longitudinal shifting of the rafters with respect to the roof itself. Wherever it was fully adopted, this expedient consisted of two separate features. One of these was the NOTCHING OF THE PURLIN-PLATE to contain the width of the rafter at its mid-length point of bearing, and thus to fix the interval it made with adjacent rafters (Dwg. 9 at G and H). The other feature was the transverse groove in the top of the wall plate, cut to receive a COG AT THE FOOT OF THE RAFTER (Dwg. 10 at A). Of these two features, the latter was the more common, and probably the more useful. The former was perhaps less essential because there an oak pin secured both the alignment and the positive attachment of the rafter to the purlin-plate. At the foot of the rafter, however, there was no positive attachment, as we have seen: the horizontally cut end of the rafter merely rested on the wall plate without any pin or fixed tenon (Plate 51). Consequently it was useful, at the time of erection when the pairs of rafters were first swung into their upright position, to have their spacing and vertical alignment firmly established, until the roofers came to be nailed across them. Subsequently, after the roof had been finished, the cogs prevented any pivoting action from taking place at the point where the rafters were supported; that is, on the purlin-plate. Such pivoting action, if allowed to develop, could have racked the roof under wind action and induced the rafter-pairs to sway in concert, folding down together in parallel collapse.

Although the general scheme of the framing and layout of New World Dutch barns is *remarkably uniform*, there is nevertheless considerable variety with respect to their overall size and proportions, as well as their individual treatment of common features and typical details. Some of these differences are due to geographical location and perhaps to the conformation of the site; some are certainly due to the particular species of wood employed. Some differences in layout may be the result of dissimilarities in the numbers and kinds of animals to be housed, and perhaps in the nature of the crops that were to be stored. Undoubtedly, some differences reflect the relative unproductiveness or prosperity of the farm they served. And some differences are clearly due to the quality of the workmanship, the skill with which the timbers were fashioned and the barn executed.

It is not surprising, too—since all the timberwork was hand-hewn and hand-assembled—that there is a certain amount of scarcely noticeable *variety among similar or corresponding features* in a single barn. In most cases, however, the discrepancies are not readily apparent, compared to similar situations in English and Continental examples, for two reasons. One is that the timbers of contemporary Old World barns, particularly those in Holland, are hewn from smaller trees; thus each timber follows the natural bends and irregularities, as well as the size, of a particular tree trunk. Early Dutch barns in this country, on the other hand, were cut from virgin forests where the trees grew tall, straight, and large; consequently all their *timbers are straight and true*. The other reason for lack of uniformity among similar features in the same barn, in foreign examples, was the complexity of their framing. Lacking an abundance of tall, straight trees of large size, the Old World structures used shorter members that were frequently built up into massive complexes of major transverse frames supporting a number of purlins on each of the roof slopes. These complexes incorporated curving members of various sorts; whereas the much *simpler framing* of the New World structures consisted universally of straight members.

All but a very few New York Dutch barns were built as either three- or four-bay structures; the surviving examples are quite evenly divided in this respect. Normally there is not much individual variation —perhaps not more than 2 or 3 inches—in the length of bays in any given building. Yet among the many barns investigated, there is no standard dimension for a bay's length; it may be as little as 10 feet or as much as 14 feet. Thus the total length of a three-bay barn varies from

32'-0" (Adriance) to 40'-11" (Larger Bradt). The difference in the length of bays is even greater in the case of four-bay barns, where the total length of the building may be as short as 40'-3" (East of Sharon) or as long as 56'-6" (Wemple).

There is a similar wide range of size in the transverse direction, in spite of the fact that the overall dimension encompasses three aisles in all cases. Total widths vary from 42'-6" (Cure) to as much as 54'-0" (Deertz), with the width of the central threshing floor varying even more, proportionately: from an exceptionally narrow 16'-3½" (Adriance) to a maximum of 28'-6" (Van Wie) in the clear. Most examples, however, measure well over 20 feet between the inner faces of the columns.

Column sizes, too, present remarkable variation in section, in different barns. Examples measure, in inches: 8 x 14 (West of Ft. Plain), 8½ x 11¾ (Kaufman), 9 x 13 (Indian Castle), 9½ x 9¾ (Bronck), 9½ x 11 (Sagh), 9¾ x 12 (Wemple), 10¾ x 11½ (Deertz), and 11 x 13¾ (Larger Bradt). Here, too, the columns of a given barn are not always identical in section. Where variations in them do occur, the transverse thickness remains constant: it is the greater dimension (that is, in the longitudinal direction) that is not the same (e.g., 9¾ x 9, and 9¾ x 11 [South of Germantown]).

There is also great variation in the cross-section of anchorbeams, from one barn to another. Again, measuring in inches: 9 x 15¼ (Cure), 9½ x 14½ (Kaufman), 9½ x 21½ (Kinderhook), 9¾ x 18 (Ripking), 10 x 19 (upper range, Deertz), 10 x 24 (lower range, Deertz), 10½ x 14 (South of Germantown), 11 x 19 (South of Stuyvesant Falls), 11 x 22 (Larger Wemp), 11½ x 14 (Numrich), 11½ x 18 (Wyncoop), 11¾ x 17 (Acker), 11¾ x 19½ (Van Bergen), 11¾ x 23 (Wemple), 12 x 23½ (Larger Bradt). The differences in section are influenced by the species of wood, by the span length of the anchorbeam, and sometimes by the width of the column-faces it abuts. But in all cases the greater dimension is always that of the depth; that is, the vertical dimension.

There is customarily a particular and characteristic variation in the depth of the anchorbeams in a given barn. But this is an intentional variation and stems from a recognizable cause. What is here referred to is the case of the gable-end anchorbeams: they are appropriately shallower than the other anchorbeams, for two reasons. One reason is that they have only half as much to carry in support of the loaded hay scaffold. The other reason for their shallower depth is that, unlike the other anchorbeams that span from column to column without intermediate support, these gable-end timbers receive additional support from the two stout posts that act as jambs for the wagon doors. The latter swung on hinges fixed to these jambs, which consequently had to be particularly sturdy. As recognition of this latter requirement, some barns have door posts of oak in a structure that consists generally of pine throughout. (The Larger Wemp barn is an example.)

JOINTS

It is curious to note that, in a considerable number of instances, *tenons are off-set* and do not align with the axis of their own timbers. Examples are depicted in Dwg. 7 at C (for a lower transverse tie); in Dwg. 8 (for rafter connections at the peak); in Dwg. 6 at F and particularly at D (for anchorbeam tongues). There seems to be no valid structural reason for these nonalignments. Actually, in most cases (as in the first and third instances just cited), the structural connection is somewhat weakened by the eccentricity of the tenon's projection, for it sets up rotational strains at the joint.

Eccentricity in the location of the *mortice* of a timber does not necessarily accompany a corresponding eccentricity in the tenon it houses. In other words, a tenon that is axial to its own timber is frequently received into the *off-set mortice* of another timber (as at A in Dwg. 7). Here the reason may be at times an aesthetic one. For example, the left-hand strut at C in Dwg. 7 shows a horizontal shelf on which the shoulder of the timber rests; it is gained into the lateral face of the column on this side; but it is *housed* on the inner face of the column so that it does not show from the threshing-floor area of the interior of the barn. (A similar housing of a timber's shoulders, this time on both faces of an anchorbeam, is indicated in plan at E in Dwg. 6.) Sometimes there was a practical reason for the mortice being off-set. For example, the various members making up the assemblage of a side wall were framed so that their outer faces were all flush, in order to secure an even bearing in a single plane for the outside cladding of weatherboarding. Nevertheless, eccentricity in the location of mortices did not create the strongest or most secure joint. Even though such eccentricity was not as critical as that of tenons, it was obviously less sturdy and dependable than a symmetrically centered void. And at times, the extreme one-sidedness of its position (as at D in Dwg. 6), which appears to have been both unnecessary and undesirable, is quite impossible to account for.

Fire, either from lightning or from the hand of man, has undoubtedly been the most frequent cause of destruction of barns. Few if any New York Dutch barns have collapsed because of structural weakness or instability, as have so many barns of much more recent date. There is no indication that any surviving Dutch barns have been deformed solely as a result of either high winds or the weight of excessive amounts of snow on their roofs. In those few instances where some degree of distortion has occurred from natural causes, it seems invariably to have been caused by subsidence in part of the foundation (as at the pier under the northwest corner of the Larger Wemp barn, Plate 6), or to the disintegration and falling away of the coursed stone piers at intervals under the wall-sill (as on the east side of the Route 20, East of Sharon barn). Even in the case of these examples of neglect, the barns in question are remarkably secure, thoroughly sound, and undeniably serviceable.

In existing Dutch barns, it is surprising how few and slight are the deformations that have come about because of man-made alterations, removals, and amputations, however numerous and varied. Many of the Dutch barns that are still in use have had major side entrances cut into them. This has invariably necessitated the permanent removal of the longitudinal head-height link between the columns bounding the bay into which the new side-wall wagon doors open. The Larger Wemp barn is a case in point; here the original south-gable doors have been repositioned, wooden hinges and all. Both of the Bradt barns and the Glen Road barn are other instances. Sometimes a side-wall entrance has been furnished with its own gabled ell whose roof intersects the original barn structure. The Wemple barn has one on the southeast side. It affords entrance, via a high ramp of earth on the exterior, at a level some four feet below the tops of the anchorbeams, from which its floor, one bay in extent, is suspended by iron hangers. Some Dutch barns have had many if not all of their upper transverse side-aisle ties—those linking the columns with the wall-tops—cut away in order to facilitate the storage of hay there; yet their structure appears to have survived this severing of ligatures without appreciably giving way (as in the Glen Road barn, south of Route 5-S). One of the massive anchorbeams in the Indian Castle barn has been completely removed; yet this barn is in constant use today and seems to be perfectly sound.

Two Dutch barns in the Hudson Valley west of Kingston, near Hurley, have been more severely mutilated. The Kaufman barn on Hurley Mountain Road has had its west side-aisle, nearest the road, removed.

The smaller barn on the Suydam estate, off Route 209 north of Hurley, has had both its side-aisles removed: thus the tongues of the anchor-beams have all been sawed off flush with the exterior faces of the columns in order not to interfere with the subsequent clapboarding of its walls.

In both the Indian Castle and the Larger Bradt barns of the Mohawk Valley, most of the ground-floor level has been drastically altered to accommodate many head of cows, and furnished with a cement floor, metal stanchions, and a low ceiling. This ceiling is the soffit of a new floor, in the loft above, that has been established at a level well below the underside of the anchorbeams. In the Bradt barn, the columns have been cut off at the ceiling level; these columns now bear upon built-up wooden girders that are supported at intervals by slender modern pipe-columns. One enters these barns through the low-ceilinged "cow palace," and it is only by climbing a ladder to the loft that one comes upon the original barn, with its impressive spaciousness, its integrity of structure, and its distinction of craftsmanship.

REBUILDING AND LATER CONSTRUCTION

Some New York Dutch barns have been extensively rebuilt. Apparently this rebuilding has been due, as often as not, to the early removal of the barn to a new site. The Nelliston barn (recently destroyed) is a case in point. Another instance is the three-bay barn just east of Fonda, up a bank on the north side of Route 5, close to the road. Here, entirely new mortices have been cut in the columns on account of a higher positioning of the anchorbeams. One of the latter—the one between the center and the western bay—is a former column, with all its previous notches and mortices for anchorbeam, lateral ties, and diagonal braces still evident.

Three examples of rebuilding are to be noted in the Hudson Valley. One, the Van Bergen barn on Vedder Road southwest of Leeds, has a quite redundant framing system for the roof. Here the column-top purlin-plate no longer supports the rafters, which are removed from it by some eighteen inches or so on account of their steeper pitch. Instead, the rafters are now supported on higher plates, somewhat nearer the middle of the building, that are held in place by inward-canted struts that take their bearing on longitudinal sills laid across the anchorbeams where they abut the columns.

A second Hudson Valley instance is the unusually large barn on the Suydam estate west of Kingston. Here the framing system is quite atypical: less simple, direct, and economical than in the normal Dutch barn. This giant structure is said to have been combined from the reassemblage of parts of three other barns, which would perhaps explain the lateness of the date (1796) that is chiseled on the side of one of the anchor-beams.

Another Hudson Valley example is that of the Wyncoop barn just west of Hurley. Here the columns have been heightened by splicing additional vertical pieces to the existing members, thus raising the level of the purlin-plate (and therefore presumably increasing the pitch of the roof).

Although not strictly a matter of *re*-building, it is worth noting that a number of New York Dutch barns proved to be inadequate in size, some time after they were built, and were consequently increased in length by the later addition of one or more bays. This has made them considerably longer than they are wide. At an early date, apparently, the Larger Wemp barn was extended to the south by the addition of two bays. Here there is no anchorbeam stretching between the intermediate columns. But at the boundaries of the new portion there are tongued and wedged anchorbeams, one close against what had formerly been the south gable-end of the original four-bay barn, the other in the added south-gable wall. All the members of the newer portion are slighter than those of the original structure, and the craftsmanship is cruder and less adept.

There are other Mohawk Valley barns that have been increased in length. These include one on the Glen Road south of Route 5-S, the barn where Route 288 meets Route 161 south of Auriesville, and the barn on the Logtown Road west of Glen. In each case the additional bay (the first to the southwest, the second to the north, the third to the southwest) is much longer than those of the original construction, and of lighter members and flimsier workmanship. The splices in the column-top purlin-plates are clearly evident in all three examples.

Some New World Dutch barns are rather difficult to identify from a distance by their shape alone, not only because they have subsequently been increased in length, but also because of later construction; that is, other farm buildings that have been added to them, abutting, intersecting, or projecting from them to form a cluster of connected barn structures. One case in point is the Larger Bradt barn with its ensemble of many different roof lines and disparate masses. Again, an extensive adjacent structure has been added to the Wemple barn, abutting against the southwest gable-end just to the right of the double wagon doors. Silos and attached side pavilions have been built onto the Van Bergen barn, while two of the barns near Glen have connecting structures which form, with the original barn, two sides of the farmyard, to west and north. None of these later additions, however, has interfered with the structural integrity of the original building. Amazingly, one Dutch barn that is now the core of a large ensemble of later structures (just off Route 9-H at Lower Post Road) retains its full complement of H-frames but has had its roof reconstructed at right angles to its original orientation!

Later barn construction in New York State reverted to transverse timbers that were more or less square in section, with tenons that were contained within the column mortice and did not protrude beyond the far face of the supporting columns.[3] After the decline of Dutch barn construction in America, at first the diagonal braces were relied on to augment the vertical support given the main transverse beam at each end by its narrow tenon. For its shoulders were not received into the columns, nor provided with a shelf that was notched into the column, to give some direct bearing at the bottom of the beam's total thickness. These shallower transverse beams—often of oak—usually carried all the way across as a single span between columns that were set in the outer walls of the building: no longer did the three-aisled scheme prevail. Consequently, barns that were built in the period subsequent to that of the Dutch barns came to be of quite a different shape. They were narrower: thirty to thirty-five feet wide instead of about fifty feet. Being in one span, transversely, instead of three-aisled, they were longer in relation to their width, with the big double wagon doors almost invariably placed midway along one or both sides, rather than at the gable-ends.

Loaded hay wagons now came into the barn in a crosswise direction, and the hay was pitched up into the lofts to right and left, at either side of the wide, high central bay. Much later, a metal track was installed just below the ridge, inside, continuing outside at one of the gable-ends, sometimes with an extension of the roof at the peak to support and protect this projection of the track. Here, high in the peak, a pair of large doors, hinged to open out, came to be installed in some Dutch barns in order to give access within to the loaded hayfork that raised large clutches of hay up to this level. With the hay wagon driven up close to the gable-end of the barn, outside, the crop was hoisted mechanically and deposited within the loft wherever it was desired to place it throughout the length of the interior. Thanks to their freedom from collars and other high transverse timbers, a number of Dutch barns came to be furnished with these hayfork tracks when the latter replaced manual pitching of hay from wagon to loft. However, some barns that have a metal track installed under the ridge have never included an extension of it through the gable-end peak (the Larger Wemp, for example); instead, the hay wagon had to be driven in the side entrance and unloaded by the hayfork from inside the barn. In any case, the unencumbered area of the loft space in New York Dutch barns, as originally built, made possible the subsequent installation and operation of a metal track under the ridge, from which a mechanical hayfork could raise and distribute the crop throughout the loft.

Conjectural Procedures of Erection

NOWADAYS, whenever a strut or brace or secondary member is to be installed between two major timbers, the carpenter measures the clear distance between them, saws the piece to be inserted, and nails or spikes it between the major members. In the past, because of all-wood joints, it was not so simple. Secondary members had their ends shaped as tenons, and these had to fit snugly into mortices cut to receive them, in the timbers they joined.[1] Since their length (because of the tenons) was always greater than the distance between the timbers they secured, only one of the latter could be permanently fixed before the strut was set in place. The other timber had to be kept apart to accommodate the insertion of the strut's tenon into the timber's mortice, then shifted into its permanent position and secured by one or more oak pins.

This absolute and invariable requirement of all-wood construction conditioned the entire structural system, imposing a stringent control over the order and sequence of the work throughout the entire period when New York Dutch barns were being built. It is therefore appropriate to speculate on the problems and probable solutions of the erectional operations that had to be followed. And speculation it must be, for there is complete silence in all written records of early timber construction. The equipment employed and, most of all, the procedures adopted were practical considerations in which the knowledge and experience of the carpenter, relying on custom and example, served in lieu of any manual or written set of instructions.

FRAMING OF SILLS

New World Dutch barns always have longitudinal sleepers running beneath the range of columns on each side of the threshing floor, and each column has a stub tenon that engages into a sinkage in the upper face of its sleeper. In the framing of the sills, it is clear that the work proceeded from the center outward; that is, from the threshing floor area to the side aisles. According to the evidence of those barns whose ruinous state permits observation of the details, the sill assemblage was framed differently in different barns.

For example, in a five-bay barn south of Sharon it is clear that the lowest—and very heavy—transverse members were the first to be laid, stretching across the central area at bay intervals, to rest on a single large rock placed solidly beneath the point at which each column was to rise (Dwg. 11 at D). Long heavy timbers were set in wide flat notches across these transverse sills: one under each range of columns, one as the median timber of the threshing floor, and one on each side of the latter, midway between it and the column sills. The mud-sill at the gable-ends of this same barn (C in Dwg. 11) was horizontally morticed to receive the tenoned ends of four of these longitudinal timbers; and a dovetailed sinkage was cut to accommodate the end of the median floor timber. This latter attachment locked the whole framework together. The locking was accomplished when the gable-end sill—in length the full width of the barn—was eased sideways into place and then secured by dropping the shaped end of the median timber's dovetail into its wide slot.

Another, probably more common scheme of framing the sills, was that in which the transverse members were tenoned into horizontal mortices cut into the side of the column sill (E in Dwg. 11). Here the longitudinal timber on which a range of columns was to be seated is supported on a plinth of two large flat stones under each column. In this scheme the framing procedure would have been somewhat more complicated. First, one of the longitudinal column-sills had to be established in place on its stone plinths. Then, having inserted the tenons of the transverse members into their mortices, the other column-sill would have been brought up, laid across its plinths, and carefully eased sideways until the tenons of the transverse timbers on that side were fully engaged into its mortices. (In this particular barn, the entire threshing floor has been removed, including the central section of the mud-sills at either gable-end. So it is not clear whether there was a median floor-sill or not. In all likelihood there was, since one is invariably present in all the barns that retain their original flooring. If indeed there was a median floor timber in this barn, the framing could probably still have been assembled as just described, with this one intermediate step in addition. In any case, the mud-sills would doubtless have been slipped in sideways over the tenons of the longitudinal sills in order to make the frame complete and secure.)

This same scheme was certainly analogous to the usual practice followed in assembling the sills of the side walls. As shown at B in Dwg. 11, the wall-sill would have had to be pushed inward to allow the mortices at its ends to engage the tenons that terminated the mud-sills at the corners of the barn. Many barns did not have floored side aisles. Where they did (as at F in Dwg. 11), the transverse beams that were framed to support the planking there may have had outer tenons: those would also have had to be threaded into mortices in the wall-sill when it was shoved into place. In any case, the corner detail shown at B indicates conclusively that the entire side wall—sill, studs, braces, and plate—could not have been framed on the ground as a complete assemblage, and tilted up into its destined vertical position all at once. Incidentally, the joints of all sill assemblages are always without pins or any form of wooden pegs. In this respect they are unlike all other framed connections throughout these barns, which are secured by one or more oak pins.

H-Frames

Once the sills had been framed together in place, resting evenly and firmly on their stone plinths, the next operation in building a New World Dutch barn would have been the erection of the H-frames. It is possible that the sill assemblage might have been managed, under the direction of the carpenter, by the farmer and his Negro, with the aid of levers and probably a team of oxen. But the erection of the H-frames could not have been undertaken without more human assistance. Even supposing that these frames were already assembled and in convenient position for their sequential raising, it would have taken a number of men, along with some special equipment, to erect them. They could have been skidded readily enough to the precise spot at which they were to be raised. But it seems most unlikely that they could have been tilted up from a horizontal to a vertical position,[2] as was the customary procedure followed in the case of English cruck construction and other heavily membered timber framing in England and on the Continent.

Two considerations militated against this common Old World practice. One was the presence of the stub tenons at the base of each column, which, as pivot points, would certainly have been injured if not actually broken off in the process, in view of the weight of the H-frames. The other reason had to do with the shape and make-up of these frames, and the location in this assemblage of their heaviest member. In many barns, the anchorbeam—much the largest and bulkiest member in the entire structural complex—together with its short but thick diagonal braces, weighed almost twice as much as its two column supports combined. Moreover, the columns were weakened at about half their height by being cut through for the mortices that received the big anchorbeam tongues. In an H-frame where the horizontal member was not only so much heavier than the uprights, but considerably longer too, a tilt-up procedure would seemingly not have been feasible. With only two widely-spaced column feet as pivot points, the columns themselves might well have proven to be too weak and in danger of breaking at the points where so much of their substance had been voided to receive the ends of the anchorbeam, when the tilt-up process got to be above the level at which heaving hands could crowd together along its length.

Of course it is possible that the anchorbeams were hoisted up first, vertically; that their diagonal braces were pinned to their soffits; and that the columns, one at either end, were then raised and slipped sideways over the anchorbeam tongues and the lower tenons of the braces. But this piecemeal procedure would have taken more raising equipment than would the erection of the frame as a single unit. It would also have necessitated the most accurate and careful adjustments in the sidewise securing of each suspended column to the suspended anchorbeam, with precise settings for each of four hoisting apparatuses. The threading of the head-height longitudinal links would have occasioned a further complication. And the total operation would have been the more difficult because of the weight and size of the members that had to be separately raised and individually interlocked while in their suspended positions.

It would seem much more likely, therefore, that the H-frames were assembled on the ground and raised as a complete unit, not by the co-ordinated manual efforts of a score or so of men, but by the application of mechanical means to assist their undertaking. Of course, the individual members of the frame were cumbersome enough to begin with, and their widely spaced supports—the columns—made a particularly awkward assemblage for the maneuvering that had to take place in raising the frame from a horizontal to a vertical position. Particularly, inasmuch as the exposed verticals of the H were so much slenderer and more vulnerable than the long heavy cross-member. But the relative flimsiness of the assemblage, subject to racking action during erection, was rendered less unstable by the nature and extent of the columns' connections to the anchorbeam. It has already been pointed out that the braces were essential in resisting swaying in the plane of the H-frame (Dwg. 12 at

A). These same braces were also useful, along with the anchorbeam tongues, in another capacity. During the process of erection, they stiffened the connection between the columns and the anchorbeam so that the entire frame could be handled as a unit without its racking or twisting apart at the joints. In this situation, the depth of the anchorbeams, and the presence of the wedges that usually supplemented their pinned joints, were further assurances of stability at these critical junctures.

Assuming, then, that the H-frames were raised mechanically as single ensembles, it is important to note that the lifting slings would have had to be secured not to the columns but to the anchorbeam. This being the largest, heaviest, and often the longest member of the H-frame ensemble, it would have been the part that needed to be raised vertically. Sufficiently long poles would have had to be supplied in each of two three-legged gins to raise the anchorbeam slightly above its destined position (in order to insert the stub tenons that terminated the base of the columns into the mortices of the sills). The total weight of the largest H-frames would have been around 5,000 pounds; so each gin would have had to raise about a ton and a quarter. This was not an excessive load, but it did require two sets of block-and-tackle with long strong ropes and a number of men pulling on them, or perhaps a team of oxen. Since the anchorbeam was joined to the columns at roughly half their height, there would have been little danger of breaking or straining the columns unduly while the frame slowly rose to its vertical position. For the upward pull would have been concentrated exclusively on the anchorbeam. The cumbersome H-frame, with its slender, awkwardly outstretching extremities, was thus reasonably manageable because no special strain was put upon these extremities, the columns. They were not actively implicated in the process of erection but were carried along as inert adjuncts to the great anchorbeam as it was being hauled up. During the course of this lifting operation, moreover, the upper and lower arms of the columns, each balanced across its attachment to the heavy anchorbeam, could be used to rotate the beam gradually from its supine to its upright attitude, somewhat in the manner of a windlass. And when the frame had been raised to its upper limit, it was easy for one man at each dangling column to insert the horizontal head-height linkage into the side face of the column, and then to direct the latter's tenon into the sill's mortice as the ropes were slackened off and the frame was lowered a few inches into its final position.

The first and last H-frames—those at the gable-ends—had an additional feature to contend with while they were being set in position.

This was the pair of oak jambs that framed each side of the big wagon doors, and on which these doors hinged. They were tenoned into the end sill, below, and the anchorbeam, above. But we have already noted that, at the time of their erection, the H-frames would have had to be hauled up a few inches higher than their ultimate position, in order to be able to have the tenons of their columns inserted into the mortices of the sills. So nothing that required exceptional treatment was encountered here; only a few more hands to set the door posts and maintain them in precise vertical alignment as the anchorbeam was lowered over their tenoned tops.

The end frames, too, unlike the normal situation in the case of the other H-frames, always had a high transverse timber linking the two end columns together. This member was usually set at a level a few inches down from the top of the columns it linked. Moreover, in some instances it was framed with diagonal braces similar to those of the anchorbeam, lower down. But these braces were lighter than those of the latter, in keeping with the slenderness of the upper tie to which they were attached. The studs that were set between this tie and the anchorbeam—usually five of them, if they were evenly spaced—were tenoned into both lower and upper member (that is, the anchorbeam and the high transverse tie) but not pinned to either. They would have been installed after the gable-end frame was raised, either by being let into a deeper mortice above, or by being swung sideways from above into a grooved mortice below. In either case, the subsequent clapboarding would have secured them from shucking about.

The insertion of the longitudinal head-height members would have presented no problem. For, with its suspension from above, the about-to-be-placed H-frame would have merely needed to be swayed slightly away from the adjacent, previously set frame, in order to allow the tenons of the struts to be inserted into the mortices of the columns.

Sway-Bracing and Purlin-Plate

Probably the next operation that was undertaken in a New York Dutch barn raising was to consolidate the series of H-frames longitudinally; that is, to link the tops of all the columns in each range to provide resistance to tilting deformation in their upright alignment. Once this was done, it completed the rigid core so essential to the overall stability of the skeletal structure of the barn (Dwg. 13). Thereafter, all other members were adjuncts which depended to a greater or lesser extent upon this central complex, and derived their alignment and/or support largely from its integrity of stability.

The first step in implementing rigidity in the longitudinal direction was to insert and pin the diagonal sway-braces into their mortices high up in the side faces of the columns. Although the pattern of the sway-braces varied (See Dwg. 5), the erectional procedures were similar. Where short diagonals were employed, it may have been possible to maintain their proper degree of slope, when they were first installed, via the snug fit and the pinned connection at their junction with the column. But longer, heavier diagonals (as in the case of the Wemple and Bradt-Mabie barns, for example) would have had to be temporarily held in their proper position by short lengths of rope. Sometimes these would have been merely cinched about the column near its top (C in Dwg. 14). But frequently, so-called raising holes may have been utilized in this connection, as indicated at A in Dwg. 14. The main purpose of the raising holes, however, was quite different.

First of all, the raising holes always pass through the upper part of the column transversely. The level at which they occur varies a good deal: sometimes it is down only some six to eight inches below the top of the column (Acker); sometimes a foot (Indian Castle); sometimes about eighteen inches (Adriance). Again, the holes are some three feet down in the Larger Wemp barn, and almost four feet in the Route 20, East of Sharon barn.

Although a few barns lack raising holes altogether, there are a number of instances in which each column is furnished with *two* raising holes, one above the other (A, D, and E in Dwg. 14). Where this is the case, they are not of the same diameter, and the upper is usually the smaller. For example, the Larger Bradt barn has 1- to 1¼-inch-diameter holes, down 9 or 10 inches below the purlin-plate, with 2- to 2¼-inch holes some 20 to 22 inches farther down. But the Wemple barn, exceptionally, has 1¼-inch-diameter holes 30½ inches above the top of the anchorbeams and 2-inch holes 26 inches above them, and these latter are set at 46¾ inches below the soffit of the plate.

It would seem that these raising holes—or rather, the rods that passed through them—served two related functions in connection with the process of installing the purlin-plate (See Dwg. 14). One was to form brackets on which sapling poles could be laid horizontally, against which one or more ladders could be leaned, and on which a man could stand. The other function of the rods was to act as a temporary resting place for the purlin-plate before it was settled into its final position atop the columns.

It will be remembered that the purlin-plate was always a single, unspliced beam, running the full length of the barn. It was probably hauled up vertically on the outside of the columns by the sustained efforts of a sufficient number of men. It would have come to rest, first, on the protruding tongues of the anchorbeams. For it was at this level that stable footing was already provided for the lifters by the anchorbeams themselves. For the second, higher haul, however, some sort of temporary platform or scaffold would have had to be devised. The simplest way of providing such a platform—one that required the least expenditure of time, labor, and materials—would seem to have been via poles resting on temporary rods passing through the column at some convenient level, as suggested above. Such a platform—a mere foot support—would have been reached, as well as held in place, by the ladders leaning against it; yet it would have been sufficient as a footrest for the job in hand.

Some such higher staging was essential at this point in the erection of the barn. For, without it, the top of each anchorbeam would have constituted the highest horizontal shelf from which the men could work, and such a shelf was much too far below the tops of the columns for them to be reached from this level. A conveniently located high ledge on which the men could perch was the more necessary because of the accuracy required in engaging all the tenons into the mortices of the purlin-plate. There would need to have been certainly one, possibly two men stationed at each column: first, to raise the purlin-plate aloft; second, to lift it up and over the tenons of the columns and the sway-bracing. This second step required both strength and precision in the coordinated efforts of the team that undertook the seating of this long, column-top member.

The advantage of having gone to the trouble of pre-assembling the columns, sway-bracing, and purlin-plate on the ground, previous to erection, is particularly evident in the case of the purlin-plate's installation. On the one hand, all the morticed joints of the diagonals had to create snug fits in order to be effective in their sway-bracing capacity. On the other hand, this very snugness of fit made the installation of the purlin-plate an especially ticklish job, involving as it did the simultaneous alignment of a large number of tenons exactly opposite their mortices in the purlin-plate. It was hard enough just to lift the long purlin-plate by hand the final foot (or feet) up over the tops of the columns. But to do this with the necessary precision in the coordination of multiple insertions, when it had to be executed high up in the air where the footing was rather precarious and human brawn was the only motive power, demanded a high level of performance. Obviously, the more hands there were available, the more expeditiously and unblunderingly the job could be done. In any case, a team of many men would have had to contribute their skill and muscle in this operation.

Group Cooperation

This latter consideration—the number of men required to do the job—was a major factor in the erection of one of these early Dutch barns. Actually, it would seem to have had a profound influence on the very nature and make-up of the structural system that was adopted. It is therefore worth noting some of the circumstances under which these barns came into being.

Generally, it may be said that the early Dutch barns of the New World were built in a pioneering era by hardy and determined settlers. The land had to be reclaimed from the wilderness, as explained by Crèvecoeur and other early writers. The forests had to be cleared, the tangle of brush and vines burnt off, the swamps drained, and the fields put into production. It was a hard life of constant, back-breaking toil. And so the barns, essential from the start to preserve the produce of all this toil, were constructed at sites removed from populous communities and, as often as not, at locations that were also distant from individual neighbors. Until his fields were in production, his barn built, and his husbandry firmly established, the farmer and his servant may have lived quite primitively in either a log cabin or a cellar-hole hut.

Because his neighbors were often so far removed from his farmstead, and because they themselves were as busy as he in the struggle of agricultural pioneering, a farmer had to rely very largely on himself; that is, on his own industry and that of his servant. Laborers were few and hard to come by. Moreover, one farmer could not expect the help of others who were quite as occupied and as hard working as he, except in special circumstances such as a barn raising. Even here, however, there was a stringent limitation on the amount of time he could ask his neighbors to give. So he had to have all in readiness before they arrived to help him. The trees would have been felled, the logs cured, and then snaked to the site; so much, he could have managed himself. But unless the farmer also happened to be a skilled carpenter, the shaping of the timbers and the cutting of mortices in accordance with a carefully laid out plan would have been the work of a professional and experienced carpenter. The craftsmanship of these old barns is generally much too expert, too finished, to have been the work of untrained men, however self-reliant and handy they may have been. So the preparation of the timbers and their test assembling would have been done by the carpenter, along with whatever assistance the farmer was competent to give. At the start of actual construction, too, the carpenter's direction, at least, would have been essential when the foundation stones were dragged in and set firmly in place. And this same professional direction would have been required during the heavy but precise work of assembling the framework of sills on top of these accurately leveled foundation stones. But at this point both the carpenter's direction and the toil of the farmer would have come to a standstill without the help of additional hands: a considerable number of men who were needed for the operations of raising the heavy H-frames, and of setting the purlin-plates. In what took place thereafter, as we will see, the rest of the barn's erection—even including the roof construction—could have been handled by the farmer and his servant, plus either the carpenter or a competent hired man.

So it is clear that both the ordering of the work and, much more significantly, the very structural system itself, were pervasively affected (at least in pioneering situations) by the necessity to concentrate all group activity with respect to the barn's erection into the shortest possible period of time: two days at most, and perhaps only one long day, from dawn to dusk, in most cases. In this respect, the American situation was quite different from that of contemporary Europe, where communities were not so widely separated and there was usually an adequate number of nearby neighbors who could be called upon for assistance as needed. In America it would seem that whole families set out, sometimes long before dawn, to make the trek to the site, bringing essential gear and perhaps additional oxen. The women would have been occupied throughout the day in preparing and serving quantities of food. Even some of the children would have been called upon from time to time to fetch a tool or run up a ladder or hold onto a length of rope. A "raising bee" was a social event in that it brought together a considerable number of people of all ages. But the infrequency and brevity of such an event were conditioned by the utilitarian purpose that occasioned it. In Europe, on the other hand, no such extraordinary status attached to a barn raising. Nor did it have to be accomplished, there, in such self-reliant isolation save for a single day or two of concentrated team effort.[3]

SIDE WALLS

Probably the next operation in building a New World Dutch barn (after the rigid central core had been achieved, and the neighbors who had helped to erect it had departed) was to raise the side walls. It seems probable that this was done piecemeal rather than in terms of tilting up a complete assemblage that had already been framed horizontally in its entirety on the ground. One detail that provides some evidence for this assertion is that of the framing of the sills: for example, the corner condition in the Van Wie barn, as shown in Dwg. 11 at B. If the entire side-wall framing (including its sill) had been pre-assembled in this instance, it could have been set in place only by raising it to a vertical position, then joining it to what was already built only by shifting this wall-assemblage laterally in a maneuver that would have involved sliding the wall sill horizontally over the tenons of all the transverse sills that engaged with it: those at the gable-ends and those in line with the columns. This would seem to have been an unnecessarily cumbersome and tricky operation, greatly complicated by the need to maneuver other pairs of tenons—those of the upper and lower side-aisle struts—into their wall-stud mortices. Again, it is just possible that, with the side-wall sill already in place, the entire frame except for this sill may have been assembled on the ground and pivoted up to a vertical position, the studs all dangling from their pinned connections to the wall-plate, to be lowered a few inches in order to engage their tenons into the mortices of the wall sill. But such a procedure would appear to be most unlikely: too rickety an assemblage to be tilted up in this fashion, and too subject to twisting and being wrenched apart at its unstayed joints. In addition, the erection of such a large-scale assemblage, all at once, would have required the assistance of many hands; and we have just made the point that, in these early American barn raisings, everything possible was done to limit to a minimum those procedures that required cooperative effort on the part of a considerable number of men.

It seems most probable, therefore, that the side-wall members were raised and secured one at a time. First to be erected in this sequence would have been the main wall posts opposite each column, starting at a gable-end corner. Their placement would have involved the insertion of the two side-aisle links, one at head-height, the other six feet or so higher up. With one man holding the wall post nearly vertical, two other men would lift the head-height strut, and one of them would insert and pin its tenon in the wall post. (Alternatively, and more probably, the wall post may have been held upright by a few not-too-tightly-strung guy ropes.) Then they would rock the post to a vertical position, thereby engaging the other end of the strut in its column's mortice, but without pinning it there. Next, standing on this head-height strut, they would raise and hold the upper transverse strut aloft, and one of them would pin its outer tenon to the wall post, having rocked this member sufficiently out of plumb to insert the high strut's tenon, but not enough to disengage the lower strut's column-linking tenon. With the installation of both lower and upper side-aisle struts completed, their column ends would then have been permanently secured.

Longitudinal stability against swaying or racking of the wall posts could have been temporarily assured, at this stage in the building operation, perhaps by ropes but more probably by a few sapling poles laid across the side-aisle struts, above and below. These temporary poles, secured to the wall posts, would have been useful in aligning the ordinary wall studs that were next to be installed. The unnumbered ordinary studs, set between the wall posts, could thus have been held in a vertical position by securing them temporarily to the sapling poles. Moreover, the precise spacing of their tops could also have been adjusted so that their tenons would accurately align with the mortices of the wall plate. That long horizontal member that capped the wall would therefore have been much more easily installed than the purlin-plate, thanks to the dual role of the sapling poles. For these poles, especially the upper ones, would have temporarily held all the vertical members in exact position, and at the same time would have provided a convenient staging from which a few men could raise and maneuver the wall plate up over the tenons of the many wall members, diagonals as well as verticals, that had to engage with it.

Roof

With the fixing of the wall plate above each side wall, the stage was set for the erection of the roof. Here, too, sapling poles would have been called upon to provide a temporary staging. Not many poles would have been needed, however, since most of the operation of raising the rafters could have been handled by a man standing on or sitting astride the purlin-plate, one on each side. The sapling poles would have been useful as a high-level temporary bridge to allow passage on the part of the workmen from one side of the central space to the other, at the column-top level. Mostly, however, this bridge was needed as a staging from which a man could pin together a pair of rafters, and from which he could help to maneuver them into position, high up across the void.

The first step in erecting the roof would have been to haul up two rafters, one for each slope, that had previously been shaped; that is, tongue-and-forked where they were to be joined, notched near the middle of their length, and cut off diagonally (with or without a cog) so as to provide a horizontal bearing on the wall plate, at their feet. These rafters would have been laid out askew across purlin-plates and sapling poles, and pinned together in chevron fashion above the center of the void. Because the rafters were balanced about their mid-length notch, a pair of them could easily be rotated on the purlin-plates at these points. Whether they were rotated so that their feet swung clockwise or counterclockwise, as seen from the side, would have made little difference. For, with the usual five-foot spacing of the rafters, there was sufficient clearance to prevent the interference of a previously set pair of rafters, in either case. Dwg. 15 shows a schematic view of this rotation procedure, where the peak of a new rafter-pair is about to be swung up under that of a previously set pair. This drawing is purposely made out-of-scale (i.e., all the timbers are shown much too thick for their spans) in order to clarify the nature of the operation.

In the roof framing of New York Dutch barns, one or both of two features are frequently omitted. Namely: a notch, the width of the rafter, in the outer vertical face of the purlin-plate (Dwg. 9 at C, E, G, and H); and a projecting cog at the foot of the rafter (Dwg. 10 at A, B, F, H, and L). It is evident, however, that these two details were useful at the time of erection in establishing and maintaining both the spacing of the rafter-pairs and their precise alignment in a vertical plane. These features were also effective supplements in preventing any racking movement in the roof as a whole, after it had been built.

Neither of these details was absolutely essential, however, even though they are usually included in those barns that manifest the most accomplished craftsmanship. The indispensable oak pin that secured the rafter at its bearing on the purlin-plate came to serve the purpose of the higher of these two features, once the pins were in place. And the nailed roofing boards, starting at the eaves, came to substitute for the other, to a considerable extent. In the meantime, ropes could have stayed the rafter-pairs in their vertical planes while each successive pair was being raised into position.

It was this roof construction that constituted such a remarkable and apparently unprecedented characteristic of the New World Dutch barns. In spite of their large size—as much as fifty-four feet wide—and their exceptionally capacious space-volume in the haylofts, the roofs could be erected by as few as two or three strong men. This feature, then, quite as much as the more conspicuous anchorbeams, manifests the outstanding and probably unique structural characteristic of these early barns.

The above conjectural comments complete the erectional account of the main structural framework of a New York Dutch barn. Certain adjunct features would have presented no special difficulties of framing or installation; at least, it is clear that they could have been both fashioned and put into place by two or three men. Such features include the planking of the central threshing floor (Plate 41), the doors and their hinges (Plates 47 and 48), the mangers (Plate 40), the eaves gutters (Dwg. 18), and the pentices over the barn doors (Dwg. 16).

Aesthetic Character

NEW YORK DUTCH BARNS are of *noble proportions* on the exterior: broad, capacious looking, spreading expansively to either side of the central wagon doors above which the roof rises in uncomplicated symmetry. These barns are big, but not overwhelmingly so. The simplicity of their shape is frankly utilitarian, but not impersonally or austerely so. Doors—even the Dutch doors of the wagon entrances—are for human use too; and both these and the martin holes above them combine usefulness and concern for good husbandry with an unselfconscious sense of good design. The shape of these barns is neither squat and sunken looking nor narrow and tall. Even when they are viewed from a distance there is a quality of integrity about them: an integrity of purpose, of materials and craftsmanship, of complete adaptation to the conditions of their being.

If one can admire the superior quality of their exterior appearance, the interior is even more noteworthy. One hears much, these days, about *revealed structure* in architecture, and about the visual quality and *expressiveness of interior space*. With respect to both of these considerations, New York Dutch barns are unusually distinguished.

Within these barns, the entire structural system was exposed to view; and so it is, today, in most of the surviving examples. Except for the threshing-floor planking that obscures the framing of the sills, there are no screens, no wall-board or lath-and-plaster partitions, no coverings to clothe or hide the structural framework. Every timber of the entire skeleton lies open to view. The dimensions of its length and cross-section, its means of attachment, its function and relative size in the ensemble—these can be freely observed. Its species of wood, its details, its degree of finish—all lie open to examination. Such an opportunity for unlimited inspection is presented only by barns; almost all other building types hide their structural members beneath plaster or paneling, behind wainscoting or ceiling finishes, except perhaps in cellars and attics. In buildings other than barns, one gets to see their structural skeleton only by chance, and briefly; namely, either during the course of their erection, or at the end of their useful life, when these buildings are being demolished.

Generally, it is of the very nature of barns that their structural framework remains consistently and permanently disclosed, inside the building. This is absolutely true in New York Dutch barns. It is somewhat less true in most Old World barns. For in these latter, a part of the barn served as residence for the farm family, whose living quarters required differentiated rooms for various purposes, separated from the animals and the fodder of the barn proper. It is highly significant (if difficult to account for) that in New Netherland, right from the start, the living quarters of human beings were never accommodated in the barn. The New World barns, therefore, did not have to be as tight against wind and cold as did the early settlers' dwelling, however rude the latter may have been. If, on certain occasions as at harvest time, an excess of hired hands slept in the hayloft, their meals were served elsewhere; no provision had to be made in the barn for cooking. Even in the wintertime, the body heat of the animals quartered there was sufficient to sustain them, insulated as they were by the store of hay above and around them, and protected as they were from wind and snow by the walls and roof that sheltered and preserved both them and their food supply. Hence, New World barns were partitionless, stoveless, unheated by artificial means. Which meant that, seen from within, their great structural framework could and did remain fully exposed to view.

The interior of these barns is extraordinarily impressive as *expansive and ordered space*. The sense of vastness and yes, of grandeur, even, is heightened by the uneven light, mostly from an open door. On a bright summer day, with both leaves of the wagon doors open, there is certainly abundance of natural light on the threshing floor for whatever tasks take place there. But even then, the upper reaches of the loft seem huge and cavernous, pierced by a few slender shafts of sunlight slanting down from the martin holes. At choretime in the early morning or at twilight, or during heavily overcast days, there could have been only faint light throughout the barn in its original windowless state, and then the place seemed vaster than ever. Whether in much or little light, however, the vastness was an ordered spaciousness, with the stable landmarks of columns to right and left, and the anchorbeams overhead. And so the framing members—purposeful, ordered, and clearly differentiated—played their part in visually organizing and subdividing the space contained within the barn's geometrically simple envelope, at once unifying it and giving it appropriate, expansive scale.

Undoubtedly, this impressive organization of visual space was an unpremeditated result of the impressive organization of a sound structural system. But in meeting the practical and engineering requirements so effectively, the anonymous craftsmen created buildings that had a rich complement of expressiveness, too. Their work is a striking demonstration of aesthetic Form developing out of utilitarian Function.

NOTES

HISTORICAL INTRODUCTION

1. See the fold-out maps facing the following pages in E. B. O'Callaghan, *The Documentary History of the State of New York* (Albany: Weed Parsons & Co., 1850), Vol. III, p. 690 ("Beatty's Map of Livingston Manor, 1714"); p. 917 ("Bleecker's Map of the Manor of Rensselaerwyck, with the Homesteads Thereon, 1763"); and p. 834 ("Wigram's Map of the Towns of Livingston, Germantown, and Clermont in the County of Columbia, with the Several Homesteads Thereon, 1798"). In all three cases the scale is sufficiently large to allow a little houselike symbol, labeled with the name of the inhabitant, to be included. But of barns there is no indication, even though in actual dimension the big barn would have been larger than any of the dwellings of the time, with the possible exception of the Manor House. Barns simply do not figure pictorially in any of the maps and charts and land surveys of the times.

2. There is a minimum of historical coverage of any sort concerned with the barns of America. Perhaps the only substantial accounts that have achieved publication in this country to date are those that deal not with New York but with Pennsylvania Dutch barns. These works include two books and one lecture, as follows:

> Charles E. Dornbusch, *Pennsylvania German Barns* (Allentown, Pa., 1958). Published by the Pennsylvania German Folklore Society as [Yearbook] Vol. 21. (Chiefly illustrations, but with an instructive 16-page introduction by John K. Heyl.)
>
> Alfred L. Shoemaker *et al.*, *The Pennsylvania Barn* (Lancaster, Pa., [1955]). Published by the Pennsylvania Dutch Folklore Center.
>
> M. D. Learned, "The German Barn in America," *University Lectures* Delivered by Members of the Faculty in the Free Public Lecture Course, 1913–14, Philadelphia (published by the University of Pennsylvania, 1915), pp. 338–49.

It is not altogether surprising—because of their conspicuous appearance and their freedom from destruction by Indians and other hostile groups—that there has been some treatment of and interest in Pennsylvania Dutch barns. As far back as 1913, Professor Learned called attention to their significance as valuable records of colonial life and as instruments of the well-ordered farming practices established in the areas settled by these German and Swiss immigrants. In 1902, in fact, there had been an ethnographical survey—the first of its kind in America—whose purpose was to collect accurate statistics on the early Swiss and Palatine settlements in Pennsylvania, including studies on the history and development of the German barn in America.

What is remarkable, however, is that there is almost nothing of a comparable nature concerning the corresponding contributions of the early Dutch settlers. They too established an agricultural economy adapted specifically to the conditions of the New World. The Holland Dutch, indeed, were quite as influential in these respects in the areas they settled as were the Germans in Pennsylvania; and their contributions to agriculture and farm economy generally in the New World predated by a number of generations those of the Germans to the southwest of them. Yet the New World Dutch achievement in agricultural excellence, though acknowledged at the time, has had but the scantiest notice in our time.

For example, in the most recent of the popular books of Eric Sloane (*An Age of Barns* [New York: Funk & Wagnalls, (1966)]), there is only a two-page spread on the early New York State Dutch barn, marred by errors in the text and inaccuracies in the drawings. These shortcomings are all the more unfortunate and misleading because of the attractiveness and seeming authority of the author's strong, effective pen-and-ink illustrations. Sloane's obvious interest and enthusiasm for his subject partly make up for the book's errors, however. And at least this is an attempt to present the entire range and variety of early American barns, together with the ancillary structures of early farming, for the first time.

Another but very brief review of the variety to be found in American barns of the past is Mary Mix Foley, "The American Barn," *Architectural Forum*, Vol. XCV (Aug., 1951), pp. 170–77, with 41 small photographic illustrations. Here the New York Dutch barn is represented by the Verplanck-Van Wyck example (Plates 13 and 14), whose gable forebay makes it exceptional and atypical. (Sloane's example is the now-destroyed Teller-Schermerhorn barn [Plate 15], whose very steep-pitched roof makes it similarly exceptional.)

Earlier, the Verplanck-Van Wyck barn had been pictured as Plate 9 in Helen Wilkinson Reynolds, *Dutch Houses in the Hudson Valley before 1776*, 2 vols., for the Holland Society of New York (Payson and Clarke, 1929), from which Foley got her information. [There is a one-volume reprint by Dover, 1965.] Reynolds' one-sentence comment on this single example of a Dutch barn included in her important and erudite work states that the gable overhang of the second story is "typical of the Dutch barns of the eighteenth century". The present writer's investigations have not corroborated this assertion.

Peter O. Wacker, *The Musconetcong Valley of New Jersey* (New Brunswick: Rutgers University Press, 1968) covers the historical geography of this New Jersey valley area in detail and the whole state more generally. Parts of Chapters 3, 4, and 5 of this commendable book discuss the presence of the early Dutch in New Jersey and their pioneering contributions there. The work includes one photographic illustration of a surviving Dutch barn near Pluckemin. It also maps the location of Dutch barns and Dutch barracks that were extant in the state from 1749 to 1782 (p. 96), and from 1730 to 1782 (p. 100), respectively.

From the nineteenth century there is a fair number of American publications that covered rural structures in the form of model books (with many illustrations) or treatises (with diagrams) describing how to design fences and gates, how to provide for the ventilation of storage barns and cattle barns, how to secure and distribute a water supply on the farm, or how to arrange the layout of farm buildings. But such publications are not historical in their approach and hence do not concern us here.

However, for an informing and generally accurate description of a New York State Dutch barn, that of John Burroughs, the American essayist and literary naturalist (1837–1921) is a welcome rarity. It is found as a part of Chapter III, "Phases of Farm Life," in his *In the Catskills* (Boston and New York: Houghton Mifflin, The Riverside Press, 1910), pp. 49–52. Here is what he writes from his native Roxbury, near the headwaters of the Delaware River in the Western Catskill region:

> Many of the early settlers of New York were from New England, Connecticut perhaps sending out the most. . . . But the State early had one element introduced into its rural and farm life not found farther east, namely, the Holland Dutch. These gave features more or less picturesque to the country that are not observable in New England. The Dutch took root at various points along the Hudson, and about Albany and in the Mohawk valley, and remnants of their rural and domestic architecture may still be seen in these sections of the State. A Dutch barn became proverbial. . . . The main feature of these barns was their enormous expansion of roof. It was a comfort to look at them, they suggested such shelter and protection. The eaves were very low and the ridge-pole very high. Long rafters and short posts gave them a quaint, short-waisted, grandmotherly look. They were nearly square, and stood very broad upon the ground. Their form was doubtless suggested by the damper climate of the Old World, where the grain and hay, instead of being packed in deep solid mows, used to be spread upon poles and exposed to the currents of air under the roof. Surface and not cubic capacity is more important in these matters in Holland than in this country. . . .
>
> The Dutch barn was the most picturesque barn that has been built, especially when thatched with straw, as they nearly all were, and forming one side of an inclosure of lower roofs or sheds also covered with straw, beneath which the cattle took refuge from the winter storms. Its immense, unpainted gable, cut with holes for the swallows, was like a section of a respectable-sized hill, and its roof like its slope. Its great doors always had a hood projecting over them, and the doors themselves were divided horizontally into upper and lower halves; the upper halves very frequently being left open, through which you caught a glimpse of the mows of hay, or the twinkle of flails when the grain was being threshed. . . .
>
> The large, unpainted timber barns that succeeded the first Yankee settlers' log stables were also picturesque, especially when a lean-to for the cow-stables was added, and the roof carried down with a long sweep over it; or when the barn was flanked by an open shed with a hayloft above it, where the hens cackled and hid their nests, and from the open window of which the hay was always hanging.

Then the great timbers of these barns and the Dutch barn, hewn from maple or birch or oak trees from the primitive woods, and put in place by the combined strength of all the brawny arms in the neighborhood when the barn was raised,—timbers strong enough and heavy enough for docks and quays, and that have absorbed the odors of the hay and grain until they look ripe and mellow and full of the pleasing sentiment of the great, sturdy, bountiful interior! The 'big beam' has become smooth and polished from the hay that has been pitched over it, and the sweaty, sturdy forms that have crossed it. One feels that he would like a piece of furniture—a chair, or a table, or a writing desk, a bedstead, or a wainscoting—made from these long-seasoned, long-tried, richly toned timbers of the old barn. . . .

3. As might be expected because of their extensive forests, the Scandinavian countries have a continuous and many-centuries-old tradition of building in wood; and for these areas there is a considerable body of literature, quite apart from that devoted to religious buildings, that deals comprehensively and in detail with the common, unpretentious vernacular buildings. An excellent example is Gerda Boëthius, *Studier I: Den Nordiska Timmerbyggnadskensten en undersökning Utgående Från Anders Zorns Samlingar* (Stockholm: Fritzes Hovbokhandel I Distribution, 1927), which contains many photographs as well as a very large number of plans, sections, and details of the construction, layout, and decoration of the buildings. But the most persistent, penetrating, and comprehensive investigations of rural buildings, and particularly of barns, are those concerned with the areas of northwestern Germany and the whole of Holland. Only a small sampling of these publications is mentioned here. However, as often as not such literature includes extensive bibliographies that indicate the degree to which research has been carried on in this field by many writers and for many years. Here are some representative works, both books and articles, most of which include some coverage of anchorbeam construction:

S. J. Fockema Andreae, ("Stad en Dorp"), E. H. Ter Kuile ("De Architektuur"), R. C. Hekker ("De Ontwikkeling van de Boerderijvormen in Nederland"), *Duizend Jaar Bouwen in Nederland*. Deel II: *De Bouwkunst na de Middeleeuwen* (Amsterdam; Allert de Lange, 1957).

Karl Baumgarten, "Probleme mecklenburgischer Niedersachsenhausforschung," *Deutsches Jahrbuch für Volkskunde* / Herausgegeben vom Institut für deutsche Volkskunde an der Deutschen Akademie der Wissenschaften zu Berlin / durch / Dr. Wilhelm Fraenger. (Berlin, Akademie-Verlag. Erster Band. Heft 1/2. Jahrgang 1955.) pp. 169–182. 11 line drawings.

———, *Zimmermannswerk in Mecklenburg: Die Scheune*, (Berlin: Akademie-Verlag, 1961).

Wilhelm Bowmann, *Bäuerliches Hauswesen und Tagewerk im alten Niedersachsen*, mit 212 Tafeln und Bildern. Dritte Auflage, Volksausgabe. (Weimar: Verlag Hermann Böhlaus Nachfolger [Dec., 1926], [Oct., 1933].)

W. H. Dingeldein, *Het 'Losse Hoes' Groot Bavel*, Rijksmuseum Twenthe (Enschede: 2e geheel emgewerkte druk, 1947).

Gerhard Eitzen, "Das Gefüge des niederdeutschen Bauernhaus im Lichte einer ältischen Bauweise," *Westfalen*, Hefte für Geschichte Kunst und Volkskunde, (Münster Westfalen, Aschendorffsche Verlagsbuchhandlung, 28. Band. Heft 1. 1950). pp. 26–38. 17 line dwgs. & map.

Jan Jans, *Landelijke Bouwkunst in Oost-Nederland* (Enschede, N.V.: v/h Firma M. J. Van Der Loeff, 1967).

Clemens V. Trefois, *Ontwikkelings Geschiedenis van Onze Landslijke Architectuur* (Antwerpen; De Sikkel, 1950).

Cl. V. Trefois, "La Technique de la Construction rurale en bois: Contribution à l'étude de l'habitat en Flandre et dans les contrées voisines," *Folk* (Leipzig: Verlag von S. Hirzel, Janv. 1937), Vol. I, No. 1, pp. 55–73. 27 Plates.

Adelhart Zippelius, *Das Bauernhaus am unteren deutschen Niederrhein,* (Wuppertal: Verlag A. Martini & Gruttefien GMBH, 1957). Series: Landschaftsverband Rheinland / Werken und Wohnen / Volkskundliche untersuchungen im Rheinland / Herausgegeben von Matthias Zender / Leiter der Volkskundlichen Arbeitsstelle des Landschaftswerbandes Rheinland beim Institut für geschichtliche Landeskunde der Rheinlande an der Universität Bonn. Band I. 99 text figs., 126 Plate figs.

In addition to such studies as those listed above, some of the northern European countries have established outdoor museums in which large numbers of buildings are displayed (transferred there from their original sites) as characteristic examples of the country's traditional wooden architecture. The Openluchtmuseum at Arnhem, Holland, and the Maihaugan at Lillehamar, Norway, are outstanding representatives of the national building inheritance. Aside from its remarkable assemblage of actual buildings brought together from all the provinces of Holland and displayed to the public in beautiful surroundings, the Openluchtmuseum is a repository for all sorts of information relating to these and similar authentic structures, including extensive collections of photographs.

In America, until fairly recently, this sort of activity has taken a different turn, as at Valley Forge and at Fort Ticonderoga, where reconstructions of wooden structures have been built following the style of the originals. However, a few places, such as Old Deerfield, Massachusetts, are preserving not only individual wooden buildings but whole groups of them in their original settings. Aiding in this belated process is the outstanding work of the Historic American Buildings Survey (HABS). In this program, under the National Park Service, eminently significant houses and other pre- and post-Revolutionary buildings are being measured and recorded with trained skill and assiduous thoroughness. But there are many important buildings yet to be covered in this nationwide survey, and it is quite understandable that the extraordinarily exhaustive recordings of the HABS have not yet been made of early barns.

In recent years steps have been taken to preserve examples of early Dutch barns for posterity. At Coxsackie on the west bank of the Hudson River the Bronck barn, on its original site, is maintained by and is on the property of the Greene County Historical Association, whose headquarters are in the old brick house adjacent to the barn. A few old Dutch barns have been moved and reestablished as permanent exhibitions in connection with some historical site: for example, at the Sleepy Hollow Restorations on the Tappan Zee at Tarrytown, where the barn was dismantled, moved across the river, and reassembled downstream from its original site in Hurley. At Upper Canada Village west of Cornwall on the north shore of the St. Lawrence River two relocated Dutch "Schoharie" barns now house the agricultural museum in this extensive collection of authentic early buildings. Hopefully, before their time runs out, other early Dutch barns will be preserved and permanently cared for.

4. One of the very few admirably technical descriptions dating from the nineteenth century is that of Rev. Robert Willis, *A Description of the Sextry Barn at Ely, Lately Demolished* (Cambridge: Cambridge University Press and London: John W. Parker, 1843).

Among Walter Horn's various scholarly studies of English and Continental barns, only the most recent (Walter Horn and F.W.B. Charles, "The Cruck-built Barn of Middle Littleton in Worcestershire, England," *Journal of the Society of Architectural Historians*, XXV (December, 1966), pp. 221–39) analyses the structure in detail and attempts to recreate the order and procedures followed in the erection of the timberwork of this "base-cruck" type of structure.

Two noteworthy recent works, both appearing in 1967, are undoubtedly the most specifically detailed and the most thoroughly reasoned out presentations to date. These are: (1) Cecil A. Hewett, "The Barns at Cressing Temple, Essex, and Their Significance in the History of English Carpentry," *Journal of the Society of Architectural Historians*, XXVI (March, 1967), pp. 48–70, and (2) F.W.B. Charles, *Medieval Cruck-Building and Its Derivatives: A Study of Timber-Framed Construction based on Buildings in Worcestershire* (The Society for Medieval Archaeology: Monograph Series: No. 2, London, 1967). Both include numerous photographs and many excellent drawings.

All four of the works listed above are concerned with English examples, however, and their applicability to New World Dutch barns is therefore limited.

5. Lucius Junius Moderatus Columella, *On Agriculture*, with a recension and an English translation by Harrison Boyd Ash. The Loeb Classical Library (Cambridge, Mass.: Harvard University Press, 1941), in three volumes. Vol. I, *Re Rustica* I–IV.

6. William James Audsley and George Ashdown Audsley, *Popular Dictionary of Architecture and the Allied Arts* (New York: G. P. Putnam's Sons, 1882), III, p. 13.

The outstanding architectural dictionary in the English language gives the entry "BARN" scarcely more than a half-page column of text, without references or figures: *The Dictionary of Architecture*, 8 vols. in 5 (London: The Architectural Publication Society, 1853–92), I, p. B-25.

There is not much more than a single page of text (although four drawings spread the account over parts of five pages) on "GRANGE" (Vol. VI, pp. 43–47) in Viollet-le-Duc's great 10-volume *Dictionnaire raisonné de l'architecture française du XIe au XVIe siècle* (Paris: Librairies-Imprimeries Réunies, 1854–68).

One of the longest dictionary accounts on the subject of barns is in Abraham Rees, *The Cyclopaedia; or, Universal Dictionary of Arts, Sciences, and Literature*. 47 vols., including 6 vols. of plates (Philadelphia: Samuel F. Bradford & Murray, Fairman & Co., [1810–24]). "First American Edition, revised, corected, enlarged, and adapted to this country." In Vol. III, there are a number of two-column pages of text on "BARN, in Rural Economy," and on "BARN FLOOR, in Rural Economy" (none of the pages is numbered), most of which deal with English practices, though there is an appended account of the different conditions and usages found in America, "in Pennsylvania, particularly."

7. Sidney Oldall Addy, *The Evolution of the English House* (Social England Series, edited by Kenelm D. Cotes) (London: Swan Sonnenschein & Co., 1898). 42 illus. (Later editions, 1905 and 1933.)

8. Professional carpenters would unquestionably have been needed to lay out the barn building, to cut the mortices, shape the tenons, and superintend the work throughout. Yet the records are completely and universally silent about both their identities with respect to a given structure and their specific activities. It is clear that there were indeed professional carpenters, however. For example, a few of the passenger lists of colonists arriving as "Early Immigrants to New Netherland, 1657–1664" are on record with respect to their trades. Such lists are given in O'Callaghan, *op. cit.*, pp. 52–63 (See *Historical Introduction*, Note 1, for complete reference). Here are masons, bakers, tailors, and shoemakers, along with a few who are designated rope-maker, cooper, glazier, painter, wheelwright, hatter, malster, etc. Many of the immigrants are identified as farmer, or "agriculturist," or "agriculturer." Of the thirty-six civilian sailings reported (some with as few as one or two passengers, some with as many as ninety or so including children and infants), there is mention of only six carpenters: three "house carpenters" arrived in 1658; two carpenters and one house carpenter in 1662. It should be noted, however, that the lists for 1663 and 1664 identify only one or two immigrants by their trade, so it is possible that there may have been a carpenter or two among these latter groups of colonists. Incidentally, there is no mention of a thatcher in any of these lists.

Another early mention of carpenters occurs in a letter (O'Callaghan, pp. 679–81) from R. Livingston to Mr. Lawrence Smith, dated April 2, 1712. The ice having broken the sluice of the corn mill on his Manor, Livingston wrote, "I have had 6 carpenters at work Ever since ye Gutter went away, & 6 horses, Dayly Rideing ye timber out of ye woods, & hope to have it ready in 3 weeks if ye water abates in ye River . . ."

I. N. Phelps Stokes, *Iconography of Manhattan Island* 6 vols., (New York: Robert H. Dodd, 1915–28), records the following item from the *New York Post-Boy* of 26 February 1759: "Since our last a company of Carpenters consisting of 60 men, arrived here from Philadelphia, on their way to Albany." These could have been either Dutch or Swedes, and hence men skilled in barn framing, though the entry does not indicate their country of origin.

DESCRIPTION

1. There is remarkable variety in early barn types throughout Holland. From this rich variety, only those examples have been selected for inclusion herewith which most closely resemble New World Dutch barns in terms of their structural system (shown in transverse section). All are approximately contemporary with New World Dutch barns, since they date from either the seventeenth or the eighteenth century. These revealing little sketches are from R. C. Hekker, "De Ontwikkeling van de Boerderijvormen in Nederland", *Duizend Jaar Bouwen in Nederland*, 1957, and are reproduced here by the kind permission of the publisher, Allert de Lange, Amsterdam.

All the plans are at the same scale, indicating far more variation in size than occurred in the New World Dutch barns. Identification has been retained in the Dutch language, where *deel* designates the threshing floor, *stal* the cattle stalls, *tas* the hay mow, and *w.k.* the wash-kitchen.

None of these examples is Frisian. The provenance of #44 is North Brabant, just northwest of Nijmegen; #48 is from the eastern portion of the same province. Both #50 and #60 are from farther north, in the western portions of Drenthe and Overijssel. #77 is from the southernmost part of Zuid Holland, in the Over-flakkee section of Goedereede Island.

The transverse sections show (1) tongued anchorbeams; (2) collars under the ridge; (3) roofs, usually in two planes between ridge and eaves; (4) no upper transverse ties from column to outer wall; but, (5) a scaffolding of poles to support the hayloft in most cases. The plans show a number of ways in which barn and human residence are combined. The perspectives indicate the three-dimensional mass of each example, the roof and eaves treatment, the presence of windows, and the prevalence of masonry walls.

With respect to their structural framing systems, the old barns of Germany's Niederrhein region (from Duisburg to the Dutch border) are far more consistent and similar than those of any equivalent area in neighboring Holland. Most of these northwestern German types are symmetrically three-aisled, with tongued anchorbeams; invariably they have collars under the ridge; and invariably there is but one transverse strut from column to outside wall. Often the pitch of the roof is steeper above the threshing-floor than it is over the side aisles; and the column bases are raised on individual stone plinths rather than being linked by a framework of timber sills.

2. Note the many examples of this enlargement at the top of timber columns that are indicated in detailed drawings of early *house* construction in America—in Connecticut, for example, in Plates I–VI, pp. 213, 218, 220, 222, and 226–27, of Norman M. Isham, and Albert F. Brown, *Early Connecticut Houses, an Historical Study*, [1900] (New York: Dover Publications, 1965).

3. Peter Kalm (see *Description*, Note 9, for complete reference) frequently notes and comments on the roof coverings of buildings of all sorts he encountered on his travels in the New World. Repeatedly he has much to say about *shingled* roofs, noting their superiority in eastern Pennsylvania and New Jersey, when of red cedar (p. 50, etc.), and farther north, around Albany, when of white pine

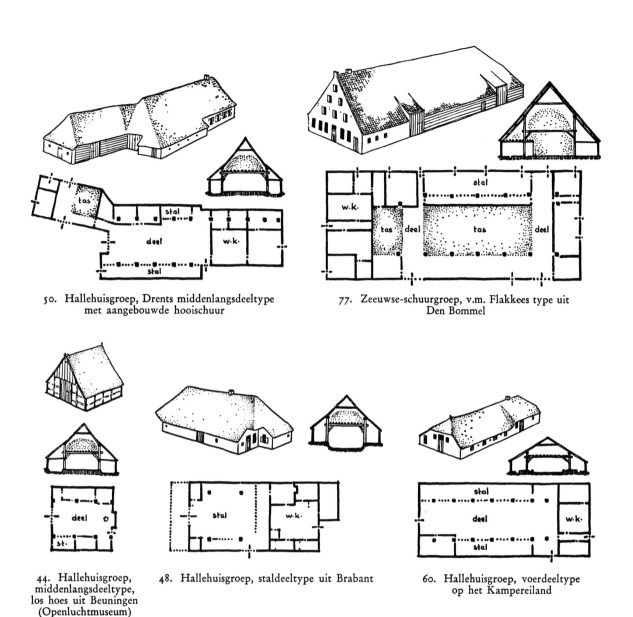

50. Hallehuisgroep, Drents middenlangsdeeltype met aangebouwde hooischuur

77. Zeeuwse-schuurgroep, v.m. Flakkees type uit Den Bommel

44. Hallehuisgroep, middenlangsdeeltype, los hoes uit Beuningen (Openluchtmuseum)

48. Hallehuisgroep, staldeeltype uit Brabant

60. Hallehuisgroep, voerdeeltype op het Kampereiland

(pp. 336, 618, etc.). Both of these woods, he says, make longer-lasting shingles than do other woods (for example, white cedar [p. 292]). Kalm also comments on roof coverings of tile (p. 20), slate (pp. 172 and 617), lapped boards (p. 430), and bark (p. 591). Yet only in Canada does he report seeing instances of "thatched" roofs (in Quebec, p. 560) and of "straw" coverings (in and near Montreal, pp. 400, 430, and 537), along with slate roofs as well as roof boards set perpendicular or parallel or at an angle with the eaves (p. 430).

Kalm's numerous observations, wherever he traveled, on roof coverings suggest that his conscientious and informed comments on the subject should be accepted as accurate.

Nevertheless, it has been reported to us that west of the lower Hudson, in the Nyack area, there is a Dutch barn whose roof is still thatched today. We have not located it. If true, this would agree with Burroughs' statement (see *Historical Introduction,* Note 2, second paragraph of quotation) about Dutch barns and their dependent sheds in his area being usually "thatched with straw." Some comment is therefore needed.

The roof covering of any building is its most perishable feature, the part which needs repair and renovation most frequently. Neither roof shingles nor thatching can be expected to last much longer than perhaps twenty years, in the climate of New York State. So there would have had to be many repairs and/or complete replacements during the generations between original construction and the present day. Somewhere along the line the Dutch barns that may originally have been thatched might have had their roof coverings changed to shingles, when nails became cheap and readily available. This could account for Kalm's unawareness of any thatched buildings in America south of Canada at the time of his travels (fairly late with respect to the Dutch barn building era).

One thing seems to be reasonably certain. For those barns furnished with eavestroughs (as evidenced by the slightly sloping range of bracket holes just below the wall plate), the roofs would never have been thatched, even at the start (see pp. 24, 30 and Dwg. 18). But thatching *could* formerly have been the roof covering on those fairly numerous barns whose wall posts are without these transverse bracket holes. Whatever may have been the prevalence of thatching— not only on barns but on other rural buildings—during the era of first settlement, certainly this kind of roof covering has long since disappeared totally from the American scene.

4. For example, cf. the following excerpts from Crèvecoeur, *Journey:*

> p. 39. The next day, impressed by the size and beauty of his barn, I asked him how it happened that it was a fine frame construction, while his house was only of hewn logs. "My father-in-law," he said, "insisted that I postpone building a proper dwelling until after the ninth harvest."
>
> p. 74. We were making our way slowly through a heavily wooded swamp, when one of our guides who was walking ahead stopped suddenly and called our attention to the faint light of a clearing, and soon after we discovered a dwelling of tree trunks known as a log cabin . . . It belonged to a Dane who had two cows and some chickens . . .
>
> p. 484. We found . . . a family of recent settlers. They had flour, pork and beans, two cows, two yoke of oxen, and a few chickens . . .; but they were still without a house. Since we planned to make this spot our headquarters, we resolved to come to their assistance, for there were seven of us; and within four days they had a shelter 14 feet wide by 25 feet long. It is true, this building was crude, constructed as it was of logs; but it was snug enough, with a good roof of oak bark which our hunters pitched on the rafters with great dexterity and willingness.
>
> p. 485. As we approached the junction of the little Owasco with the Seneca we spied a dwelling, a crude one, to tell the truth, a mere shelter, but with a shingled roof. The mistress of the house . . . was polite enough to lead our horses in under what she called a shed. This was a roof of bark, mounted

on four poles and weighed down with stones to prevent the wind from carrying it away.

Among eighteenth-century writers concerned with the contemporary scene in America, undoubtedly the most wide-ranging, detailed and circumstantial accounts are given by Crèvecoeur. J. Hector St. John Crèvecoeur, also known as Michel-Guillaume St. Jean de Crèvecoeur, was a Frenchman who as a young man traveled extensively in America, became a naturalized citizen, married an American wife, and settled on a farm in what is now Orange County, northwest of New York City. His keen observations and lively comments on life in rural America, on the husbandry of the pioneer farmer, on early travel and the character of the land, are to be found in the form of letters he wrote to a fictitious friend in Europe. Though first published abroad, his chief works are more recently available in the following editions:

> *Journey into Northern Pennsylvania and the State of New York* (Ann Arbor: University of Michigan Press, 1964). (Referred to as *"Journey."*)
> *Letters from an American Farmer* (New York: Duffield & Co., 1908). (Referred to as *"Letters."*)
> *Sketches of Eighteenth Century America:* More *"Letters from an American Farmer"* (New Haven: Yale University Press, 1925). (Referred to as *"Sketches."*)

Crèvecoeur wrote at a time—namely, just previous to the Revolutionary War—that was rather late for his observations to be entirely pertinent to the subject of the erection of early Dutch barns. However, since much of what he describes has to do with pioneering and the life of early farmers establishing homesteads in the wilderness (removed from the settled valley communities along the main rivers), his comments relate to conditions and situations that had had to be faced and overcome by settlers before his own time. (cf. *Conjectural Procedures of Erection*, Note 3)

5. A single exception is that of a 1681/82 deed, published in *Early Records of the City and County of Albany and Colony of Rensselaerwyck* [Albany, 1916], Vol. II, p. 154, which reads in part as follows: (I am indebted to Mrs. James K. Gibbons of Oneonta for calling my attention to this reference.)

> As rental of the said land, the said And⁵. and Hendrik Janse, at the end of ten years, shall deliver a proper dwelling house of twenty-two and a half feet square, covered with shingles and having a stone cellar as large as the house, which house shall be delivered over, glass, roof, floor, and wall, tight; likewise a barn of fifty-two and a half feet long and as wide as the barn which Marte Gerritse has built there which they shall deliver over in substantial and good repair as to wall and roof; with a proper protecting fence about the arable land, that is to say about the half of the nearest land, according to the judgment of impartial persons; likewise to plant an orchard which must consist of two hundred fruit trees, but the lessor is holden to furnish the trees which they at the end of the lease must deliver over in a good fence; also a good fence about the homestead; in like manner as a yearly quit rent 25 pounds of butter to commence in May, 1683.

6. Thus we have nothing more detailed than Crèvecoeur's off-hand remarks (*Letters*, p. 115) about a pioneer house-raising: ". . . In the afternoon the logs were placed with skids, and the usual contrivances; thus the rude house was raised."

The nearest thing to a circumstantial account of an early barn's erection in America is to be found in the essay referred to in *Historical Introduction*, Note 2, "Phases of Farm Life," pp. 56–58 of *In the Catskills*. Burroughs' observations read like an eyewitness description of a barn raising, though he does not identify it as such and he may well be putting into his own words the accounts related to him by old-timers. Although his essay was published long after the time when Dutch barns ceased to be built, and although his description does not appear to apply to a Dutch barn in any event, what he reports is worth quoting here as a vivid account by a sympathetic but unprofessional observer.

> When the farmers made "bees," as they did a generation or two ago much more than they do now, a picturesque element was added. There was the stone bee, the husking bee, the "raising," the "moving," etc. When the carpenters had got the timbers of the house or the barn ready, and the foundation was prepared, then the neighbors for miles about were invited to come to the "raisin'." The afternoon was the time chosen. The forenoon was occupied by the carpenter and the farm hands in putting the sills and "sleepers" in place. . . . When the hands arrived, the great beams and posts and joists and braces were carried to their place on the platform, and the first "bent," as it was called, was put together and pinned by oak pins that the boys brought. Then pike poles were distributed, the men, fifteen or twenty of them, arranged in a line abreast of the bent; the boss carpenter steadied and guided the corner post and gave the word of command. . . . When it gets shoulder high, it becomes heavy, and there is a pause. The pikes are brought into requisition; every man gets a good hold and braces himself, and waits for the words. . . . Slowly the great timbers go up; louder grows the word of command, till the bent is up. Then it is plumbed and stay-lathed, and another is put together and raised in the same way, till they are all up. Then comes the putting on the great plates,—timbers that run lengthwise of the building and match the sills below. Then, if there is time, the putting up of the rafters.
>
> In every neighborhood there was always some man who was especially useful at "raisin's." He was bold and strong and quick. He helped guide and superintend the work. He was the first one up on the bent, catching a pin or a brace and putting it in place. He walked the lofty and perilous plate with the great beetle in hand, put the pins in the holes, and, swinging the heavy instrument through the air, drove the pins home. He was as much at home up there as a squirrel.
>
> Now that balloon frames are mainly used for houses, and lighter sawed timbers for barns, the old-fashioned raising is rarely witnessed.

Much nearer our own day, we have the testimony of an author who says that he has helped in the erection of at least a dozen timber barns. Victor C. Dieffenbach contributed one of the articles, entitled "Barn Raisings," found in *The Pennsylvania Barn*, pp. 40–45, published by the Pennsylvania Dutch Folklore Center, 1955. Illustrated with thirteen photographs, this article deals mainly with a barn-raising in northern Lancaster County about 1905, and a more recent raising of an Amish barn. These are informing eye-witness accounts with specific and authentic progress photographs. But both the twentieth-century date and the type of barn structure illustrated have little in common with the New York Dutch barns of more than two centuries before.

7. The difficulties encountered in dating barns are not confined to this country or to the present century. Note the following remarks made well over a century ago in an English publication, John Henry Parker, *Some Account of Domestic Architecture in England, from Edward I to Richard II* (1853), Vol. II, p. 151:

> There are probably many barns existing in England of great antiquity, though from the plainness of structure and absence of architectural detail it is most difficult or sometimes impossible to assign them any date.

Our own New York Dutch barns are probably not sufficiently ancient to allow their exact ages to be determined by the radiocarbon dating method. And apparently the tree-ring method of dating has not been employed here in the East as it has with success in the southwest of our country—perhaps because the pattern here is more uniform than it is there, with less variation due to recurring seasons of drought.

Lacking documentary evidence for assigning a date of erection for our barns, the historian awaits the development of some intrinsic means for ascertaining their age with unassailable accuracy.

8. As stated elsewhere in these pages (e.g., see *Conjectural Procedures of Erection*, Note 3), only those barns are here considered that have survived to our time. During all eras of history some structures have been well built, some poorly or shoddily built. Irrespective of the accidents that have occurred either from natural causes or through man's carelessness or vindictiveness, any Dutch barn's survival throughout two to three centuries could have happened only in the case of a structure that was soundly and ruggedly built at the outset.

9. Peter Kalm was a Swedish naturalist sent to this country by the then newly founded Swedish Academy of Sciences to make observations on useful plants and trees that could benefit the mother country. He traveled in Pennsylvania, New Jersey, New York, and southern Canada from September, 1748, to February, 1751. The account of his journey and his observations on whatever of interest he saw—which included people and buildings and customs as well as nature—was published in 1753, in Stockholm. The first exclusively American edition, in English, is *Peter Kalm's Travels in North America*, 2 vols. (New York: Wilson-Erickson, 1937).

While traveling between Trenton and New Brunswick, in the vicinity of Princeton, New Jersey, Kalm encountered some barns which he described in his travelogue (p. 118 of the American edition cited above) as follows. (They appear to have been Dutch barns of the type indicated in transverse section in Drawing 4, at K, L, and M.)

> "The barns had a peculiar kind of construction in this locality, of which I shall give a concise description. The main building was very large almost the size of a small church; the roof was high, covered with wooden shingles,

sloping on both sides, but not steep. The walls which supported it were not much higher than a full grown man; but on the other hand the breadth of the building was all the greater. In the middle was the threshing floor and above it, or in the loft or garret, they put the unthrashed grain, the straw, or anything else, according to the season. On one side were stables for the horses, and on the other for the cows. The young stock had also their particular stables or stalls, and in both ends of the building were large doors, so that one could drive in with a cart and horses through one of them, and go out at the other. Here under one roof therefore were the threshing floor, the barn, the stables, the hay loft, the coach house, etc. This kind of building is used chiefly by the Dutch and Germans, for it is to be observed that the country between Trenton and New York is not inhabited by many Englishmen, but mostly by Germans or Dutch, the latter of which are especially numerous."

Later, on his trip north from Albany into Canada, Kalm records the following observations:

p. 350–51. "On the west bank of the river [the Hudson, about six miles north of Albany] we saw several houses, one after another, inhabited by the descendants of the first Dutch settlers, who lived by cultivating their grounds . . . The barns were generally built in the Dutch way, as I have before described them; for in the middle was the threshing floor, above it a place for the hay and straw, and on each side stables for horses, cows, and other animals. The barn itself was very large. Sometimes the buildings of a farm consisted only of a small cottage with a garret above it, together with a barn upon the above plan."

p. 356. "This night we lodged with a farmer who had returned to his farm after the war was over. All his buildings except the big barn had been burnt."

p. 359. "The inhabitants [at Saratoga] are of Dutch extraction . . . We lay overnight in a little hut of boards erected by the people who had come to live here."

10. In Crèvecoeur's *Journey*, p. 254, an early settler speaks as follows:

Only one misfortune has befallen me since my arrival here: the fifth year lightning struck my barn a few days after I had filled it with a full harvest. Inattentive, like so many others, to the use of lightning rods, I had ignored helpful advice that the venerable Franklin often used to insert in his famous *Poor Richard's Almanach*, as well as his urgent solicitations to protect our barns and houses. I know not why, but the former are much more subject to being struck by lightning when they are filled than when they are empty.

11. Although it does not describe a Dutch barn, judging by the dimensions he cites, one of Crèvecoeur's more illuminating passages that deals specifically with the barns of his day is that found on p. 141 of his *Sketches:*

The barn, with regard to its situation, size, convenience, and good finishing, is an object, in the mind of a farmer, superior even to that of his dwelling. Many don't care much how they are lodged, provided that they have a good barn and barn-yard, and indeed it is the criterion by which I always judge of a farmer's prosperity. On this building he never begrudges his money. The middle-sized ones are commonly 50 x 30 feet; mine is 60 x 35 and cost $220.00. They are either shingled, clap-boarded, or boarded on the outside. Therein we lodge all our grain, and within many operations are performed, such as threshing, and cleaning of flax and husking the corn, etc. Therein the horses are stabled and the oxen stall-fed. In the summer the women resort to it, in order to spin their wool. The neatness of our boarded floors, the great draught of air caused by the open doors, which are always made wide enough to permit a loaded wagon to enter, and their breadth afford [the women] an opportunity of spinning long threads, of carding at their ease. Many farmers have several barracks in their barn-yards where they put their superfluous hay and straws. Nor ought the subdivisions of these yards to pass unnoticed. They require great judgment, demand attention and expense. All classes of our cattle, our sheep, our calves, must be placed by themselves, and have in each division convenient racks and bars in order to communicate easily from one to another.

12. Born in 1755, Mrs. Grant spent her childhood in America. It was only many years later, after she had returned to Scotland with her parents, that she wrote down her recollections and published them in 1808, in London. These recollections are so vividly recalled and so specific that it seems appropriate to reproduce here what she had to say about a barn—quite obviously a Dutch barn—and the life and activities that it sheltered. Following is her Chapter XVIII entitled "Description of Col. Schuyler's Barn, the Common, and Its Various Uses." It is found in her book *Memoirs of An American Lady, with Sketches of Manners and Scenery in America, as they existed previous to the Revolution* (New York: D. Appleton & Co., 1846), pp. 87–90.

Adjoining to the orchard was the most spacious barn I ever beheld; which I shall describe for the benefit of such of my readers as have never seen a building constructed on a plan so comprehensive. This barn, which, as will hereafter appear, answered many beneficial purposes besides those usually allotted for such edifices, was of a vast size, at least a hundred feet long, and sixty wide. The roof rose to a very great height in the midst, and sloped down till it came within ten feet of the ground, when the walls commenced; which, like the whole of this vast fabric, were formed of wood. It was raised three feet from the ground by beams resting on stone; and on these beams was laid, in the middle of the building, a very massive oak floor. Before the door was a large sill, sloping downwards, of the same materials. A breadth of about twelve feet on each side of this capacious building was divided off for cattle; on one side ran a manger, at the above-mentioned distance from the wall, the whole length of the building, with a rack above it; on the other were stalls for the other cattle, running also the whole length of the building. The cattle and horses stood with their hinder parts to the wall, and their heads towards the threshing floor. There was a prodigious large box or open chest in one side, built up for holding the corn after it was thrashed; and the roof, which was very lofty and spacious, was supported by large crossbeams. From one to the other of these stretched a great number of long poles, so as to form a sort of open loft, on which the whole rich crop was laid up. The floor of those parts of the barn, which answered the purpose of a stable and cow-house, was made of thick slab deals, laid loosely over the supporting beams. And the mode of cleaning those places was by turning the boards, and permitting the dung and litter to fall into the receptacles left open below for the purpose; thence in spring they were often driven down to the river, the soil, in its original state, not requiring the aid of manure. In the front [by the front is meant the gable end, which contains the entrance] of this vast edifice there were prodigious folding-doors, and two others that opened behind.

Certainly never did cheerful rural toils wear a more exhilarating aspect than while the domestics were lodging the luxuriant harvest in this capacious repository. When speaking of the doors, I should have mentioned that they were made in the gable ends; those in the back equally large to correspond with those in the front; while on each side of the great doors were smaller ones, for the cattle and horses to enter. Whenever the corn or hay was reaped or cut, and ready for carrying home, which in that dry and warm climate happened in a very few days, a wagon loaded with hay, for instance, was driven into the midst of this great barn; loaded also with numberless large grasshoppers, butterflies, and cicadas, who came along with the hay. From the top of the wagon, this was immediately forked up into the loft of the barn, in the midst of which was an open space left for the purpose; and then the unloaded wagon drove, in rustic state, out of the great door at the other end. In the mean time every member of the family witnessed or assisted in this summary process; by which the building and thatching of stacks was at once saved; and the whole crop and cattle were thus compendiously lodged under one roof.

The cheerfulness of this animated scene was much heightened by the quick appearance and vanishing of the swallows, which twittered among their high-built dwellings in the roof. Here, as in every other instance, the safety of these domestic friends was attended to, and an abode provided for them. In the front of this barn were many holes, like those of a pigeon-house, for the accommodation of the martin—that being the species to which this kind of home seems most congenial; and, in the inside of the barn, I have counted above fourscore at once. In the winter, when the earth was buried deep in new-fallen snow, and no path fit for walking in was left, this barn was like a great gallery, well-suited for that purpose; and furnished with pictures not unpleasing to a simple and contented mind. As you walked through this long area, looking up, you beheld the abundance of the year treasured above you, on one side the comely heads of your snorting steeds presented themselves, arranged in seemly order; on the other, your kine displayed their meeker visages, while the perspective, on either, was terminated by heifers and fillies no less interesting. In the midst your servants exercised the flail; and even while they thrashed out the straw, distributed it to the expectants on both sides; while the "liberal handful" was occasionally thrown to the many-colored poultry on the sill. Winter itself never made this abode of life and plenty cold and cheerless. Here you might walk and view all your subjects, and their means of support, at one glance; except, indeed, the sheep, for which a large and commodious building was erected very near the barn; the roof containing a loft large enough to hold hay sufficient for their winter's food.

Colonel Schuyler's barn was by far the largest I have ever seen; but all of them, in that country, were constructed on the same plan, furnished with the same accommodations, and presented the same cheerful aspect. The orchard, as I formerly mentioned, was on the south side of the barn; on the north, a little farther back toward the wood, which formed a dark screen behind this smiling prospect, there was an enclosure, in which the remains of the deceased members of the family were deposited. A field of pretty large extent, adjoining to the house on that side, remained uncultivated and unenclosed; over it was scattered a few large apple trees of a peculiar kind, the fruit of which was never appropriated. This place of level and productive land, so near the family mansion, and so adapted to various and useful purposes, was never occupied, but left open as a public benefit.

13. For illustrations and descriptions of all sorts of early tools used for felling trees, shaping logs, and preparing joints for timber-framing, see Henry C. Mercer, *Ancient Carpenters' Tools* (Doylestown, Pa.: The Bucks County Historical Society, [1929]), 3rd edition, 1960.

14. It may be that this soundness—this paucity of splits and shakes and other imperfections—was due to the methods utilized by the early builders in cutting the trees and curing the logs. Crèvecoeur and others speak of the proper time of year, and even the phase of the moon, when trees should be felled. There is much of lore and legend in these matters.

For example, one of the prescriptions encountered from time to time in the early accounts is that of curing logs by immersing them in water for up to three years. It is hard to verify whether this was ever done by the early barn builders. But at least some interval of immersion may have been resorted to, and with some justification for such a practice. In this connection see William F. Fox, "History of the Lumber Industry in the State of New York," *Sixth Annual Report of the Forest, Fish and Game Commission of the State of New York* [Report for 1900] (Albany, N.Y.: James B. Lyon, State Printer, 1901), pp. 237–305. On p. 254 Fox writes: "It was claimed by many of the old-time lumbermen that rafted lumber was better than any other, because the soaking of the boards diluted the sap and resinous matter so that when piled again in the yards it would season better and quicker."

Fox's article (with 23 photos and a double-page map of "First Settlements in the State of New York") has much of interest about the primeval forest cover, and about pioneer lumbering in the State, based on a very thorough search of early published records. For example, (p. 251), he quotes Mrs. Grant's description of "Rafting on the Upper Hudson"; and later (p. 255), he remarks that "Hewed timber, as well as boards, was floated to market in rafts. . . . The hewed timber was thought to be more valuable; it was stronger and would last longer than sawed timber whenever it was used." He lists a very large number of first sawmills and their builders, by place and date, throughout the state (pp. 286–305). Some of these mills date from the seventeenth century, although unfortunately the earliest records for the Dutch-inhabited counties of the state are incomplete. It would seem that much of this sawn timber was exported to England and to Holland. In any case, it is doutbful that any substantial amounts of it went into the construction of early Dutch barns locally (except perhaps for clapboards and roofers), since generally it is patently apparent in the surviving barns that their timbers are not sawn but are hewn.

15. The only exceptions so far encountered to the rule of no positive attachment at the feet of the rafters are in two barns southwest of Middleburg. In one of these cases, vertical oak pins, in the other, pins driven perpendicular to the roof slope, have been used to secure the rafters' feet at the eaves. This practice is most abnormal, even in the Middleburg area. Two other barns in the same vicinity can demonstrate the almost universal prevalence of non-attachment at the eaves. One, the Forrest Lape barn on the northeast outskirts of Middleburg, had its walls replaced in 1963. During this protracted operation the original roof remained intact (even when some high winds struck the area) while an entire gable-end wall and one whole side wall were removed, leaving the lower half of the rafters suspended out over the void. The other nearby barns, on the southwest outskirts of this same community, perpetuates a similar situation that is recorded in the photographic illustration, Plate 51. Here it can be seen that there are no pins that ever secured the feet of these suspended, far-oversailing rafters to the wall plate.

Other examples where this same lack of positive attachment at the base of the rafters can be ascertained are in two barns where part of the side wall has settled, creating a void of a few inches between the wall plate and the hanging rafter-tails. These are the Rte. 20, East of Sharon barn, east side; and the Larger Bradt barn, above a non-original wagon-door entrance cut through the middle of one of the side walls.

One is tempted to guess that the two exceptions mentioned above were not part of the original framing but were subsequent applications, installed during later repairs to the eaves and the lower portions of the roof. This speculation may be the more likely because of the fact that in one of these barns not all the rafter feet are pinned to the wall plate.

STRUCTURAL CONSIDERATIONS

1. There are many technical reports that deal with the properties of different species of wood. Though not recent, one of the best—at the same time compact and comprehensive—is found in G. Lister Sutcliffe (ed.), *The Modern Carpenter, Joiner, and Cabinet-Maker, A Complete Guide to Current Practice*, 8 vols. (London: The Gresham Publishing Co., 1902–1904). This work was published in England at a time when timber framing was still to some extent being practiced. Many of the tests recorded in it were conducted in America, however, and many of the data refer to American species. For our purposes Vol. IV, "Part II: Practical," is the most useful. The headings cover the following:

> Chapter I: Physical and Mechanical Properties Affecting the Strength of Timber (pp. 331–38)
> 1. The Percentage of Moisture in Timber
> 2. The Specific Weight of Dry Timber
> 3. The Method of Seasoning
> 4. Other Conditions Affecting the Strength of Timber (including The Nature of the Soil, and Climate)

Chapter II: Tensile and Shearing Strength (pp. 338–41)
Chapter III: Compressive Strength (pp. 341–54)
Chapter IV: Transverse Strength and Elasticity (pp. 354–63)
Chapter V: Factors of Safety (pp. 363–65)

2. More has been written on the early timber roofs of England than on those of the Continent, doubtless because there is so much more variety in the former than there is in the latter. The standard English works that deal comprehensively and specifically with timber roofs are the following:

Raphael and J. Arthur Brandon, *The Open Timber Roofs of the Middle Ages* (London: David Bogue, 1849).

Reginald A. Cordingley, "British Historical Roof-Types and Their Members," *Transactions of the Ancient Monuments Society*, New Series Vol. IX (1961), pp. 73–117.

F. E. Howard, "On the Construction of Mediaeval Roofs," *Archaeological Journal*, Vol. LXXI (1914), pp. 293–352.

J. T. Smith, "Medieval Roofs: A Classification," *Archaeological Journal*, Vol. CXV (1960), pp. 111–49.

However, in connection with general descriptions of timber buildings as a class, or of individual timber-work structures, there is a good deal of information on the framing of the all-timber roofs of Europe to be found in a large number of publications in various languages. The following are a few examples:

For Holland and northwestern Germany: See *Historical Introduction*, Note 3.

For England:

Francis B. Andrews, "Medieval or 'Tithe' Barns," *Birmingham Archaeological Society, Transactions XXVI* (1901), pp. 10–31.

Fred H. Crossley, *Timber Building in England from early times to the end of the Seventeenth Century* (London, Batsford, 1951). Chapter VI, "Timber Roofs," pp. 56–67.

Walter Horn, "The Great Tithe Barn of Cholsey, Berkshire," *Journal of the Society of Architectural Historians*, Vol. XXII (1963), pp. 13–23.

Walter Horn and Ernest Born, *The Barns of the Abbey of Beaulieu at its Granges of Great Coxwell and Beaulieu-St. Leonards* (Berkeley: University of California Press, 1965).

C. F. Innocent, *The Development of English Building Construction* (Cambridge: University Press, 1916). For early timber roof construction see Chaps. IV, V, and VI; but there is much else of value, including "The Carpenter" and his tools (Chap. VIII), "Thatching" (Chap. XIII), etc.

For France:

Walter Horn, "Les Halles de Crémieu," *Evocations*, Bulletin du Groupe d'Études Historiques et Géographiques du Bas Dauphiné, Crémieu (Isère). No. 3, 17ᵉ année (Jan.–Fev. 1961), pp. 66–90.

———, "Les Halles de Questembert (Morbihan)," *Bulletin de la Société Polymathique du Morbihan* (Vannes, 1963), pp. 1–16.

Antoine Moles, *Histoire des Charpentiers* (Paris, Librairie Gründ, 1949). Chap. VIII, "La Charpente du Moyen Âge," pp. 151–81.

E. Viollet-le-Duc, *Dictionnaire raisonné de l'architecture française du XIe au XVIe siècle* (Paris: Librairies-Imprimeries Réunies, 1858–68). Article "Charpente," Vol. III, pp. 1–58.

Elsewhere:

L. Dietrichson, *De Norske Stavkirker: Studier over Deres System, Oprindelse og Historiske Udvikling* (Kristiania og Kjøbenhavn, Alb. Cammermeyers Forlag, 1892).

J. G. E. F. Heinzerling, *Constructions-elemente in Holz* (being pp. 94–138 in Vol. I of division 3: "Hochbau-constructionen," in *Handbuch der Architektur*, 24 vols [Darmstadt, 1880–93]).

Josef Strzygowski, *Early Church Art in Northern Europe*, with special reference to timber construction and decoration (London: Batsford, 1928), see Chaps. II, III, IV.

3. Perhaps the best place to study how New York barn structures first departed from the true New World Dutch form is in the Middleburg area, a locale that had a strong tradition of Dutch barn building. Here are to be found a considerable number of early barns, both those that followed the scheme of framing discussed in this study and those that immediately superseded them.

CONJECTURAL PROCEDURES OF ERECTION

1. One of the very few American publications that describes in clear and specific detail the steps to be followed in fashioning joints for timber construction was first printed in 1830 in Boston, subsequently appearing in at least ten other editions up to 1876. This manual is

Edward Shaw, *Civil Architecture*, being a complete theoretical and practical System of Building, containing the fundamental principles of the art. . . . 6th ed. (Cleveland, Ohio: Jewett, Proctor, and Worthington, 1852).

It is worth quoting this book's article on "Framing," in order for one to appreciate some of the procedures that would have had to be followed in the structural assemblage of New York Dutch barns. The effort required to follow the instructions given herewith is an index of how far removed we are, nowadays, from this kind of carpentry-work.

(p. 116). *Framing*. This mechanical science is divided into two principles—the Scribe and the Square Rule.

The Scribe Rule.

1. First, the mortises should be made, and the faces got out of wind [i.e., free from bends or crooks; perfectly straight]. Second, after finding the length of the timber in which the tenons are to be made, for convenience apply the two foot square. Third, take out the size of the mortised timber on the end of the square; suppose 10″ the one to be mortised, then 14″ remain on the square; make a distance mark at the end of the square, which is called

the 2-foot mark. Fourth, measure from this mark, for the shoulder, 15″, which leaves 1″ to be scribed; after the tenon is made and entered, the mortise and the shoulders are brought together or to a bearing; then cut the shoulders to a scribe, and when put together they will remain out of wind, as when scribed. The process is generally applied to sills, posts, and principal rafters.

2. A process called *tumbling*, is applied to timbers, both ends of which are to be tenoned, as girders, etc.; also to sides and ends in section framing. The girder should be placed so that both ends shall come directly over the lower end of the mortises. For the tenons you are about to strike, place the lower edges of the girder to the line of the lower end of the mortises; make a scratch on the girder at both ends, exactly to the face of the mortise. Cant the girder so as to leave those marks up; fetch the girder again over the mortise, and apply the edge of the square to the face of the mortise, the square extending above the girder. Move the girder by a hammer for that purpose, until the scratch on the corner of the girder is brought to the outer edge of the square. Then with your compasses draw a line across the girder by the edge of the square; then move the square on the opposite side of the girder, and draw another line; in the same manner draw lines at the other end of the girder. Strike a line across the top and bottom of the girder, meeting the end of those which give the exact length of the shoulders; then strike the tenons.

3. Cant or plumb marks are those which are applied to all principal timbers that are to be employed in section framing, after having been put together in the sides. At some part of the post try on the square, and fit that part (which may be up, in the laying out of the section) to a right angle with the level plane of the side framing, provided the section should be at right angles with the sides. But if the section should be required at any other angle with the side, the plumb should be made according to that angle. The angle should be taken with a bevel set for that purpose; and on these fittings of the posts a right angle should be struck, to guide the direction of the square across the section framing. The posts should be brought by means of wedges in a horizontal plane across the section.

The Square Rule.

This principle is considered more simple than the Scribe Rule, as it can be applied in many cases with less help and more convenience. In order to make a good frame of any considerable magnitude, it should be the first care of the master workman (after examining the plan of the frame with care) to make out a proper schedule of the various sizes of the timber. Set down their appropriate marks on the schedule; and when you have finished Nos. 1, 2, etc., check them on the schedule. It is of importance that all mortises, tenons, pin holes, etc., should be struck with a pattern. All the timber should be lined to its proper size, and the mortises faced to the same. Care should be taken in applying the pattern; for striking, it should be governed by the appropriate lines. This method has the preference in detached framing; the timber admitting of being framed in different places, and not tried together until its raising.

2. Although assiduous search for them has been made in some of the barns whose craftsmanship in wood is most accomplished and whose timber surfaces are most evenly finished, we have not been able to find any tell-tale scars on the

smooth faces of columns or anchorbeams that would indicate the use of pike-poles in their erection. If this method of erection had indeed been employed, the size and weight of the anchorbeams would certainly have created more than inconspicuous pin pricks on the part of any iron-pointed pike-poles in the tilt-up process of erection.

3. If undue emphasis appears to be given in this study to the remoteness of early barn sites and the consequences of their isolation, it is because so many of the early Dutch barns that have survived to our day are located now, as in the past, in out-of-the-way places. The more populous settlements would have been more vulnerable to the burnings recorded in the reports of raiding parties and military expeditions, just as these more populous settlements have also succumbed to the march of "progress" throughout the intervening years.

But the present study is concerned with those early Dutch barns that are still in existence, that still can be examined. It seems appropriate, therefore, to comment and speculate on the evidence of *actual survivals* rather than on former examples that have long since disappeared and are known now only as statistics in the military accounts of their destruction.

From observations he made in the middle of the eighteenth century, Kalm gives reasons why New York was much less populous than Pennsylvania (p. 143, and again on pp. 615–16). He sums up with the statement that "It is not to be wondered, then, that so many parts of New York are still uncultivated, and that it has entirely the appearance of a frontier land."

Even in New Sweden (a colony situated along the Delaware River, south of Trenton, N.J.), Kalm recounts that (p. 265):

> Now and then I came upon swamps in the valleys. Sometimes there appeared, though at considerable distances from each other, some farms, frequently surrounded on all sides by grain fields. Almost on every field there yet remained the stumps of trees, which had been cut down, a proof that this country had not been long cultivated, having been overgrown with trees forty or fifty years ago. The farms did not lie together in villages, or so that several of them were near each other in one place, but were all unconnected. Each countryman lived by himself, and had his own ground about the house separated from the property of his neighbor. The greatest part of the land, between these farms so far apart, was overgrown with woods, consisting of tall trees . . . The old Swede, whom I came to visit . . . said he could very well remember the state of this country at the time when the Dutch possessed it, and in what circumstances it was in before the arrival of the English. . . . He still remembered to have seen a great forest on the spot where Philadelphia now stands . . .

On his voyage up the Hudson River to Albany, Kalm noted the sparsity and separation of the farms. For example:

> p. 330. "The eastern side of the river was much more cultivated than the western, where we seldom saw a house. The land was covered with woods though it was in general very level. About fifty-six English miles from New York the country is not very high; yet it is everywhere covered with woods, except for some pioneer farms which were scattered here and there."

p. 331. "The country on the eastern side was high, and consisted of well cultivated soil. We had fine plowed fields, well-built farms and good orchards in view. The western shore was likewise high, but still covered with woods, and we now and then, though seldom, saw one or two little settlements."

p. 332. "The country on both sides of the river [but nine English miles from Albany] was low and covered with woods, only here and there were a few little scattered settlements."

DRAWINGS
AND PLATES

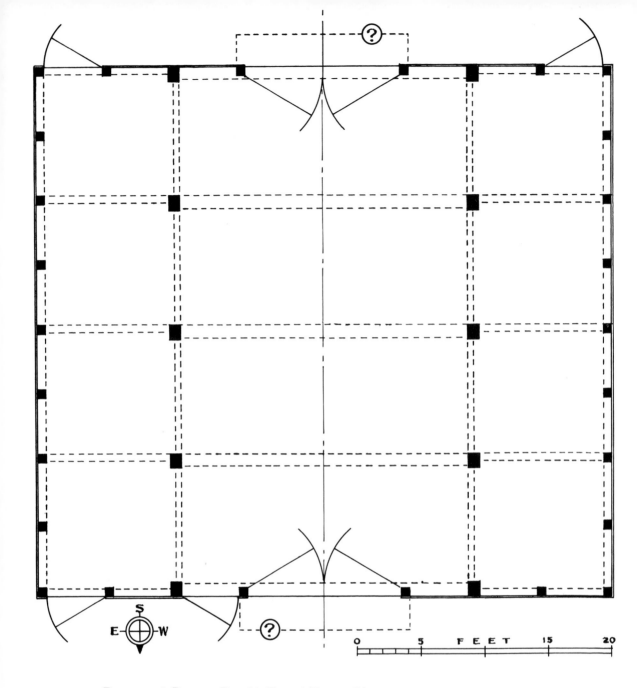

DRAWING 1: *Barn on Rte. 20, East of Sharon: Plan*

This plan is typical in its regularity and simplicity. Double wagon doors, swinging inward, are on axis at both north and south gable-ends; doors for humans and/or animals swing out at the corners of the south end; one corner door and one next to the wagon entrance swing out at the north end. Typical also are the outside studs in the form of wall-posts that are evenly spaced and heavy. Longitudinal dotted lines indicate the eastern and western wall-plates and the head-height column links. Transverse pairs of dotted lines designate the lower side-aisle struts from column to wall-post on either hand and the anchorbeams that span the central threshing floor. The amount of projection for the pentices is conjectural. The orientation is closely approximate.

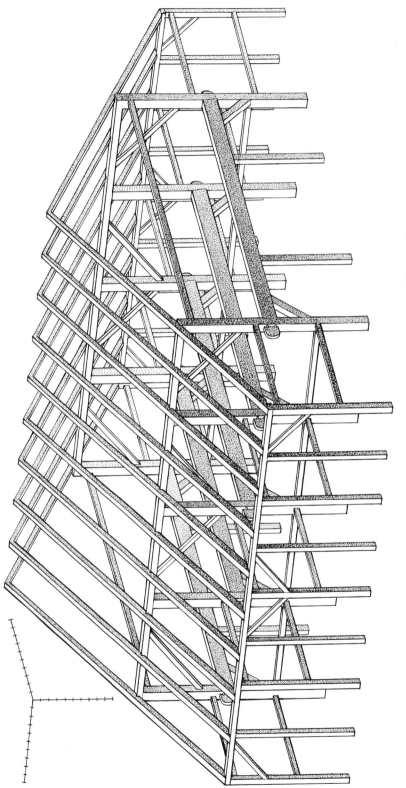

DRAWING 2: *Larger Wemp Barn: Axiometric Drawing of Timber Skeleton*

Encompassing the east side and the north gable, this drawing reveals the essential structural timberwork of this barn: here is what needed to be erected as the indispensable
skeleton. The ensemble represented here, including the location, span, and size of each
member, is that of the Larger Wemp barn, with one exception; namely, the spacing of
the studs in the sidewalls. The drawing shows the spacing to be even and regular, which
is the usual arrangement—the spacing of the studs in the Wemp barn, however, is quite
irregular. The sill pattern, obscured under the floor in this barn, is not shown here; nevertheless, the sills are certainly in existence and operate as the framework that both supports and consolidates all the vertical members of this barn at their base.

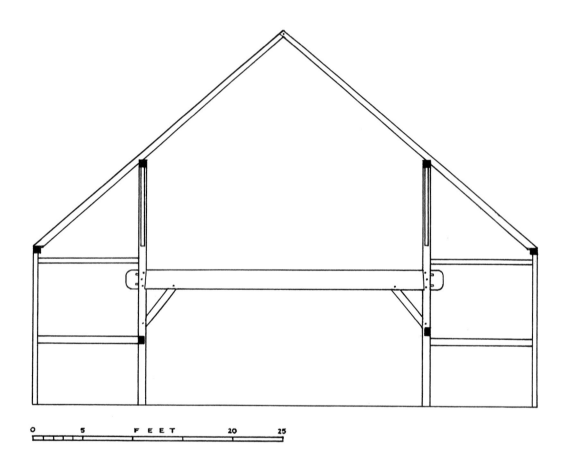

DRAWING 3: *Larger Wemp Barn: Transverse Section, Looking South*

This is a drawing of the barn's timberwork framing, omitting such surface features as (1) flooring, (2) weather-boarding, (3) roofers and shingles, as well as (4) the horizontal sapling poles laid across the anchorbeams of the two northern bays to provide an aerated floor for the hayloft. This fine barn is in a good state of preservation, so the sills and their framing, obscured under the flooring, cannot be examined.

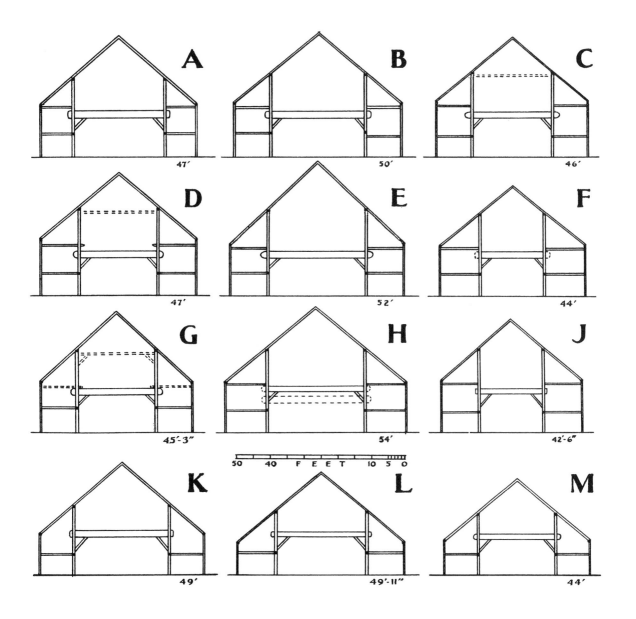

DRAWING 4: *Representative Transverse Sections*

(A) Wemple; (B) Larger Wemp; (C) Indian Castle; (D) East of Indian Castle; (E) Van Wie; (F) Acker; (G) East of Sharon; (H) Deertz; (J) Cure; (K) Van Alstyne; (L) Verplanck-Van Wyck; (M) Ripking. The last three are variants of the normal scheme in that they lack upper transverse ties across the side-aisles, which permit lower side walls. Only a small number of barns (all in the Hudson Valley) have been found to follow this latter scheme, but these three are well-preserved examples of it.

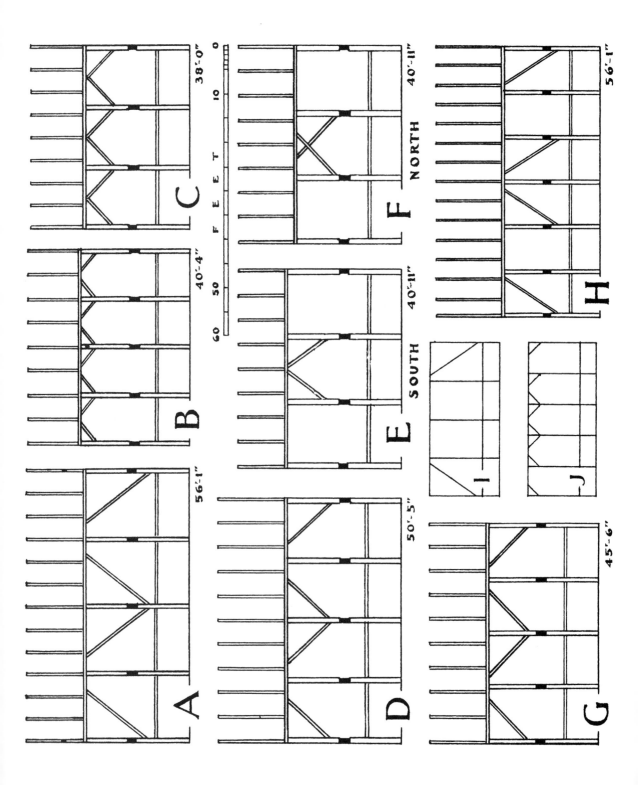

DRAWING 5: *Longitudinal Sections*

(A) Wemple; (B) East of Sharon; (C) Smaller Wemp; (D) Van Wie; (E), (F) Larger Bradt; (G) Larger Wemp; (H) Van Alstyne; (I) Bradt-Mabie; (J) Marte Gerretse Van Bergen.

It will be noted that the rafters (indicated only from ridge to purlin-plate, though of course they do continue down to the eaves) are consistently spaced at wide intervals except for the six-bay barn at Kinderhook (H). The three-bay Larger Bradt barn is unique in that, although the gable ends are symmetrical, the side-aisles are not of equal width: this results in a higher purlin-plate on the south side than on the north (where the narrower side-aisle is located). The system of short, high sway-bracing in the Sharon barn (B) is the most commonly encountered one. The Wemple (A), Van Alstyne (H), and Bradt-Mabie (I) barns are unusual in having their sway-braces branch out from a point below the level at which the anchorbeams are framed into the columns. The roof structure of the Van Bergen barn (J) has been radically altered and is at present redundant; however, the sway-bracing shown here is that of the original system.

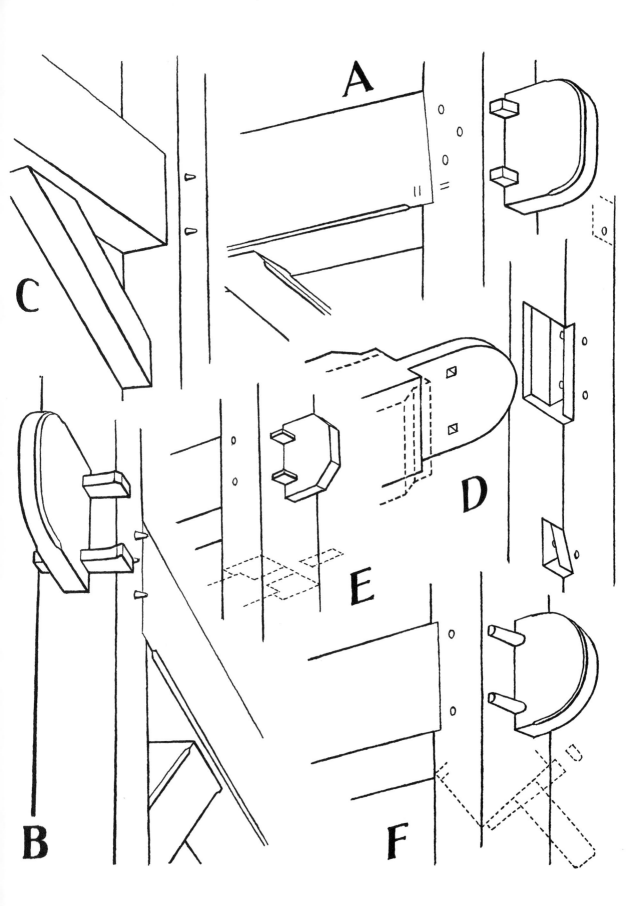

DRAWING 6: *Anchorbeam Attachment to Columns*

The great size of the anchorbeams, together with their protruding tongues, furnish the most striking features of the interior. There is considerable variety in the shape of the tongues (sometimes in the same barn) and in their projection, although in the finest barns they are uniform throughout.

A and B are of the Larger Wemp barn, showing the unusual feature of neat chamfering on the braces, the lower edges of the anchorbeam, and the curving part of its tongue. The big wedges are spaced 15½″ apart. 3¼″-thick tongues, projecting 16″, are centered on both the 11¾″ x 22″ anchorbeams and the 9½″ x 11¾″ columns, as are the stout diagonal braces.

Sometimes the anchorbeam's shoulders are housed in the column, as in the Kaufman barn (E), with its thin angularly-profiled tongue of 11″ projection, and wide thin wedges. Here the 9½″ x 14¼″ anchorbeam is much narrower than the face of the 8½″ x 11¾″ column that receives it.

The Indian Castle barn (D) has tongues that project an exceptional 21″ beyond the far face of the column, with shoulders housed on one side only. Here the tongue is not centered on the 11½″ x 19½″ anchorbeam, nor is its mortice symmetrically cut through the 9″ x 13″ column. (The Slater barn has a practically identical mortice-and-tenon arrangement, except that the shoulders of the anchorbeam are sloped).

The 12″ x 23¼″ anchorbeam of the Larger Bradt barn (F) is housed in the 11″ x 13¾″ column on one side, but its tongue (15″ projection) is off-center. Wedges here are slight, and rounded on the outer side.

C is a frequently-encountered condition where the vertical faces of column, anchorbeam and brace are flush on one side. This is the normal practice in all barns at the gable-ends, of course, to provide a regular surface for the weather-boarding.

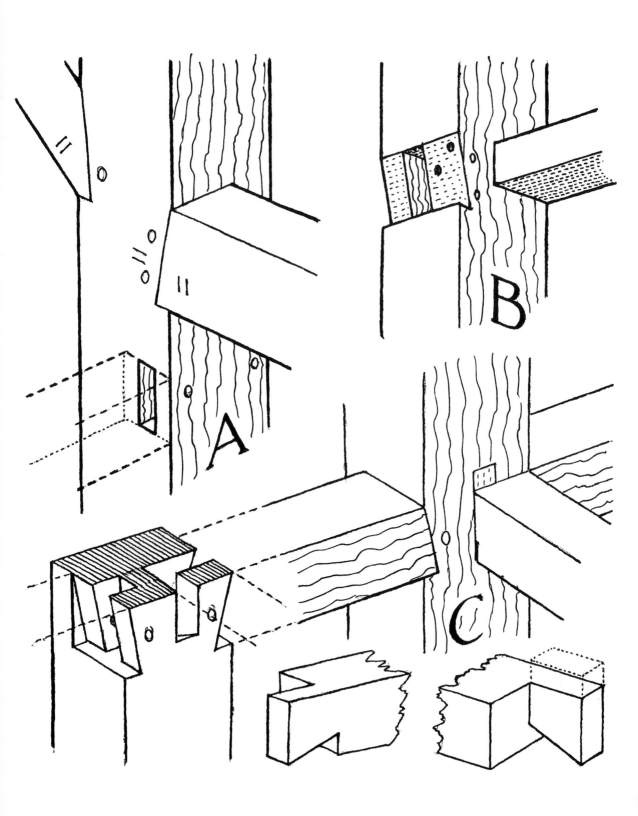

DRAWING 7: *Head-height Framing of Struts to Column*

In each case, a lateral face and the side-aisle face of a column are shown here. A typical scheme is indicated at A (west side of Verplanck-Van Wyck barn) where the Roman numeral chisel-marks are shown. Here the transverse link to a wall stud is at a higher level than the longitudinal strut, whose mortice alone shows in the drawing. Sometimes these levels are reversed, particularly in the side-aisle that was originally used to accommodate oxen or horses.

Two unusual instances in which both longitudinal and transverse struts are at the same level are sketched at B and C. The detail at B shows the east column in the northeast gable wall of the Wemple barn. Here the wider-than-deep transverse strut had to be pinned in place before the tenon of the longitudinal strut was inserted into the column's mortice.

In C, details of the east side of the Larger Wemp barn are delineated. At the left, the column is shown in plan section at the top of the longitudinal mortices, indicating how much of the column's substance has had to be cut away. When it came time to put the transverse strut in place, its dovetail end (about a third of the strut's width) was raised about two inches for insertion into its somewhat higher mortice hole. Slid into position, it was made snug and unretractable by a wood plug inserted into the upper portion of the mortice.

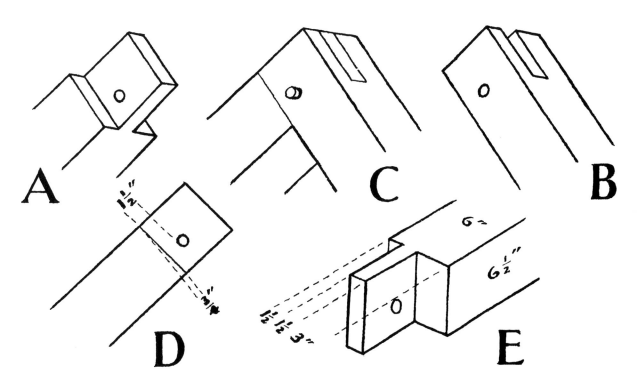

DRAWING 8: *Rafter Connection at the Ridge*

None of the New York Dutch barns has a ridge beam. Instead, the rafters are separately paired; and their connection invariably consists of a tongue-and-fork arrangement. The examples here illustrated are from the Van Wie barn, where the tongue or tenon is off center. Other examples have an evenly-spaced symmetrical joint; always of the tongue-and-fork scheme, never the half-lap scheme.

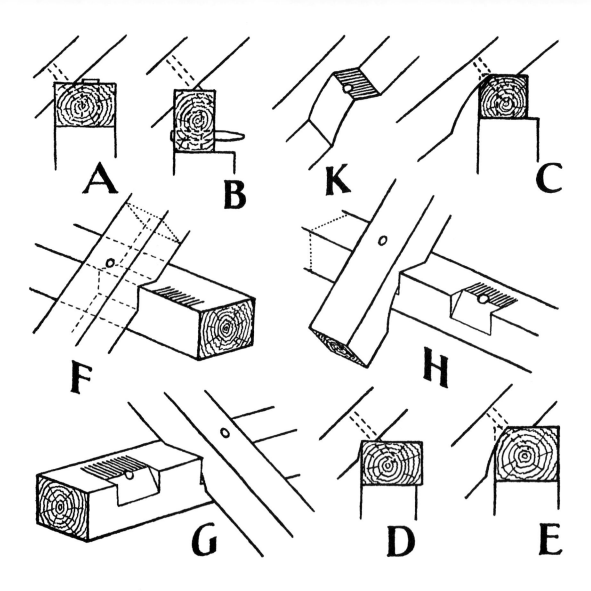

DRAWING 9: *Rafter-Bearing on Purlin-Plate*

At K, and at one side in F, G, and H (though not at the proper spacing from the designated rafter), hatch lines indicate the amount of bearing the rafter has on the purlin-plate. It should be remembered that this constitutes the entire area of direct support for each rafter. As shown in F and D (Indian Castle) this can be as little as 2″ (times the width of the rafter) on the 7¼″ x 10″ plate. G and E (Van Wie) shows a 4″ bearing; here, fully half the depth of the rafters (7¼″ at this point) is cut away. C, H, and K show the condition in the Verplanck-Van Wyck barn; where again, half the depth of the rafters has been cut away, this time in a sweeping curve. A (Lape) shows 5″ x 5½″ rafters and the 7″ x 10″ purlin-plate above which the column's tenon projects. B (Nelliston) has a 8″ x 5″ purlin-plate above an 8″ x 13″ column, the tenon of which is secured by two protruding pins. Here, the rafter pin is apparent from the nave side, between the soffit of the rafter and the top of the purlin-plate.

Each rafter is secured by a single oak pin, which is often roughly octagonal in section—a chamfered square. The hole is bored normal to the roof's slope. Only one instance (a couple of rafters in the very much cut up and altered barn north of Claverack on Rte. 9) has been noted of a *vertical* hole bored through the rafter and into the purlin-plate.

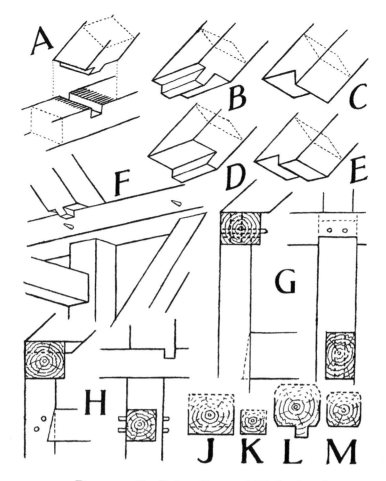

DRAWING 10: *Rafter Feet and Their Attachment*

Rafter feet are normally unsecured to the wall-plate, either by pinning, or by mortice-and-tenon, or by metal spikes. However, numerous examples are fashioned with a cog that fits into a transverse slot notched in the plate. A, B, and F show this system at the Larger Bradt barn; D and H are details from the Larger Wemp barn. The cog does not, of course, prevent the rafter's foot from kicking out. Rather, the cogs assure a fixed spacing of the rafter feet along the wall-plate.

Sometimes the rafter feet are fish-tailed as at C (Deertz) and E (Smaller Wemp), although both varieties may occur in adjacent rafters of the same barn. Many instances are found where there is neither cog nor fish-tail, as at G (Verplanck-Van Wyck). Here the diagonally-cut feet of the rafters merely rest upon the wall-plate.

Unlike most other structural members, rafters sometimes vary considerably in section in a single building. For example: Smaller Wemp (J), 7″ x 8″, 7½″ x 9″, spaced 61″ center-to-center; Cure (K), generally 4¼″ x 5″, spaced 41″; Larger Bradt (L), 7½″ x 8½″, spaced 59½″ to 61″; Verplanck-Van Wyck (M), 4¼″ x 7″, 5″ x 6½″, 6½″ x 6½″, spaced 52″, 56″, etc. (J, K, L, and M are combination drawings, showing both (1) the rafters' transverse section and (2) the cog or notch of their section in a vertical plane (lower portion)). In the Wemple barn, rafters measure 6″ x 6½″, 6″ x 8¼″, 8″ x 8½″, etc. at the butt, and are spaced about 56″ center-to-center, the same as the wall studs. More often than not, rafters are not completely squared in section. In the Smaller Wemp, Cure, and Wemple barns, however, all are sharp-edged, like the rest of the timberwork.

The upper transverse tie (linking column to wall stud) occurs 6″ below the soffit of the wall-plate in H (Larger Wemp). There is 17″ of clearance above the *Lower* tie in G.

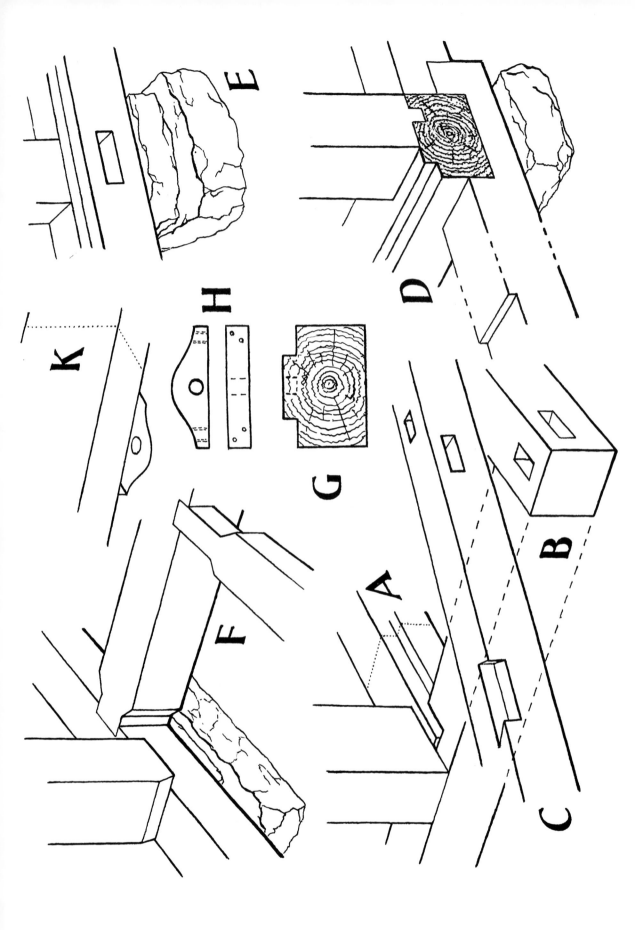

There is considerable variety in the foundation framing schemes of New York Dutch barns.

A is the northern-most column of the eastern range in the Van Wie barn, showing the junction of the column sill (rebated to receive the floor planks) with the transverse end-wall or gable sill. B shows the north end of the west wall sill in the same barn, morticed from the top to receive the corner post's tenon. Here, the horizontal mortice goes all the way through the timber, to house the tenon end of the north wall's sill.

C is the central portion of the end-wall sill in the Slater barn. The dove-tailed rebate received the end of the axial floor beam; and the horizontal mortice housed one of the secondary floor supports that ran longitudinally under the planking. Inward from the gable wall, this secondary beam lay in the shallow notch (to the left, under the letter D) of the heavy cross beam that was one of the transverse supports for the column sills in the same barn. Here, at D, a column sill is shown in darkened section, rebated (2″ deep, 2½″ wide) to receive the stub of the column's tenon, which runs the full longitudinal dimension of the column. The side-aisle sill is notched to sit upon the top of the through-projecting transverse sill, the former's upper face being flush with the top of the column sill.

E shows the two-stone support for the column sill in the Lacko barn, where a transverse beam, framed into the mortice beneath the column, linked column sill with axial floor beam.

F is the side aisle floor framing in the Deertz barn at one of the columns in the western range, where the loose floor boards are removed. G is a section of the barn's axial beam in the threshing floor, rebated 4¼″ x 2″ on each side to receive the planking. At one point it has a 2½″ round hole bored into it to receive the lower end of a vertical threshing pole. The upper end of this pole or arbor turned in a similar hole through an oak cleat (plan and elevation at H) nailed to the side of one of the anchorbeams (diagonal upward view at K). This was a very common feature. More rarely (as in the Wemple and larger Wemp barns) a hole drilled in the soffit of one of the anchorbeams answered the same purpose.

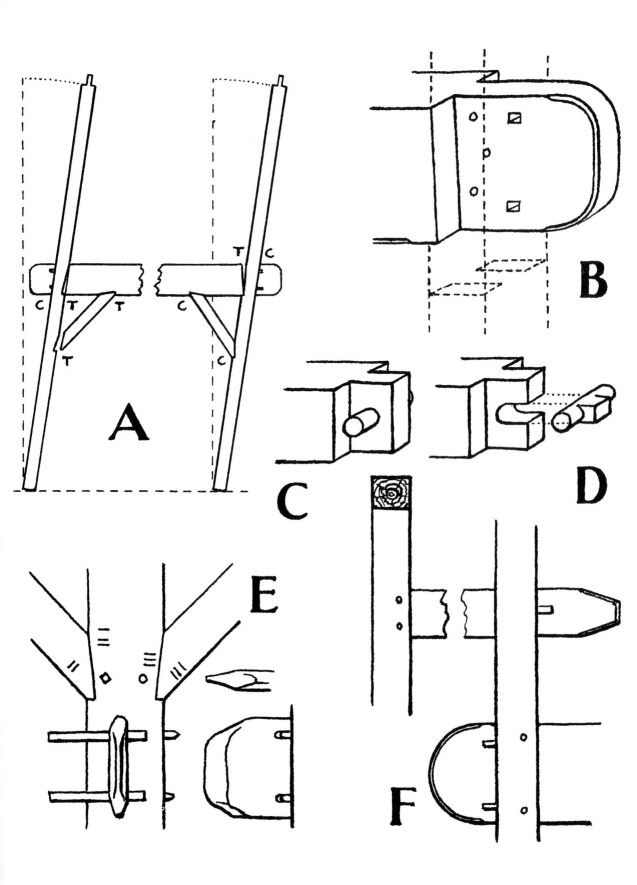

DRAWING 12: *Tenons, Protruding Tongues, and the Rigid Frame*

At C, a wooden pin is shown inserted through a short tenon. When a joint of this type undergoes tension, failure occurs when the pin pulls out along the grain, shearing away that portion of the tenon against which the pin bears (D). Obviously, the longer the tenon, the more resistance there is against shearing. Thus (at F) the 9″-deep transverse link between wall stud and column (barn on Rte. 5, east of Indian Castle) is secured to the 8″ x 14″ column by a long, single-wedged tongue. A similar situation, with different spacings and proportions, is found in the middle frame of the East of Sharon barn (see Plate 33). The great anchorbeams have protruding tongues for the same reason. Whether they have wedges (the normal condition) or are secured by oak pins alone, the tenon's length beyond the perforations for pins and wedges is important. For this length provides assurance that the wooden pieces driven through their appropriate slots are not likely to pull out under tension by ripping along the grain. (B is the tongue in the Larger Wemp barn; E is the less elegant and cruder condition in the Verplanck-Van Wyck barn, looking at the outer or side-aisle face of the column.)

A is an exaggerated diagrammatic view (for the Larger Wemp barn) of what happens when an H-frame tries to sway transversely in its own vertical plane. C and T designate the principal points that undergo compressive and tensional stresses respectively, in this situation. Obviously, the right-hand diagonal strut, here in compression, is more effective than its opposite number, here in tension.

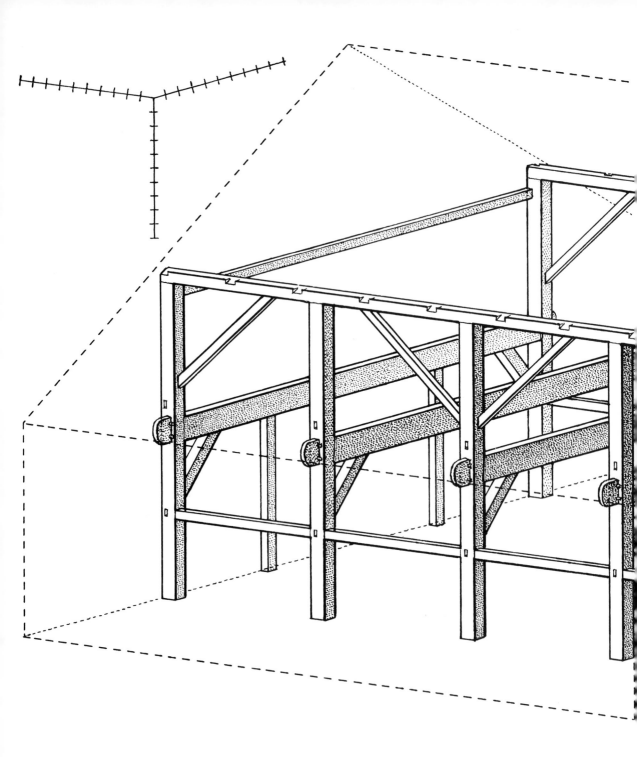

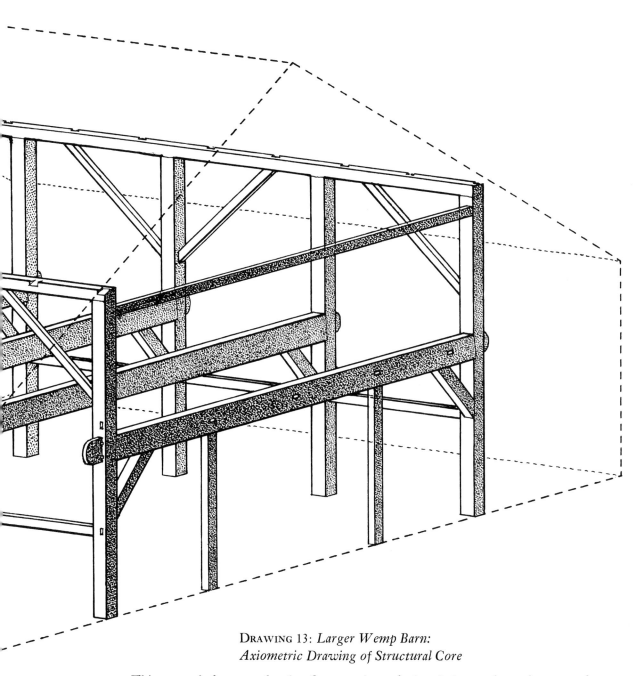

DRAWING 13: *Larger Wemp Barn:*
Axiometric Drawing of Structural Core

This central framework, the first portion of the timberwork to be erected, constitutes the rigid core on which the stability and security of the entire barn depended. The total space-volume of the building, indicated by broken lines, was subsequently attached to this core: the side walls, framed of stout posts; the gable walls of somewhat slighter studding; and the roof, in two slopes, on long tapering rafters in separate, widely-spaced pairs. This view is from the northeast, and is to the scale indicated in the upper left corner, where each of the major directions is calibrated in feet.

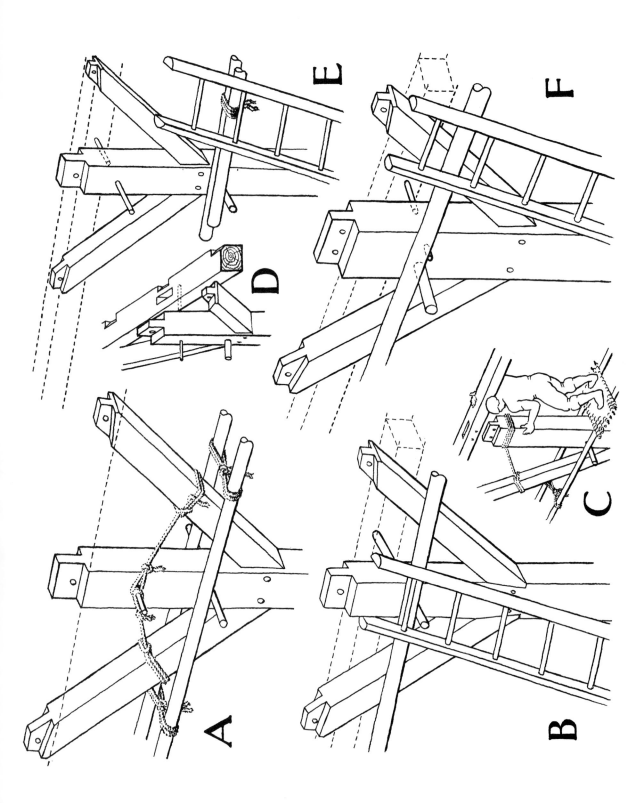

DRAWING 14: *"Raising Holes" and Their Probable Utilization*

Many of the columns in New York Dutch barns are pierced transversely by a hole—rarely by two holes, as at D, E, and F—which are located in the upper portion of the columns, one or more feet down from their tops. Nothing significant has been discovered remaining in any of these holes. However, this series of drawings shows examples of some of the levels at which the holes occur, together with a conjectural reconstruction of how they may have been utilized as scaffolding supports at the time of the purlin-plate's erection.

DRAWING 15:
Rafter-Raising Scheme

This sketch is purposely drawn out of scale with the intention of showing more clearly and compactly the probable way in which a pair of rafters was erected. Hauled up separately to the level of the purlin-plate, two rafters of a pair would have been laid askew, each resting on its purlin-plate and a temporary bridge of poles; they would have been pinned together in this horizontal attitude; then they would have been swung up to a vertical position, pivoting on the purlin-plates at their notched points of balance. Whether they were swung in the direction here shown (up from under a previously set pair of rafters), or in the opposite direction (the lower ends of the rafters swinging down past those of a previously installed pair), there would have been sufficient clearance in either case.

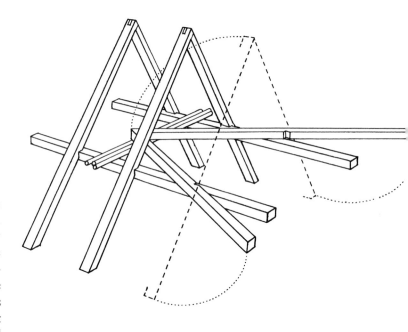

DRAWING 16: *Pentices: Survivals and Conjectures*

A, B, and part of C show actual conditions; the other drawings are conjectural. A is the long wedged tenon of one of the pentice's horizontal brackets, viewed from the interior, above the south door of the East of Sharon barn. The Larger Wemp barn has similarly wedged tenons still in place above its north door. B is one of the 3¼″ x 4¼″ mortice holes through the south door's anchorbeam, viewed from the interior, in the Van Wie barn; here the hole is shown in its relationship to the right-hand, six-inch-wide oak door-post.

None of the sheltering pentices that exist today above the wagon doors of New York Dutch barns is original. So neither the amount of projection nor the angle of slope, as orginally built, is certain; all the outdoor portions have long since rotted away. Although lacking both clapboarding and the roofers with their shingle covering, the drawing at C is a conjectural reconstruction of the Larger Wemp barn's north pentice. Direct evidence (including thin mortices for the upper ends of the pentice's rafters) survives only for the portion to the left of C. Whatever the roof pitch and the projection may have been, this assemblage

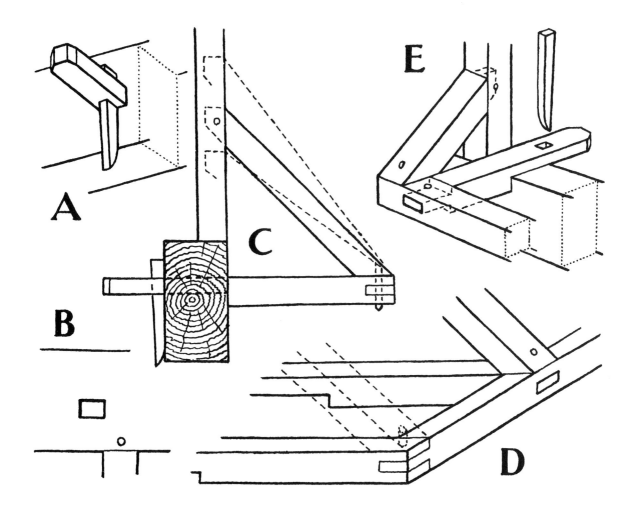

could easily have been installed by shoving it horizontally into place from the exterior. D shows part of the outer portion of the same scheme, although the outrigger-rafter units are here shown too close together, in the interest of clarity. Such a scheme might have been followed in those numerous examples where rectangular pentice-holes (usually three in number) are found cut through the end anchorbeams above the wagon doors.

E shows a very much compressed scheme that may have been followed in the Sagh barn. Here, uniquely, the surviving pentice-holes (nothing else of the pentice remains) are cut through the clapboards immediately *above* the wagon doors' anchorbeam.

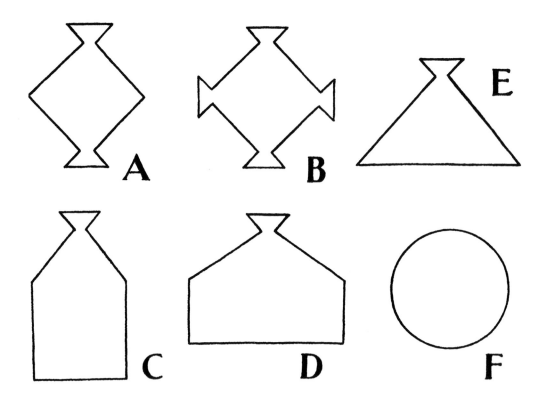

DRAWING 17: *Martin Holes*

All New York Dutch barns that retain their original weather-boarding have one or more martin holes in at least one of their two gables. Sometimes there is but one, high up under the peak. Two martin holes, widely spaced but at the same level, is a fairly common occurrence, and there are a number of cases where three are found in a triangular arrangement. At least three instances have been encountered where there are six widely-spaced holes in a one-over-two-over-three pattern. Occasionally there are other combinations. With few exceptions, all the holes in a given gable are of the same shape.

The commonest shapes are those indicated in C and D, though the proportions vary considerably. D may be as much as eleven or twelve inches wide (Indian Castle). C is found in East of Sharon (north gable), Larger Wemp (two in each gable), Van Bergen (two in west gable), and in barns north of Middleburg (one with six in south gable), and on Rte. 10 north of Cobleskill (one with three in north gable). A occurs in a barn on the Logtown Road; B is found in a barn nearby on the Glen Road and in another barn many miles away, near Conesville. E occurs in a number of barns southwest of Middleburg. Often a simple circle, F, is used as a martin hole, some six inches in diameter. North of Middleburg, particularly, there are instances of six of these circular holes to a gable.

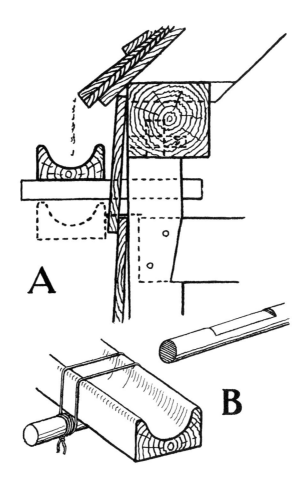

DRAWING 18: *Reconstructed Eaves and Gutter Detail*

Only one pair of original eaves-troughs has been discovered. These occur in the ruinous barn one mile south of Hurley, where the east-side trough is still in place. That to the west is fallen to the ground and broken into two pieces (one is 21'-3" in length); but the long slanting break makes it obvious that the eaves-trough was originally fashioned and installed as a single member.

The roof shingles shown in this drawing are conjectural, but the other known details are those of the Larger Wemp barn. These include the double-pegged upper transverse tie, and a 2"-diameter oak rod inserted through the wall-post as a gutter support, the stub of one being found *in situ*. There were five of these oak brackets along each of the eaves of this barn, from corner to corner, in a length of some forty-five feet. The wide weather-boarding was nailed just above the lap, to allow for across-the-grain expansion of the boards without splitting them. It is somewhat unusual that the pins securing wall-plate to studs do not show on the interior of this barn.

How the wooden eaves-trough was attached to its round oak supports is not known. The use of raw-hide lashing for this purpose, as shown here, is both conjectural and somewhat doubtful.

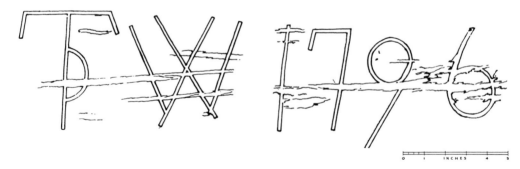

DRAWING 19: *Larger DeWitt-Suydam Barn: Carved Date*

This cypher, TDW, and date, 1796, are reduced from a rubbing made from the inscription that appears on one of the anchorbeams of this huge barn. The barn is said to have been assembled from parts of three Dutch barns formerly located nearby on the same DeWitt-Suydam property. The cypher presumably refers to Tjerck DeWitt, son or grandson of Tjerck Andriesen DeWitt; and the date is probably that of the rebuilding.

PLATE 1: *Barn on Route 20, East of Sharon: South Gable-End* (33)*

Along with the wagon entrance (whose western door-post is missing, as are the doors themselves), there are small doors at each corner of this end. Two of the three mortice holes for the wagon entrance's pentice are clearly evident, and although the clapboarding is old, it is not original. A narrow unglazed window high in the peak replaces one or more martin holes that were doubtless cut through the former cladding. The milk house to the east and the small windows flanking the wagon entrance are later additions.

The number in parentheses indicates the location of the subject on the Check-List and the Map of Barn Distribution.

PLATE 2: *Barn on Route 20, East of Sharon, North Gable-End* (33)

The clapboarding of most of this end is original, although the central portion at the peak is not; neither is that portion above the wagon entrance, where formerly a pentice projected above the double doors. A small door remains just to the left of the wagon doors; and a single martin hole survives in the gable above it. The negligible projection of the roof at the eaves and up the rakes of the gable is characteristic of early New York Dutch barns.

PLATE 3: *Larger Wemp Barn: South Gable and East Wall* (31)

At an early date, this barn was lengthened to the south by the addition of two bays. Subsequently (also at an early date), a wagon entrance was installed in the east side, giving access to what was originally the southernmost of four bays. This side-wall wagon entrance can just be made out in the photograph, about midway in the building's length. Two martin holes show in the peak of the near gable, whose unpainted clapboards have been burned dark by the weather. The barn lies beyond and below the foreground rise in the land.

PLATE 4: *Larger Wemp Barn: North Gable-End* (31)

Here the original clapboarding is still extant, showing some degree of variety in the width of its generally wide boards. Two characteristically shaped martin holes remain. The upper one is slightly off center because of the presence, within, of a central stud reaching to the peak. Lower down, holes through the clapboarding reveal where the original pentice rafters were attached. (The existing pentice is a small rebuilt one). Instead of the usual three, there is an additional rafter hole to the right, as well as a horizontal mortice hole below it, indicating that formerly the pentice extended west to give protection above the small Dutch door immediately adjacent to the wagon entrance. The leaves of this door still swing on their original iron hinges; unlike the wagon doors of this barn, this one swings out. Another door, for humans and animals, is set at the extreme right corner. Formerly, this one gave entrance to the animal stalls that apparently were located only on the west side, within this particular barn.

PLATE 5: *Larger Wemp Barn: View from Northwest* (31)

Notches which formerly accommodated the wooden hinges of one of the wagon doors can be seen cut into the inner edge of the far door-post. These wagon doors (the near one is still operational) swung inward. Exterior metal hinges are still extant on the little Dutch door immediately to the right of the wagon entrance. The pentice is modern; its predecessor originally sheltered both the wagon entrance and its small companion door, as indicated by the mortices. A cattle-door at the near corner opens outward, above the dislodged foundation-stones. Most of the clapboarding is original; piercing it in the peak are two characteristically shaped martin holes. The slate roof is recent.

PLATE 6: *Smaller Wemp Barn: Exterior View Looking Southeast* (30)

None of the exterior of this barn is original. The clapboarding is recent, and the wide roof projection at eaves and gable ends does not conform with the practice followed at the time this barn was originally built. Its wagon doors are also recent, as is their present location midway along the side walls. Originally, the wagon entrances were located on axis, at both gable ends.

This view is taken from within the wagon doorway on the east side of the Larger Wemp Barn.

PLATE 7: *Barn on Acker Hollow Road, off Route 145: Southeast Gable-End* (17)

Six circular martin holes show in the original clapboarding. Although the wagon doors and the overhead track they are hung on are new, the small door in the right-hand corner is original. The roof here is of rather flatter pitch than in most New York Dutch barns.

PLATE 8: *Nelliston Barn: View Looking Southwest* (27)

This Dutch barn has been considerably altered, from two causes. One, it has been moved some two hundred feet and re-erected on a site across a little stream from its original location. Two, it has been radically adapted to conform to a sloping site, the ground-level at the far gable-end being much higher than that of the barnyard in the foreground. The location of the wagon entrance, together with its pentice, is not original.

PLATE 9: *Wemple Barn: Southwest Gable-End* (32)

Later structures have been added to the right and left of the wagon entrance, whose double doors (the one to the left in two leaves, upper and lower) are still operational, swinging on their original all-wood hinges. A single martin hole is to be seen high in the peak, above the two blank openings which were made at some time subsequent to the barn's erection. Most of the clapboarding of this splendid barn is original.

PLATE 10: *Wemple Barn: Northeast Gable-End* (32)

Most of this gable-end retains its original clapboarding. Both leaves of the wagon doors are Dutch doors that swing inward on original all-wood hinges; the smaller corner doors swing outward on original wrought-iron hinges. The wagon entrance's pentice has disappeared, although its mortices remain in view. None of the windows is original, but the three martin holes remain. This is a large four-bay Dutch barn of exceptionally fine workmanship, which largely retains its authentic original state, within.

PLATE 11: *Ripking Barn: South Gable-End* (1)

This is a fine barn on the inside, of excellent workmanship and with massive timberwork of oak members. None of the exterior envelope is original; but the scheme of this south gable is an authentic one: (a) a pentice above (b) the wagon entrance which is on center and furnished with two doors, one fashioned as a Dutch door, in two parts; (c) a small door immediately to the right of the wagon entrance; and (d) an animal door in the far right corner.

PLATE 12: *Van Alstyne Barn: North Gable-End* (11)

None of the envelope of this fine six-bay barn is original, though the central location of its wagon entrance, and the near corner door, are characteristic. The lack of rafter collars and cross ties within has made it practical in the present century for some New York Dutch barns to be furnished with an outside hay-lift, peak doors of entry, and a track under the ridge within, for distributing the hay throughout the length of the loft. Hence the modern projection at the peak and the large access doors beneath it, to accommodate this modern labor-saving device. Note the unusual lack of symmetry: western eaves higher than eastern, and wagon-entrance not centered below the peak.

PLATE 13: *Verplanck-Van Wyck Barn: South Gable-End* (2)

Originally, the upper part of the gable wall projected in accordance with the existing overhang of the roof. (See Plate 14 for this feature as it is still retained at the north gable-end of this barn). Cattle doors are found here at both outside corners, to the right and left of the central wagon-entrance. This opening was formerly protected by the projecting gable above, in lieu of a pentice.

PLATE 14: *Verplanck-Van Wyck Barn: North Gable* (2)

There is a photographic illustration of this entire façade in Mrs. Reynolds book, *Dutch Houses in the Hudson Valley Before 1776*, Plate 9, p. 43. Although she speaks of the over-hanging gable as being typical and common for the Dutch barns of this region, this writer has found no other example of the feature in the New York Dutch barns he has encountered. Here, neither the doors in the peak nor the clapboarding is original.

PLATE 15: *Teller-Schermerhorn Barn: South Gable-End*

This barn, formerly located southwest of Schenectady but now destroyed, is most like an Old World Dutch barn in its proportions; that is, exceptionally steep roof pitches and very low side walls. None of the envelope of this barn—including windows, clapboarding, raking eaves' projection, and the overhead hanging of the doors—is original; the scheme, however, is thoroughly typical.

(Reyer Schermerhorn was father-in-law to Jan Wemp on whose property, some fifteen miles away, are the two Wemp barns. This photograph is supplied by courtesy of Mr. Clarence VanderVeer.)

PLATE 16: *Deertz Barn: South Gable-End* (20)

This barn has been better taken care of than almost any other New York Dutch barn. Probably for this very reason, none of the exterior envelope is original. The scheme, however, is authentic: wagon-doors on center, sheltered by a pentice, with a threshold close to ground-level, and a cattle-door at the left-hand corner. This is a very large barn: originally six bays long (sixty feet), no less than three more bays were added later, erected in a quite different framing system. The large opening shown here provides the only wagon-entrance to the interior. Both the windows and the doors, together with the hanging of the latter, are relatively modern installations.

PLATE 17: *Van Wie Barn: South Gable-End* (29)

The windows and the gabled doorway, including the doors themselves (which now swing out instead of in), are later insertions. The clapboarding, too, is not original. However, this was once a very fine barn, and an unusually large one. The pitch of its roof is steeper than that of most surviving New York Dutch barns.

PLATE 18: *Van Wie Barn: General View of Ruined Interior* (29)

View looking south, showing the interior framing of this ruinous 4-bay barn. One of the largest New York Dutch barns, it is of excellent workmanship throughout. Photographically, only in a view like this can one get some sense of the spaciousness of the hayloft whose vastness is unencumbered by rafter ties, collars, or transverse beams across the void from column-top to column-top.

The near column on the left marks the north end of this barn; the column next to it has fallen away. The horizontal piece attached to the anchorbeam at mid-span is there to receive the upper pivot of the threshing arbor.

PLATE 19: *Van Wie Barn: View Looking Southeast* (29)

A view looking southeast from within the ruins of this once splendid barn. Here are revealed the wide spacing of the slender rafters; the close setting of the roofers; an upper transverse tie, just above the anchorbeam's tongue; the long diagonals of the sway-braces that branch up to the purlin-plate, from the central column of this eastern range; and lying in the foreground, the gable-end column of the western range and some of the gable-end clapboarding.

PLATE 20: *Van Wie Barn: Detail of Interior* (29)

View facing northeast, looking up to one of the rafters (slightly bent as it crosses the purlin-plate), past the thin, unwedged, off-center tongue of two of the anchorbeams. The far column is the central one of the western range. Unlike the near column, it is linked to the side wall by an upper transverse tie. The purlin-plate is broken off at the top of this central column; originally, it continued north to link together the tops of all the columns in this range. The diagonal sway-brace, still attached to the purlin-plate above, has become dislodged from its mortice in the central column and has swung down, to remain hanging in a nearly vertical position. The fixed ladder is not original.

PLATE 21: *Van Wie Barn: Anchorbeam Tongues* (29)

View looking toward south gable-wall, where modern two-by-fours have been inserted, alternating between each pair of original studs, and later clapboarding has been installed. The fine craftsmanship of column, diagonal brace, and anchorbeam are evident in the foreground, where the thin tongue is long but without wedges. The farther tongue is characteristically smaller because its anchorbeam is shallower, being a part of the wall-framing of the gable-end.

PLATE 22: *Indian Castle Barn: Anchorbeam Connection* (25)

This anchorbeam, gained about an inch into its column, is both pinned and wedged. The anchorbeam tongues of this barn project more than those of any other Dutch barn that has so far been encountered. Slight chamfering can be seen in the rounded portion of this tongue.

PLATE 23: *Van Alstyne Barn:
Axial View of Interior
from North* (11)

Axial view of interior, as seen through
the north wagon entrance. This is one
of but two original six-bay barns discovered to date. The left-hand leaf of
the double-door wagon entrance at the
far end is a Dutch door. The sapling
poles that rest upon the anchorbeams
were the normal support for hay piled
in the loft; many of them may well date
from the time when the barn was built.

PLATE 24: *Van Alstyne Barn: West Range of Columns* (11)

The poles of the hay-loft's scaffold are clearly visible in this six-bay Dutch barn.
One of the leaves of the wagon doors in the south gable-end is a Dutch door;
each of these doors swings on all-wood hinges. Seen at the lower right-hand
corner of this view, the western side aisle is unfloored and at a lower level than
the planked threshing-floor. At the far gable-end wall, modern two-by-sixes have
been inserted between the much heavier original wall studs.

PLATE 25: *Van Alstyne Barn, Western Side-Aisle* (11)

View of three bays of the west side-aisle, near the north gable-end of this six-bay barn. The sway-bracing, seen here in the first and third bays, branches from the columns below the anchorbeam level. There are no upper transverse ties; and the lower one that was formerly framed into the first free-standing column has been removed. The second bay's above-head-height longitudinal strut has also been removed. The cattle-door in the northwest corner enters onto an unfloored side-aisle. Some of the notches for a slatted manger remain in the upper near edge of the third bay's longitudinal strut.

PLATE 26: *Van Alstyne Barn: Eastern Side-Aisle* (11)

The side-aisle bays in this eastern range are now partitioned off from the threshing-floor area by horizontally-hinged doors. The resulting enclosures are ceiled above from joists resting on the longitudinal struts that link the columns above head-height. However, the main framing members of the interior of this barn are clearly evident. A comparison of this photograph with that of Plate 25 (and a glance at the exterior, Plate 12) shows the wagon-entrance to be exceptional in that it is off-center, closer to the west than to the east side of the barn.

PLATE 27: *Larger Wemp Barn: Interior Axial View Looking North* (31)

The structure of this barn, originally of four bays, is symmetrical except that the head-height struts linking the columns longitudinally are slightly higher on the west side of the barn (the manger side), than they are on the east. The mortices cut into some of the anchorbeams to receive permanent longitudinal joists are an exceptional feature. However, most of the loft is floored with sapling poles, as was typical in New York Dutch barns. The craftsmanship of this barn is remarkably fine.

PLATE 28: *Larger Wemp Barn: East Range of Columns* (31)

The chamfering of the diagonal braces can here be discerned; and the upper transverse ties can be noted, strutting each column to the side wall. The craftsmanship of this barn is generally superior, so it is rather surprising to find marked irregularity in the spacing of the wall studs when all else is so uniform and regular. Here, a small door is rather uncharacteristically located in the side wall not far from the north corner of the building. Since the mangers were located exclusively on the other (west) side of the threshing floor in this barn, the position of this door is to be explained by the fact that the Smaller Wemp Barn as well as the farmhouse lie in this direction.

PLATE 29: *Germantown Barn:*
West Range of Columns (7)

This barn on the eastern side of the
Hudson River is exceptional in certain
respects. It is the only New York Dutch
barn so far discovered whose anchorbeam braces are consistently curved. It
is a five-bay barn of unusual height. The
depth of its anchorbeams, which is shallower than usual, is further reduced just
short of the columns; and no tongues
project on the far side of the latter. It
should be noted that all the original longitudinal struts that once linked the
columns of this western range at head-
height have been removed, leaving their
mortices revealed. High upper transverse ties from column to wall are still
in place, however, as are the unique longitudinal struts from column to column
at the level of the loft flooring of
sapling poles.

PLATE 30: *Barn on*
Route 9H South of
Stuyvesant Falls:
Column Framing (10)

Massive columns sup-
port a heavy purlin-
plate against which lean
the generally unsquared
rafters. The anchor-
beam and its diagonal
brace are framed with
their far sides flush with
the far face of the
column. There are no
upper transverse ties
across the side-aisles in
this barn.

PLATE 31: *Barn on Route 20, East of Sharon: West Range of Columns* (33)

Here the lateral faces of the columns, anchorbeams, and diagonal braces are flush on their south sides, and the head-height longitudinal struts are flush with the inner face of the columns. Above, can be seen the wide spacing of the rafters, which in this barn are squared and carefully finished. Framed into the central column, only, is an upper transverse tie; and higher up, there is a diagonally braced transverse beam spanning the central area from this column alone to its corresponding central column in the eastern range, opposite.

PLATE 32: *Barn on Route 20, East of Sharon: Wedged Anchorbeam Tongue* (33)

The anchorbeam attachment at the column between first and second bays, on the north side, is shown in detail. (The middle column, with its upper transverse tie (illustrated in Plate 33), shows in the upper left-hand corner of this view). Here, two thin but wide wedges secure the big tongue that is cut to a semicircular termination, and chamfered; and there are two stout oak pegs that hold the sloping shoulders of the anchorbeam close in against the notch that is gained in the column's inner face. The wood is pine.

PLATE 33: *Barn on Route 20, East of Sharon:*
Wedged Anchorbeam and Tie (33)

The detail of the anchorbeam connection to the center column, north range, of this 4-bay barn, shows the sloped inset of its shoulder, its 2-pin attachment, and the wedging of its big rounded tongue, slightly chamfered. Immediately above the anchorbeam is the upper transverse tie that links only the center column (in this barn) to the side wall. Like the anchorbeam below it, this tie is also both pinned and wedged.

PLATE 34: *Nelliston Barn: North Range of Columns* (27)

In this barn, the upper transverse ties of the side-aisles are exceptional in that they are at the level of, and frame into, the wall-plate. The near face of each anchorbeam and diagonal brace is flush with the near face of the column that supports them. All the anchorbeam tongues are secured with two wedges.

PLATE 35: *Nelliston Barn: South Range of Columns* (27)

The outer wall of this rebuilt barn has subsided somewhat, causing the upper transverse ties to tilt downward toward the exterior. The two nearest columns in this view define the middle of five bays: originally they supported transverse beams that spanned the central area above the level at which the sway-bracing branches up from these columns.

PLATE 36: *Verplanck-Van Wyck Barn: Column Framing* (2)

In this Hudson Valley (east side) barn, the craftsmanship is far less accomplished than in most other New York Dutch barns, but the framing scheme is familiar. However, no upper transverse ties from column to side wall were employed here. Most of the shape of a tenon can be observed in the diagonal brace where the near cheek of its mortice has torn away or been removed from the anchor-beam. The sway braces from the farther column to the purlin-plate have been removed; the mortice for one of them shows on the near face of that column.

PLATE 37: *Smaller Wemp Barn: Interior, Looking West* (30)

This is a three-bay barn of massive timberwork and of excellently finished craftsmanship. (Modern carpentry, as in the framing over the wagon doors and the intermediate two-by-six studs along the side wall, looks tenuous and weak by comparison.) The wagon entrances of this barn have been shifted to the middle of the side walls from their original locations centered at the two gable ends. Raising holes—exceptionally, not at the same level—are apparent in both columns at a point some two-fifths of the distance down from purlin-plate to anchorbeam-top. A unique but not contemporaneous feature of this interior is the windlass (for drying fish-nets, probably, from the nearby Mohawk River). The wide spacing of the heavy, carefully squared rafters is clearly evident.

PLATE 38: *Smaller Wemp Barn: Detail of Sway-Bracing Connection to Column* (30)

This is a view of the outer, side-aisle face of one of the main columns of the eastern range, showing the numbering of its connections, IIII-IIII and V-V, with the sway-bracing attached to it. The oak pins are cut off flush with the face of the column; and the braces, whose faces are flush with that of the column on this side, have shoulders that are gained into the column in sloping cuts.

PLATE 39: *Deertz Barn:*
Double Anchorbeam and
Manger (20)

After four bays in which the anchorbeams are framed at a normal height, two huge anchorbeams, one above the other, span the central area of this great barn. Beyond this point the loft rises from the level of the tops of the lower anchorbeams. This photograph shows the drop in the loft's floor at the fifth column from the wagon-entrance end of the barn, clearly showing that the lower anchorbeam is deeper than the one above it. In the lower center of the picture is an original manger, seen from the threshing-floor side.

PLATE 40: *Deertz Barn:*
Manger Detail (20)

This is a view looking diagonally inward toward the threshing floor, from the low-ceilinged "side-aisle" in which the animals were quartered. The framing of this manger stall is still original, although some features (the boarding above the tilted slats, and the chicken wire) have been added. The post at the far end of the manger is the lower portion of one of the main columns of the barn: not only is the manger construction framed into it, but both the longitudinal strut and the side-aisle link that spans the side-aisle are mortice-and-tenoned into it at head-height. It is apparent that the cattle that fed at this manger faced inward, toward the threshing floor.

PLATE 41: *Deertz Barn: Original Planking of Threshing-Floor* (20)

View looking diagonally toward the open wagon entrance at the south gable end, showing the original planking of the threshing floor. Across the center of the picture is the median floor sill (in one piece, sixty feet long). The heavy planks rest on shelves rebated into the sill, to which they are secured with oak pins.

PLATE 42: *Deertz Barn: Detail of Column Support* (20)

Here some of the loose planking of the floor has been removed in the western side-aisle, to reveal (1) the base of one of the main columns, resting on (2) its longitudinal sill, which in turn bears upon (3) a large flat rock. To the right, (4) a stout transverse floor beam is framed into the sill, which is morticed to receive the narrowed end of the beam.

PLATE 43: *Ruinous Barn
One Mile South of Hurley:
Detail of Column Support* (24)

The outer, or side-aisle face of one of
the columns in the western range is
shown here. The large flat stone that
serves as foundation for the column sill
at this point is revealed because the near
side-aisle is not (nor ever was) covered
with a plank floor. In this barn, the planking of the threshing-floor rests on the top
of the columns' sill, instead of on a shelf
rebated into its upper, inner edge.

PLATE 44: *Larger Wemp Barn:
Detail of Clapboarding* (31)

This is a view looking SW at the
column of the eastern range that marked
the south end of the barn as originally
built. With the early erection of additional bays to the south, portions of the
original weatherboarding survive in the
interior, as in these fresh-looking clapboards that have been sawn off an inch
or so from the east face of the column.

Nails that secure the boards to the
column can faintly be made out at two
points, just above the top of the split
board and at the one above it.

Plate 45: *Verplanck-Van Wyck Barn: Projecting Gable Detail* (2)

This view is looking northeast, with the over-sailing gable on the left. The wall anchorbeam appears at the lower left; its connection to the end column is obscured by the loose lumber lying across the anchorbeams. The north-south dimension of this column is partially hidden by the sheathing boards that lap it irregularly on its interior face. The northern-most rafter of the side-aisle is cut off just beyond its bearing on the purlin-plate whose soffit has been adjusted to the height of the column-top at this point. The pins that secure the sway-bracing to the purlin-plate are driven in from the far side; they do not project through, and are therefore not visible on the near side.

PLATE 46: *Verplanck-Van Wyck Barn: Projecting Gable Framing* (2)

This view is looking west, just inside the north gable wall. To the left, a rafter is shown bearing on the sway-braced purlin-plate, which projects beyond the lower face of the gable wall to support the ends of a conspicuously sagging girt into which the jack-studs are tenoned.

PLATE 47: *Wemple Barn: All-Wood Hinges of Dutch Wagon Door* (32)

This is a detail of the condition inside the south wagon-entrance, showing the oak hinges and their common pintle in the case of the closed position of the upper and lower leaves of this Dutch door. The inside of the wide clapboarding appears at the right of the door-post; and the diagonal board of the upper leaf (essential to prevent the plank door from sagging) is shown in the upper left.

PLATE 48: *Larger Wemp Barn: All-Wood Hinge of Wagon Door* (31)

This is a detail of the lower hinge of the western wagon door leaf, north gable-end of the Larger Wemp barn. The position shown is that when the door is half open; that is, when it has been swung ninety degrees inward from its closed position in the plane of the gable wall. Immediately to the left of the door-post is the small Dutch door that served as an entrance for humans. Both upper and lower leaves of this door, here shown closed, swing outward.

PLATE 49: *Wemple Barn: Wrought-Iron Hinge* (32)

This is a detail of the contemporary iron hinge on the cattle-door at the north-east corner of the Wemple barn, whose wagon doors swing on all-wood hinges that are still in use.

PLATE 50: *Barn One Mile South of Hurley: Wooden Eaves-Gutter* (24)

This photograph of the original eaves-gutter (now fallen and broken into two long portions) was taken from the west side of the ruined barn. Formerly, when it was in place, it was in one piece measuring about thirty-eight feet in length and 3½″ x 6½″ in section.

PLATE 51: *Gargeo Barn, Southwest of Middleburg* (51)

In this, one of the more spectacular testimonials to the nature of the roof construction in New York Dutch barns, the north side wall has collapsed entirely, leaving these rafters hanging without apparent support. Actually, they are cantilevered from their bearing on the purlin-plate and obviously not dependent on support at the eaves. The ends of the rafters can be seen to be furnished with cogs. This barn is unique among those so far examined in having quite narrow roofers that are widely spaced (as though, perhaps, they had originally been covered with tiles instead of shingles).

PLATE 52: *Smaller DeWitt-Suydam Barn: Carved Date* (39)

This cypher, TADW, and date, 1758, are carved on one of the anchorbeams, the figure "8" being done mechanically with a kind of router. The cypher almost certainly indicates Tjerck Andriesen DeWitt; and the date is probably that of the year in which the barn was built. Since both this inscription and that shown in Dwg. 19 are exceptional, being found only on DeWitt barns, they must be interpreted as ownership markings.

Appendixes

Glossary

Index

Appendix A

Pictorial Glossary

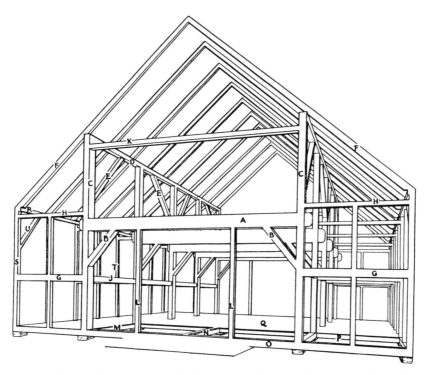

Shown here in perspective is the structural skeleton in timber-work, characteristic of a 4-bay Dutch barn. The dimensions (and most of the details) are those of the Larger Wemp barn. Omitted from this drawing are the following: (1) Roofers and roof shingles, (2) Clapboards, (3) The gable-ends' upper tiers of studs (inserted after the structural frame was assembled and in place, and installed without pins), (4) Pentice over wagon entrance, (5) Doors and their hinges, (6) Mangers, (7) Eaves troughs.

A – Anchorbeam	H – Upper transverse struts	O – Gable-end (mud) sill
B – Anchorbeam braces	J – Longitudinal head-height	P – Side-aisle transverse sill
C – Columns	strut	Q – Threshing-floor planking
D – Purlin-Plate	K – High transverse beam	R – Wall plate
E – Sway-bracing	L – Wagon-door posts	S – Corner wall-post
F – Rafters	M – Column sill	T – Wall-post or major stud
G – Lower transverse struts	N – Median floor sill	U – Side-wall sway-bracing

Appendix B

Maps of Dutch Barn Distribution
and Early Dutch Settlement

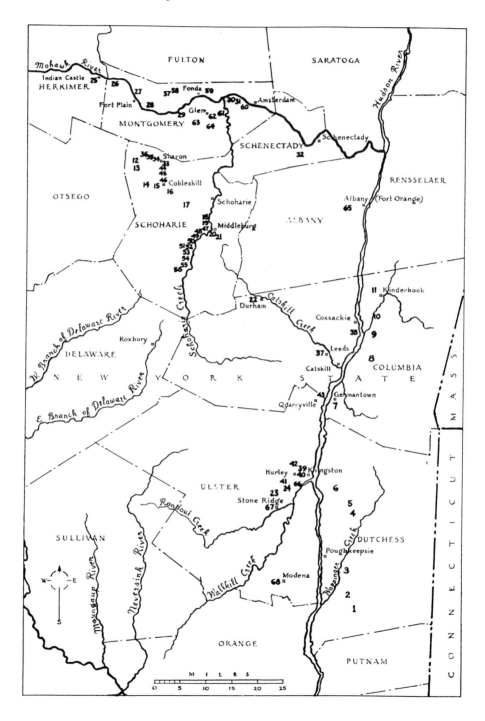

Detail Map of Eastern Central New York State, a chart of the location and distribution of early Dutch barns noted in the Check-List. (Left, on facing page.)

The center of this map is the high ground of the Catskill Mountains from which (1) two branches of the Delaware River flow southwest, (2) the Mongaup and the Neversink flow south, (3) the Rondout and the Wallkill flow northeast into the Hudson at Kingston, (4) the Catskill flows southeast into the Hudson farther north, and (5) the Schoharie Creek flows north into the Mohawk.

Modern boundaries of New York State Counties are indicated, as are the State's boundaries with contiguous New England States on the east. These latter boundaries run generally north-south near the Hudson River watershed on that side.

Although both the State and the County boundaries here designated were not finally determined until after the Colonial Period when the Dutch settled these parts of the New World, they are shown here to familiarize the viewer with the location of the areas under consideration. See the smaller map (right) for the extent of the region covered by this map.

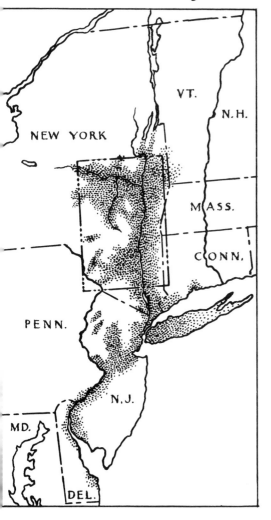

Maximum Extent of Early Dutch Settlement in America, from the first immigrants in 1624 to the outbreak of the Revolutionary War in 1775. (left)

The time span encompassed by this map makes its comprehensiveness somewhat misleading. For example, the early Dutch colony established in the Connecticut area around New Haven was under the Dutch for a brief period, then absorbed by the English. On Long Island the Dutch pulled back at an early date (also due to English expansion from New England) from their loosely scattered holdings throughout most of the island, to consolidate in the area at its western end, in the vicinity of Manhattan. Much of the New Jersey region along the eastern side of the Delaware River, from Trenton south, was shared with the Swedes (this area was even called "New Sweden"). Again, the fort community which the Dutch established at the southern side of the entrance to Delaware Bay was held by them for only a few decades. Actually, the significant geographical expansion of the Dutch was to the north, in the eastern part of what is now New York State, in the region west of the Hudson River and largely in and south of the Mohawk Valley.

It can be assumed, however, that barns were built by the Dutch at one time or another in all the areas they settled, even though the barns' survival to our time is most unlikely in many of these areas.

Appendix C

New Checklist of Dutch Barns

This appendix combines John Fitchen's original checklist of Dutch barns, first presented in 1968, with updated information for the second edition provided by Gregory D. Huber. Fitchen's original numbered barn commentaries are left intact, and each one is followed by Huber's own findings and annotations. Each author's contributions to the checklist are followed by his initials, J.F. or G.D.H.

It is not to be supposed that the following list includes all extant Dutch barns. Far from it. This is an annotated listing of those barns the author himself has visited.

Most of the data recorded here refer to the conditions found to exist in each barn at the time it was first seen. Some of these conditions have subsequently been altered; in a few cases even the barns themselves no longer survive. There would seem to be some significance, therefore, in noting the dates of first viewing:

> A: September 29, 1962
> B: June 9, 1963
> C: June 19, 1963
> D: September 3, 1963
> E: September 4, 1963
> F: September 13, 1963
> G: November 2, 1963
> H: August 7, 1964
> J: April 24, 1965

Barns are listed, not in any alphabetical or chronological sequence, but geographically in accordance with the routes which the author and his companions first followed in getting to see the barns. In the process, other barns of more or less early date were encountered, of course; but none of these, however interesting, is included here. Nor are later attached structures and other subsequently added features included in these notes, unless such features have affected the barn's structure as originally built. It is early Dutch barns alone with which we are concerned.

If some barns are given but slight notice, it is because of the exigencies encountered on barn-hunting expeditions. For it should be noted that a tour of parish churches, for example, in France or England, is inevitably quite different from a tour of barns in New York State. European churches can always be closely approached and examined on the exterior; moreover, in most cases they are open to worshipers (and to tourists) throughout the day. Our barns, on the other hand, are individually owned and are on private land; hence one is a trespasser if he approaches a barn without getting the permission of the proprietor. Furthermore, to enter a farmer's barn is somewhat like entering his house: both are his private property, and the stranger should not expect to be welcome in either without invitation.

Because the barn is a structure that is indispensable to the farmer's livelihood throughout the changing seasons, it reflects these seasonal changes by the gear or the animals or the crops it contains at one time or another. One cannot forget that any useful barn is not a public show place but a practical utilitarian building whose prime multiple function is storage. Hence an observer's visual survey of the interior of a barn is apt to be obscured or limited by the legitimate presence of machines or sacks of fertilizer or the gathered-in harvest. Only a barn that has ceased to serve its basic year-round functions can be seen and photographed without some distracting piece of farm equipment or some obscuring piles of produce in the way. These factors account for the brevity of some of the notations given below.

Where known, the names of original owners are cited; otherwise the name of the present owner or occupant (p.o.) may be given. Locations are designated on the map of barn distribution shown in Appendix B.

—J.F.

A full third of a century has passed since John Fitchen made the last of nine visits that yielded information he made of seventy-one Dutch American barns. His first visitation was to the excellent larger Wemp barn in September 1962, which was followed by six visits in 1963 and one visit each in 1964 and 1965. He recorded to varying degrees details on fifty-seven barns. Reduced viewability severely hampered his efforts with fourteen other barns. Of these, he noted only one or two traits in each of three barns and the remaining eleven barns he could not positively identify as Dutch because they were either locked or too full of hay. He visited about a half dozen barns at least twice, and he saw the magnificent Wemple barn (no. 32) three times. Two barns (nos. 27 and 44) were removed from their sites before the book was published. Barns numbered 72 to 76 apparently were never visited by Fitchen.

A significant aspect of Dutch barns today is their rapid disappearance from the cultural landscape. This circumstance applies to many of the barns that Fitchen located. Since February 1976 I have been able to track down the status of barns at each of the seventy-one Fitchen visited sites. Only twenty-two barns are extant (with two ruinous) and this amounts to an astonishing attrition rate of about 70 percent. In other words, fully two thirds of the barns John Fitchen brought to light are no longer at the sites where he observed them. It is true, however, that nine barns or parts of barns have been relocated and re-erected at new sites. Three more barns are in storage. One should bear in mind that although the structure of a barn itself can obviously be saved by dismantling and rebuilding at a new location, this process forever destroys the cultural fabric in its original locational setting in which a barn was originally fashioned and utilized. We do not know with a high degree of authority which of these barns were at their original erection sites because innumerable barns were moved for reasons related to shifting agricultural economies during the nineteenth century.

Fitchen understood that his barn list was far from complete. I have located about 570 Dutch barns since 1975. There have been seventy to eighty additional barns reported by other observers and interested parties. The total attrition rate, while not exactly known, is understood to be rather high. The disappearance of barns because of neglect that leads to their removal or to relocation seems to have occurred more in the upper river valleys of eastern New York state than in the lower Hudson River Valley and in New Jersey.

I have provided a much-expanded base of information for many of the barns that appeared in Fitchen's original list. Each barn's status is recorded: extant or nonextant, relocated (dismantled and re-erected at a new site), in storage, or nonextant but possibly saved. The last situation is noted in cases where I visited certain sites too late to know if the particular barn was relocated, in storage, or destroyed. In all cases, the status was current as of the summer of 1998. I have not attempted to cite every trait with the same level of detail in all the barns because, like Fitchen, I found that not all barns were equally accessible. Often, only a barn's most salient features are noted. In a few cases important traits that Fitchen cited are repeated. Certain barns, either because of their popularity or significant structural composition, have been discussed at length. Some original houses at some homesteads are noted. In most cases a well-educated guess based on twenty-five years of field research has been made on each barn's erection date.

The great majority of barns have changed ownership since Fitchen originally visited the sites. Only four homesteads exist where the original owners still live—barns no. 4, 37, 42, and 52. A few others may still reside at the original locations.

A few Dutch barns (including two in this checklist) appear at Dutch house sites described in two classic books that readers should consult: *Dutch Houses in the Hudson Valley Before 1776*, a book on regional Dutch house architecture by Helen W. Reynolds (n.p., 1929), and *Pre-Revolutionary Dutch Houses and Families in Northern New Jersey and Southern New York*, by Rosalie F. Bailey (New York: W. Morrow and Co., 1936). Together, these books display pictures (plates) of a combined 260 Dutch homesteads that both Reynolds and Bailey originally visited (some plated houses had already disappeared). At all these sites, I have found just nine barns (including remnants). I make several references in this appendix to homesteads that the two authors visited.

Note that the letter or letters immediately following the barn numbers refer to the date when Fitchen visited the barn in question, as indicated in the list of dates that appears at the beginning of this appendix.

—G.D.H.

1. (E) Ripking, p.o. S of Poughkeepsie on Rte. 376 just W of junction with Rte. 52.
Three-bay. N-S orientation. 36 ft. long, 44 ft. 3 in. wide, 10-ft. height of side walls from floor level. Wagon doors at both gable-ends; usual entrance at S. Wagon-entrance jambs notched at midheight to receive bar of timber to secure doors shut from inside. Anchorbeams of $9^1/_2$ x 18 in. are housed into columns on through-pin side; tongues are neatly chamfered and are double-wedged. Anchorbeams are only 10 ft. $2^1/_2$ in. in clear height from floor to soffit. Columns are spaced 22 ft. $7^3/_4$ in. trans-

versely, face to face. Anchorbeams, columns, and braces are all flush on their N faces. Rafters are big, averaging 8 x 9 in. at their fishtailed feet. Mostly oak framing throughout. Careful workmanship shown in the sharp-edged rectangularity of structural members.

Transverse section at M, Dwg. 4; S gable-end, Plate 11.

—J.F.

Extant but relocated. The first barn on Fitchen's list was deteriorating to some degree when I visited it in late 1977. It was, however, saved by a barn renovator in 1985 when he dismantled it. Later, it was re-erected southeast of Syracuse. Many of its timbers had to be replaced. Nave is 24 ft. wide. Side aisles are 10 ft. Side walls are about 10 ft. high and *verdiepingh* is 5 ft. Anchorbeam-to-post unions have both diminished haunch and square shouldering (this combination trait occurs occasionally). Roof peak height about 26 ft. H-frame braces are both hewn and milled. Marriage marks are present. No slots in wagon door posts for wooden hinges. Its two inner anchorbeams are of tulipwood (*Liriodendron tulipifera*), and three different types of contours appear on anchorbeam tenons. The barn has a fairly steep roof. Circa 1790.

—G.D.H.

2. (E) Verplanck–Van Wyck (G. L. Stringham, p.o.). Rte. 376 at Sprout Creek.
Four-bay. 43 ft. 10 in. long, 49 ft. 11 in. wide, $9^{1}/_{2}$-ft. side-wall height. N-S orientation. Wagon doors at both gable-ends; usual entrance at N. Columns $10^{1}/_{2}$ x $11^{1}/_{4}$ in., spaced 26 ft. 5 in. transversely, face to face. Five-foot 3-inch height to soffit of longitudinal links; 6 ft. 3 in. height to that of transverse struts. Very slender rafters, spaced irregularly about 4 ft. 6 in. apart on the average. Regular pattern of fairly long sway braces. Roman numeral numbering of framed members starts at N end. Anchorbeams of yellow pine, other structural members of oak. Rather coarse workmanship throughout. Unique feature: cantilevered projection of N gable (originally at S end, too), central portion, from anchorbeam level.

Transverse section at L, Dwg. 4; rafter details at G, K, and H, Dwg. 9, and at G and M, Dwg. 10; detail of anchorbeam tongues at E, Dwg. 12; exterior views, Plates 13 and 14; interior views, Plates 36, 45, and 46.

—J.F.

Extant but relocated. This is one of the most interesting Dutch barns on the list. In contrast to Fitchen's assertion that this was the only barn with gable-wall cantilevering found during his barn trips, Helen W. Reynolds claimed, in her 1929 book *Dutch Houses in the Hudson Valley Before 1776*, that cantilevering was typical of Dutch barn construction. However, four other cantilevered barns—three in Brooklyn and one in Wayne, New Jersey (see Bailey Plate 144)—are represented in old photographs. No other example of this type was known until April 1996, when I discovered an excellent barn with a three-sided cantilever in Ho-Ho-Kus, New Jersey, only three months before most of the barn was removed. In addition, two other barns, both in west central New Jersey, had some evidence of cantilevering. It is curious that Fitchen did not speculate as to the function of cantilevering except to say that the central wagon entrance was protected by the cantilever in lieu of a pentice. It probably served for ventilation of stored crops above the anchorbeams.

The Verplanck-Van Wyck barn was dismantled in 1974 by a Connecticut contractor at Sprout Creek (see Reynolds Plate 149) in East Fishkill, where a 1768 Dutch gambrel-roofed house still stands. The barn was then re-erected at Mount Gulian (see Reynolds Plate 148). Its original timbers, many of which were replaced, are slowly deteriorating with powder post beetle. In 1998 a Mohawk Valley contractor who consulted with me was hired to reconstruct the threshing floor doors and other doors. There are plans to do other much-needed renovation work in the future.

The cantilever in the Verplanck-Van Wyck barn is five sided and spans the entire width of the nave. Its side wall is 63 in. in height and is in line with the H-frame posts. The cantilever is created by both purlin plates, which extend out beyond the gable wall H-frame posts by 18 in. (The Ho-Ho-Kus barn mentioned above had a cantilever of 12 inches.) Three large sapling poles stabilize the base and stretch from above the first interior anchorbeam over and beyond the gable-wall anchorbeam and then into a mortised crossbeam that frames the base. The upper angled edge of the cantilever is formed by rafters whose feet rest on a tie that stretches between the projecting part of both purlin plates.

The existence of eight cantilevered barns in a fairly wide geographic range implies that this distinctive form originally may have been represented by several dozen or even a few hundred of its type by the late eighteenth century. It probably had European antecedents.

The barn has the rare trait of purlin braces that are riven. They attach to posts at the top level of the anchorbeams and are 80 in. long and of variable widths up to 9 in. All sixteen braces (eight per side) appear to be original with marriage marks. Only two original horizontal head height ties and one original side aisle transverse tie ($9^1/_2$ x $5^1/_2$ in.) of oak remain.

Three inner (non-gable-wall) anchorbeams of tulipwood (*Liriodendron tulipifera*) of 16-in. depth have double-wedged square tenons with broadly chamfered upper corners. Gable-wall anchorbeams of 11-in. depth are oak (one bent) and probably chestnut (other bent). All anchorbeam-to-post joints are square shouldered and double pegged. There are 2-foot scribe marks on the anchorbeams. The ten H-bent posts are all of oak. Horses were stabled on one side aisle as indicated by the presence of notches that serve as attachment points for manger boards. *Verdiepingh* 61 in., and there are no raising holes. Distance from top of anchorbeams to the nonoriginal floor is 12 ft. Gable-wall H-frame braces are both generally smaller in x-section and longer than inner bent braces.

Roof is 30ft. high. Nave is 28 ft. wide, with side aisles each 11 ft. wide. The roofline has classic proportions, with a steep pitch and quite low side walls. Circa 1765.

—G.D.H.

3. (E) Rte. 9G, $^1/_4$ mile S of Rte. 53.
A probable Dutch barn, but too full of hay to examine.

—J.F.

This barn has never been found. The location appears to be nonexistent. Fitchen may have assigned incorrect route numbers in his original notes.

—G.D.H.

4. (E) Adriance, p.o. Rte 9G, town of Clinton; E side of road.

Three-bay. N-S orientation, with wagon doors at both ends. 32 ft. long, 38 ft. 1$\frac{1}{2}$ in. wide. W side aisle is unfloored and at lower level than E. Column-sill and its stone supports lie exposed to view on this W side. (Subsequently built outer side aisle to W utilizes slope of land.) 16 ft. 3$\frac{1}{2}$ in. clear span, transversely, face to face of columns. Raising holes, down about 18 in. below purlin plate. 10$\frac{1}{4}$- x 11$\frac{1}{2}$-in. columns, 18-in. deep anchorbeams, and braces, all of oak.

—J.F.

Extant. This barn is in excellent condition and forms the nucleus of a working farm. It is in the same ownership as it was at the time Fitchen visited. It overlooks some rather uneven land and a one-and-a-half-story frame house that is circa 1815. Nave is 18 ft. wide, and *verdiepingh* is 7$\frac{1}{2}$ ft. long. Raising holes appear about 1$\frac{1}{2}$ ft. below post tops. Nine pairs of rafters fishtailed into wall plates. Purlin braces milled. Anchorbeam-to-post junction is square shouldered. Anchorbeams adjacent to gable walls have no extended tenons. The barn has the extremely unusual trait of a mowstead-like wall that stretches between H-frame posts. It is similar to many three-bay English barns and Pennsylvania Swiss-German barns. It has a rather steep roof line. Circa 1810.

—G.D.H.

5. (E) Cure, p.o. Shortly N of Rte. 55, on Rte. 9G, E side of road.

E-W orientation. 42 ft. 5$\frac{1}{2}$ in. wide, about 41 ft. long, 14 to 15 ft. high at eaves. 9- x 13-in. columns, 9- x 15-in. anchorbeams, both of oak; 6$\frac{1}{2}$- x 8-in. braces of pine. Chamfered, square-cut anchorbeam tongues project 6$\frac{1}{4}$ in. Slender, neatly squared rafters of oak, 4$\frac{1}{4}$ x 5 in. in section at their feet, are spaced 41 in. apart on the average. Raising holes occur 10 in. down from purlin plate; two pins secure the latter at each column-top. This barn is of good craftsmanship and is in excellent condition.

Transverse section at J, Dwg. 4; rafters at K, Dwg. 10.

—J.F.

Extant. For craftsmanship, a good Dutch barn in very good condition. Its orientation is 16 degrees east of north instead of the original Fitchen citation of east-west. It is exactly square with each side 42$\frac{1}{2}$ ft. long. Nave is 20 ft. wide. Anchorbeam post junction is square shouldered. Purlin braces are hewn. *Verdiepingh* is close to 10 ft. Thirteen pairs of hewn rafters are in line with side-wall posts and studs. Rafters are fishtailed into wall plates. Side walls few inches shy of 14 ft. high. Circa 1800. A gable-roofed Dutch stone house of 1$\frac{1}{2}$ story construction still occupies this site.

—G.D.H.

6. (E) Acker, p.o. (Said to have been always in one family; Beckman in 1769.) On old Rte. 9G just S of Wurtemburg Road.

Four-bay. NE-SW orientation. 41 ft. 0 in. long, 44 ft. 0 in. wide. High side walls; less than usual roof pitch. Center wagon doors on all-wood hinges are flanked by a small door at each corner of SW gable-end (facing road and across from farmhouse). Columns are $8^1/_2$ x $13^1/_2$ in. in section, with raising holes about 3 ft. 6 in. down from purlin plate, at a level just above branching of regularly patterned sway-bracing. $11^3/_4$-x 17-in. oak anchorbeams, gained 1 in. into column face. Tongue projections sawed off. 5-ft.-6-in. height to soffit of $7^1/_4$-in.-deep longitudinal links; $1^1/_4$ in. higher to soffit of $8^3/_4$-in.-deep transverse struts. Middle anchorbeam has bracket for threshing arbor attached to its NE face. A poorly carved date 1797 is incised on the SW face of one of the anchorbeams.

Transverse section at F, Dwg. 4.

—J.F.

Nonextant. This barn burned about 1980. No documentation is known. Several good photos exist. A 23-ft. charred timber $16^3/_4$ x $9^1/_2$ in. (possibly an anchorbeam) that may have come from the barn existed as late as 1993. It is particularly unfortunate that this barn was lost as it was dated (1797), and its traits could have been cross-checked with those of other barns known to be from this timeframe. It has martin holes of type C, as shown in Dwg. 17. A $1^1/_2$ story Dutch frame house sits across the street from the original barn site.

—G.D.H.

7. (E) Poole, p.o. At southern limit of Germantown, E side of road.

Five-bay. N-S orientation. 11-ft.-10-in. height to soffit of $10^1/_2$- x 14-in. anchorbeams. 25-ft. column height, with high cross-ties linking the two middle column pairs only, located 2 ft. 8 in. down from column-tops. Columns vary in section: $9^3/_4$ x 11 in., $9^3/_4$ x 9 in. 20 ft. $1^3/_4$ in. span, transversely, face to face of columns. Ends of anchor-beam tongues barely project, but are chamfered. Regular pattern of sway-bracing. Three pentice mortices, with stubs in situ, through N gable-end anchorbeam, located at center and at a foot or so beyond door posts to right and left. Steep roof pitch. Big rafters. Unique feature: all 4 x $5^1/_2$ in. anchorbeam braces are curved.

Interior view, Plate 29.

—J.F.

Extant. In excellent condition. Orientation: 20 degrees west of south. One of the rare barns with H-frame braces curved at both upper and lower surfaces. In contrast to Fitchen's assertion, the gable-wall braces are straight. An example of a small-scale regionalism is seen here as a nearby barn also has the very rare curved soffitted braces. Nave is 21 ft. 8 in. wide. One side aisle is 12 ft. wide. One purlin plate is spliced. Raising holes in H-frame posts. New weatherboarding recently installed. Pentice mortise stubs in both gable-end anchorbeams. Oak timbering. Roof is quite steep but very long *verdiepingh* (unmeasured) probably indicative of post-1790 erection date.

—G.D.H.

8. (E) Shortly N of Claverack on Rte. 9H, W side of road.
A small barn, originally four bays, very much rebuilt and hacked up. E-W orientation. Wagon entrance now on S side. Present column spacing is very irregular. At notch, at midlength bearing of rafters, some pins are set vertically, some normal to the roof slope.

—J.F.

Nonextant but possibly saved. A close scrutiny of the area has not yielded this barn's presence, and no photos or documentation are known.

—G.D.H.

9. (E) Just off Rte. 9H to W, at Lower Post Road.
The skeleton framework of a four-bay Dutch barn is now the center of a large complex of later barn structures that surround and completely incorporate it. The original barn roof has been rebuilt to run transversely, at right angles to its original N-S orientation! The tongues are rounded and far-projecting, each with one wedge.

—J.F.

Nonextant. Probably came down no later than about the mid-1980s. Some timbers were laying about in 1993. One oak anchorbeam tenon was saved. Several excellent interior and exterior photos were taken by John Stevens in late 1969. A close examination of its timbering reveals that the roof was probably not rotated as Fitchen believed. The barn was originally built with the main wagon entrances on the side walls and with H-frames parallel to the ridgeline. The nave was about 20 ft. wide. Hewn rafters. Original queen posts emanated from Dutch purlin plates that supported higher-up longitudinal purlin plates which in turn supported the roof. Anchorbeam-to-post union was secured with two pegs and had square shoulders. No raising holes in very short post extension above anchorbeams. One anchorbeam was $16^1/_2$ x $11^1/_2$ in. Circa 1810.

—G.D.H.

10. (E) Rte. 9H, S of Stuyvesant Falls, E side of road.
Five-bay, NW-SE orientation. Originally, bays were evenly spaced. Later, when wagon doors were moved from SE end to SW side, the middle bay was widened by relocating the columns of the third H-frame a number of feet to the SE, quite close to the second H-frame. 11-x 19-in. yellow-pine anchorbeams are notched $1^3/_4$ in. into their columns, with tongues far off-center of the columns. Transverse span is 25 ft. 4 in. face

to face of columns; 8-x 10-in. anchorbeam braces. Raising holes are down about 3 ft. 7 in. from column tops. Regular pattern of sway-bracing. All-wood wagon-door hinges.

Interior view, Plate 30.

—J.F.

Nonextant. When I first came to this excellent barn in mid-1979, most of the structure was sound. The barn was, however, dismantled about 1994. A few timbers, including a partial anchorbeam tenon, were saved. This barn was the rather well-known Skinkle barn. The roof was broad and sweeping and had classic proportions. Dimensions included a 51-ft. length, a 48$\frac{1}{2}$-ft. gable-wall width, low side walls at 11 ft., a peak of about 35 ft., a nave of 27 ft., side aisles of 10$\frac{1}{2}$ ft. Eight foot *verdiepingh* with raising holes 50 in. down from post tops.

There was a mixture of pine in anchorbeams and oak in H-frame braces and posts, a trait seen to a fair extent in Columbia and Rensselaer County barns. Both purlin plates of pine were spliced. There were no transverse side-aisle ties, and no 2-foot scribe marks on anchorbeams that were joined to posts with diminished haunched shoulders.

In almost all Dutch barns, layout or reference faces (where anchorbeams, posts, and braces in one bent are all flush on one side) of all inner H-frames are oriented toward or face the same direction for ease of bent assembly. Adjacent H-frame flush faces in this barn uniquely alternated in orientation. A small 1$\frac{1}{2}$ story Dutch brick gable-roofed house, circa 1760, stands 195 ft. north of original barn site. Barn is circa 1760.

Plate 30 is not the Skinkle barn, as indicated.

—G.D.H.

11. (E) Van Alstyne (Mrs. Dorothy Francke, p.o.). About three miles NW of Kinderhook, near Schodack Landing.

Six-bay. N-S orientation. 56 ft. 1 in. long, 49 ft. wide, 11-ft.-10-in. height to W eaves, about 32 ft. 7 in. to peak. Wagon doors at both gable-ends; those at S have all-wood hinges still in use. Columns are only 18 ft. 2$\frac{1}{2}$ in. high, spaced 27 ft. 7 in. apart transversely, face to face. Anchorbeams are of hard pine, 9$\frac{1}{2}$ x 21$\frac{1}{2}$ in. in section. Tongues are centered on columns: they are only 2 in. thick and only 13$\frac{1}{2}$ in. high. Anchorbeam braces, with three pins at both top and bottom, are 7$\frac{1}{2}$ x 11 in. in section and are set (as usual) at a steeper angle than 45 degrees (coordinates are 37 in. [horiz.] and 43$\frac{1}{2}$ in. [vert.]). Columns are 9 x 9$\frac{1}{2}$ in. in section. Height from floor to top of anchorbeams is 12 ft. 1 in. Height of 6 ft. 4 in. to soffit of 6$\frac{3}{4}$-in.-deep side-aisle struts (no upper struts). Somewhat abnormal pattern of sway-bracing.

Transverse section at K, Dwg. 4; longitudinal section at H, Dwg. 5; exterior view, Plate 12; interior views, Plates 23, 24, 25, and 26.

—J.F.

Extant. In very good condition, at the site of the most original condition pre-Revolutionary Dutch homestead in Columbia County. Roofline with exceptional proportions. There is an excellent circa 1760 1$\frac{1}{2}$ story Dutch gambrel roofed brick house at the site. It is a very rare six-bay barn. There are sixteen pairs of hewn softwood rafters, a few of which are recycled and all of which are flat-edged on wall plates. Each purlin plate is a single piece of softwood timber, 56 ft. long. Purlin braces attach low on posts, $1\frac{1}{2}$ ft. below anchorbeams. *Verdiepingh* is 7 ft. long. Single raising hole per post. Anchorbeams that vary in height at their midpoints, 17 to 21 in., are joined to posts with diminished haunched shoulders. Nave is 29 ft. wide. One side aisle is $9\frac{1}{2}$ ft. wide. Original oak wood hinges on threshing floor doors at one gable-end. The wagon entrance is unusual in that it is not centered below the peak. Circa 1765.

—G.D.H.

12. (D) Johnston (?), p.o. Rte. 10, S of Sharon Springs, W side of road.
Full of hay. Tongues sawed off.

—J.F.

Extant. In very good condition. Originally four bays with one bay added. Softwood timbers. A few recycled beams. Nave width of 25 ft. Both side aisles 10 ft. wide. One inner anchorbeam 18 in. in depth, and tenons extend 6 in. without wedges. Inner H-frame posts with double raising holes; all lower holes with in situ peg stubs. One unique feature is that purlin braces are hewn in both end bays (one per bay per side) and frame into the gable-wall H-frame posts $5\frac{1}{2}$ ft. below the tops, whereas the braces in the two middle bays (two per bay per side) are milled and frame $3\frac{1}{2}$ ft. below the post tops. Not a full drive through barn. Moderate to somewhat steep roof slope. Circa 1815 or perhaps earlier. There is an excellent two-story 1799 brick house at the site.

—G.D.H.

13. (D) Just off Rte. 10 on Rte. 165 toward Roseboom.
Three-bay. N-S orientation.

—J.F.

Nonextant but possibly saved. This barn was in good condition in early 1976 when I took two photographs but no measurements. Probably dismantled in early to mid-1980s. It was likely a later barn, as it had a moderate roofline. Circa 1800 or later.

—G.D.H.

14. (D) Rte. 10, E side of road.
NW-SE orientation. Extensively rebuilt, with one long bay added to NW. Oak columns, white-pine anchorbeams, one of which has been sawed out, but with tongues remaining in column mortices. NW gable-end has three martin holes of type shown at C, Dwg. 17.

—J.F.

Nonextant but possibly saved. Searches have not revealed the presence of this barn.

—G.D.H.

15. (D) Rte. 10, W side of road.
Four-bay. E-W orientation. About 45 ft. long. Heavy, thick anchorbeams except for those at gable-ends; short braces. Original (?) planking, laid flush with top of rebated axial floor beam. Barn is in fairly good condition. Wagon doors on center at both gable-ends.

—J.F.

Nonextant but possibly saved. Never found.

—G.D.H.

16. (D) Strouse, p.o. Rte. 145 about one mile N of Cobleskill, E side of road.
Four-bay. N-S orientation. Badly broken internally: center anchorbeam, eaten by woodborers, has fallen thereby breaking one of the columns. Basswood anchorbeams with semicircular tongues. Other barn structures attached to E and N.

—J.F.

Nonextant but possibly saved. I took one photo about 1979 but no measurements. Fitchen recorded that the anchorbeams were basswood (*Tilia americana*) and were worm eaten. This wood species was rarely used, and there are two extant barns in Schoharie County with similarly worm eaten basswood anchorbeams. Fairly steep roof with medium height side wall. Circa 1795.

—G.D.H.

17. (D) Off Rte. 145, toward Middleburgh, sharp right onto Acker Hollow Road, then left-hand dead-end fork.
Originally four-bay, now three-bay. NW-SE orientation. Very much remodeled. Yellow pine. High transverse beams across threshing floor at all bents. One raising hole down 8 in. to 10 in. Wide clapboards. Six round martin holes in SE gable. Barn rather dilapidated.
Exterior view, Plate 7.

—J.F.

Extant. Only a fair state of preservation of original framing. Last bay 17$\frac{1}{2}$ ft. long, whereas three other bays are 11 ft. each. Nave 23 ft. wide and side aisles 11 ft. wide. Side walls 18 ft. Softwood timbers, but all braces and some floor sills oak. One H-frame post is oak. Anchorbeams without tenon extensions and joined to posts with three pegs. Wall plates are spliced. One inner anchorbeam only 12 in. high. About 12$\frac{1}{2}$ ft.

verdiepingh. Original side wall entry. This is strictly a square rule era barn. Original 1½ story frame house on site. Circa 1830.

—G.D.H.

18. (D) Forrest Lape, p.o. Off Rte. 145, N of Middleburgh.
E-W orientation. Height to eaves 10 ft. 2 in. 10-x 10-in. columns topped by 7-in. (vert.) x 10-in. (horiz.) purlin plate. 5-x 5½-in. rafters, with cogs projecting into the wall plate at their feet.

—J.F.

Extant but in storage. Dismantled in July 1990. Four-bay construction with an 18-ft.-long added-on bay. Nave 25 ft. wide, side aisles 10 ft. wide, and side walls 13 ft. high. Raising holes present. Softwood timbers with single wedged square contoured anchor-beam tenons with sloping shoulders set into posts. Circa 1800.

—G.D.H.

19. (D) On Rte. 145, N of Middleburgh, E side of road.
A barn complex of which the portion to the S, with N-S axis, is a Dutch barn with anchorbeam tongues. Too full of hay to examine. S gable has six martin holes of type C, Dwg. 17.

—J.F.

Nonextant. Burned in June 1992. This barn was painted red and stood quite close to Route 145, 1.7 mi. north of the Middleburgh bridge. No photos or documentation are available. No estimate of date.

—G.D.H.

20. (D & C) Deertz, p.o. On Clauverwie St., southern outskirts of Middleburgh.
Six-bay (original part), 60 ft. long, 54 ft. wide, side walls about 14 ft. high. Later, three bays added in a completely different framing system, to the N end and on axis with the original barn. N-S orientation. S wagon-door opening 12 x 12 ft. Yellow-pine 10½- x 12-in. columns; oak 7½- x 11-in. braces; white-pine 10-x 19-in. anchor-beams. 28 ft. 2 in. clear span transversely, column face to column face. Two anchorbeams, one above the other, at fourth bent from S: lower one 10 x 24 in. in sec-tion, with two oak posts at third points strutting the 17-in. space between them. Rebated flush-topped floor beam in one 60-ft. length, on axis. Part of W side aisle furnished with unpegged, removable floor planks, offering access to view of sill framing and stone support of column sleeper. Unique features: (1) original manger framing still intact, E side; (2) inverted sway-bracing framed into longitudinal links above head height. This is a large barn of fine workmanship, well cared for and in ex-cellent condition.

Transverse section at H, Dwg. 4; sills, etc., at F, G, H, and K, Dwg. 11; exterior view, Plate 16; interior views, Plates 39, 40, 41, and 42.

—J.F.

Extant but relocated. A very rare six-bay barn. Nave is 30 ft. wide and both side aisles are 10 ft. wide. One bent has a 24-in.-deep anchorbeam; anchorbeams do not get any bigger in New York State. Anchorbeam tenons do not extend beyond post face. Anchorbeams joined to posts with square shoulders and three pegs. H-frame braces attach at each end with two pegs. Upper tie beams about one foot down from posts' tops at both gable-wall end bents and middle bent. Thirteen pairs of rafters. No upper transverse side-aisle ties at inner bents. As is the case in many barns, the posts at all inner H-frames are joined to the purlin plate with two pegs, whereas at the gable-wall H-frames the unions are secured with one peg. Braces in side walls. *Verdiepingh* about 8 ft. at first three inner H-frames and single raising holes in all posts. The barn's width is actually 50 ft. Bruno Deertz, who bought the farm in 1940, told me that on one side aisle every bay had intact manger framing. The last bay, however, did not have any feed rack originally. All were taken out but one. In August 1981, I witnessed the measurement of the wooden pieces and angles of the manger by people from Upper Canada Village. This project testifies to the rarity and importance of this architectural feature. The 60-ft.-long median floor sill in one piece is one of the biggest and longest timbers in any Dutch barn. Its original threshing floor is mostly intact and had an ancient, worn look with great tree knots protruding above the rest of the general floor level. The barn was dismantled in 1988 by a new owner and moved to east of the Hudson River. Not a full drive-through barn. This barn is strictly a square rule building, as wide notches at timber unions attest. Its roof slope was moderate to fairly steep. This was one of Fitchen's favorite barns. Despite its big timbers, the barn was built circa 1815 or perhaps a bit earlier.

—G.D.H.

21. (D) SE of Middleburgh, up the hill out of the "Flats" Area, off to right on dead-end dirt road.

A probable Dutch barn, but too full of hay to examine.

—J.F.

Extant but 50 percent ruinous. This barn is somewhat south of southwest, but it should still be considered the one Fitchen saw. Before about 1985, it may well have been one of the very best barns in Schoharie County. Four bays, not of equal length. Nave 25 ft. wide. Anchorbeams with superb patina vary in depth 19 to 21 in.; their tenons extend 14 in. and are double-wedged. These tenons are centered on post, which is not the norm. *Verdiepingh* is 10 ft. 2 in., and there is a full complement of raising holes down from post tops about 2 ft. Eleven pairs of hewn rafters have rare long, sweeping, cut in curves (a.k.a. curved relief) at wall plates. Sawn purlin braces. One H-frame brace is 9 x 10 in. One H-frame was moved 3 ft. toward one gable wall during major modification to accommodate side wall entry. One gable wall has all its original wide weatherboarding secured with wrought nails. At least one gable-wall wagon entrance door is of frame construction. Three martin holes of C type. All pine construction. Roof slope is rather steep. Barn is slated for removal. Circa 1790.

—G.D.H.

22. (D) Rte. 145 near Durham, about 24 miles from Catskill, up bank on right side of road.

Access to hayloft not possible, but undoubtedly a Dutch barn.

—J.F.

Extant. Excellent condition, although all inner anchorbeams have been removed. Four bays. No raising holes on posts, and there are twelve pairs of hewn rafters. Purlin braces probably riven. Very wide roof boards (nailers). Originality of threshing floor area is much changed. Quite a steep roof line. Circa 1785.

—G.D.H.

23. (D) Numrich, p.o. (Andries DeWitt, 1698?), on Hurley Mountain Road just N of Ashokan Road into Marble Town.

NE-SW orientation. $60^1/_2$ ft. long, $50^1/_2$ ft. wide, 11-ft.-10-in. side-wall height from floor to eaves. $11^1/_2$ x 14 in. oak anchorbeams spanning 28 ft. 2 in. in the clear, with semicircular tongues, some with two wedges and some with one. Regular pattern of fairly long sway braces.

—J.F.

Extant. In general, good condition. This rare six-bay barn has a storied past. The location was supposedly "out in the country" from nearby Hurley, and Andreas DeWitt, who was here about 1700, had his storage facilities at this homestead. Oak construction. Almost all barns south of this point in Ulster County are of oak, and barns to the north are of a mixture of oak and pine. Both hewn and round pole rafters are original. One H-frame post has extremely rare 33-in. peg that faces the threshing floor and is positioned 41 in. below purlin plate. Function unknown. Side wall is about $12^1/_2$ ft. high. Roof peak is about 29 ft. Anchorbeam-to-post union with square shoulders. Anchorbeams vary in height from 14 in. to almost 17 in., and their tenons extend 8 to 10 in. Nave is 30 ft. wide. Side aisles are very close to 10 ft. wide. H-frame braces are milled. *Verdiepingh* is about $7^1/_2$ ft. Double raising holes per post. No upper transverse side-aisle ties. Remnant of original threshing floor door with unusual curve on wooden hinge. Roof is quite steep with a low-to-the-ground feeling. Original $1^1/_2$ story gable-roofed Dutch stone house sits about 135 ft. southeast of barn. Circa 1785 and possibly before.

Frances Numrich, who owned the barn for about forty years (1959–99), related to me in September 1991 that she remembered John Fitchen coming up her driveway (in September 1963) to photograph her barn without prior notice. Fran at first thought all the commotion meant her barn was on fire. By the time she got to the barn, all the lighting equipment was set to start the photographing. She recalls Fitchen saying, "I'm doing a book." He was there less than one hour and then he was on his way.

—G.D.H.

24. (D) About one mile S of Hurley, E side of road.

Three-bay. N-S orientation. Extensively rebuilt, now ruinous. 38 ft. 1 in. long; side wall 12 ft. high, floor to eaves. 10-ft.-wide double Dutch wagon doors turning on original wood hinges; these doors at S gable-end only. Unfloored side aisles; that on E side is much lower than central threshing floor. Each side aisle has its own small door in S corner of gable-end. One column of oak, others of hard pine. Unique feature: Original eaves-trough of wood, W side (now fallen and broken in two pieces).

Detail of eaves gutter, Dwg. 18; photographs, Plates 43 and 50.

—J.F.

Nonextant but possibly saved. No one has been able to locate this barn. It probably disappeared by late 1960s. The barn may have had its original wooden eaves trough when Fitchen visited the site. Several Dutch barns have transverse holes in wall posts that housed pegs that held up eaves troughs, including the Bronck barn (no. 38) and the Wemple barn (no. 32). No exterior photos are known. No erection date is known.

—G.D.H.

25. (B, F) Indian Castle, N side of road. (Green [?], p.o.)

Four-bay. N-S orientation. Column height 24 ft. 9 in. from floor to $7^1/_4$-in. (vert.) x 10-in. (horiz.) purlin plate, on which notched rafters have but 2-in. bearing. $8^1/_2$- x 13-in. oak columns are spaced 23 ft. 6 in. transversely, face to face. $11^1/_2$- x $19^1/_2$-in. anchorbeams have wedged and rounded tongues of maximum projection (up to 21 in.). Anchorbeam of second bent from S has been removed, revealing details of the off-center mortice for its tongue. The center bent has a high-level braced cross-tie (about 6 in. [vert.] x $4^1/_2$ in. [horiz.] in section) framed into the columns at a level approximately one foot down from the purlin plate. Other bents have raising holes at this same level. Regular pattern of sway-bracing. Martin holes are of type D, Dwg. 17.

Detail of anchorbeam framing at D, Dwg. 6; transverse section at C, Dwg. 4; interior detail of anchorbeam tongue, Plate 22.

—J.F.

Extant. Recently reroofed and in generally very good condition. 46 ft. wide by 51 ft. long. Fitchen cites H-frame posts as oak, but there are four of softwood. Nave is 25 ft. wide and side aisles each $10^1/_2$ ft. wide. *Verdiepingh* is 10 ft. Pine anchorbeams with 2-foot scribe marks and tenons that extend up to 21 in. that were once regarded as the longest in any Dutch barn. It has since been surpassed by two barns that each have 24-in. extended tenons. Fitchen notes in Dwg. 14 that nothing significant has ever been discovered in any raising holes. Perhaps close to a dozen barns have now been found with raising holes with in situ pegs of varying length, including the Indian Castle barn and barns no. 10 and 12 (this appendix). Circa 1790.

—G.D.H.

26. (F) On Rte. 5S, S side of road, 4.8 miles E of Indian Castle barn, near intersection with Sanders Road.

Originally three-bay, with E-W orientation. Later, a much longer bay added to west end. 8- x 14-in. columns (three of which are either of maple or beech) are spaced 22 ft. 10 in. transversely, face to face. White-pine anchorbeams have semicircular tongues that are chamfered and secured with two wedges. Long-tongued, single-wedged upper transverse strut to side wall is 9 in. deep and framed into column some 16 in. or 18 in. above anchorbeam. Raising holes occur at different levels on different columns, one of which has two holes. Sway-bracing, too, is not uniform though of regular pattern. Seven pentice mortices occur at E gable-end, where wagon doors are considerably off-center (making use of end column at S door jamb!). This barn has been altered in various ways, including the insertion of wagon doors in N side wall.

Detail of transverse framing at F, Dwg. 12.

—J.F.

Nonextant but possibly saved. No barn fitting this description appears and no photographs or documentation are available.

—G.D.H.

27. (F) On Rte. 5 at NW edge of Nelliston Village in a hollow on S side of road.

NW-SE orientation, but this barn was moved and considerably rebuilt at some former time. 8-in. (vert.) x 5-in. (horiz.) purlin plate above 8- x 13-in. columns. Raising holes. Heavy upper transverse struts framed into wall plates, both side aisles. This barn was destroyed in 1965.

Exterior view, Plate 8; interior views, Plates 34 and 35.

—J.F.

Nonextant. Fairly long *verdiepingh* and hewn purlin braces. Diminished haunch shoulders at anchorbeam to post unions. Illustrated in plates 8, 34, and 35. No documentation or photographs are available beyond what Fitchen offered. Circa 1795.

—G.D.H.

28. (F) On Rte. 5, $^{8}/_{10}$ mile W of western edge of Palatine Bridge Village, S side of road.

E-W orientation. Originally three-bay, but with later very long bay added to the W (spliced purlin plates give evidence). Pentice mortices occur at both gable-ends, but chief wagon entrance is now on N side wall, facing highway. The two central anchorbeams of the original three-bay structure are now framed into their columns at shoulder height; but offset mortices exist showing the level at which they were formerly framed into the columns. Anchorbeam tongues are slightly chamfered but do not protrude. (Possibly there were protruding tongues before the reframing mentioned above.) Many of the timbers in this barn have been sawed off.

—J.F.

Nonextant but possibly saved. There is a barn exactly at this spot, but it is north of the road rather than south as Fitchen indicates. This barn has several of the traits Fitchen cites for barn no. 28, but other traits do not correspond.

—G.D.H.

29. (F, G) Van Wie, near Randall on Rte. 5S, W bank of Van Wie Creek near its junction with the Mohawk River.

Four-bay. 50$^1/_4$ ft. long, 52 ft. wide. N-S orientation. Mostly white-pine timbers. 9$^1/_2$- x 13-in. columns spaced 28 ft. 6 in. transversely, face to face. No wedges through long rounded tongues of 11- x 22$^1/_2$-in. anchorbeams whose soffits are at 11-ft.-$^1/_2$-in. height above the floor. The S gable-end anchorbeam is 10 x 18 in. in section, with inverted braces (i.e., framed above instead of below the anchorbeam). There is a 13$^1/_2$-in. (vert.) x 8-in. (horiz.) high-level transverse beam in the S gable, at a level 11$^3/_4$ in. down from top of 23-ft.-10-in.-high columns. The square rafters taper slightly, as usual; here they measure 6 x 6$^1/_4$ in. at the ridge, and about 7 x 7 in. at mid-length where a notch gives 4 in. of horizontal bearing on the purlin plate. Holes for gutter supports, E side, occur in heavy wall posts at bay intervals, for drainage to S. Three 3$^1/_2$-in. (vert.) x 4$^1/_4$-in. (horiz.) pentice mortices are cut through the S gable-end anchorbeam. The all-wood hinges of the S gable-end's wagon doors are now sawed off, but details of their former attachment are still clearly evident. The N half of this barn is now collapsed and in ruins, allowing the framing of the sills at the N gable-end to be examined. This barn was once a splendid example of large size and superior workmanship.

Transverse section at E, Dwg. 4; longitudinal section at D, Dwg. 5; rafter details, Dwg. 8 and at E and G of Dwg. 9; sill details at A and B, Dwg. 11; pentice mortice at B, Dwg. 16; exterior view, Plate 17; Interior views, Plates 18, 19, 20, and 21.

—J.F.

Nonextant. Sixty percent ruinous when Fitchen saw it. One or two anchorbeams were recycled into a resort structure at Gore Mountain in the Adirondacks. Several excellent photos were taken by Clarke Blair, who showed the barn to barn historian Dudley Witney. Hewn rafters. Anchorbeams secured to posts with double pegs and square shoulders. Raising holes down about 3$^1/_2$ to 4 ft. below top of posts. Nave was 30 feet wide and *verdiepingh* 11 ft. Long purlin braces attached more than two thirds down upper post extension and only one brace per bay per side. Circa 1790.

—G.D.H.

30. (F) Smaller Wemp, off dirt road E of Queen Anne's Chapel, near Fort Hunter and close to Mohawk River.

Three-bay, 41 ft. long. N-S orientation. $10^{1}/_{4}$- x 12-in. columns. 12- x $20^{1}/_{2}$-in. anchorbeams spanning 21 ft. 4 in. transversely, face to face of columns. Gable-end anchorbeams are only 17 in. deep. Anchorbeams are gained 1 in. into column faces. Some of the rounded tongues are secured with one wedge, some with two. Wagon doors are now centered on each side wall; originally they were centered at each gable-end, where mortices remain in the door posts for all-wood hinges, now lost. Four 2- x 4-in. pentice mortices occur through the N gable-end's anchorbeam, the westernmost hole indicating that a door for humans was originally located next to the wagon doors on this side, with the pentice sheltering both large and small openings. The upper transverse side-aisle struts, now sawed off, were originally framed into the wall plate. Big fishtailed rafters, from $7^{1}/_{4}$ x 8 in. to $7^{1}/_{2}$ x 9 in., are spaced 61 in. on centers. Two raising holes occur in each column, including those of the gable-ends, but at varying heights. The sequence of the chiseled numbering of timbers is from N to S. The basic structure of this barn consists of big timbers and is of good workmanship.

Longitudinal section at C, Dwg. 5; exterior view, Plate 6; interior views, Plates 37 and 38.

—J.F.

Extant and in generally very good condition. This barn and its "bigger brother," the larger Wemp barn, joined to form the best known double barn complex in the Dutch barn domain until 1990, when the larger barn was moved. There are only four other "double barn acts": the barns south of Middleburgh on Route 145 in Schoharie County; the Fredericks barns in Guilderland in Albany County; the nonextant DeWitt barns at the Suydam Homestead near Hurley in Ulster County; and a barn in northern Montgomery County with an end-to-end arrangement that forms a long, seven-bay complex that was taken from two Dutch barns. It is difficult to understand why two Dutch barns would appear at the same homestead when the vast majority of farms had one barn. Some farms may have needed a greater crop storage capacity because they were uncommonly prosperous, or there may have been an unusual extended family situation in which double houses and barns were originally closely arranged but then an original house may have been lost resulting in a farm with double barns and a single house.

The nave is close to 23 ft. wide, and each side aisle is 11 ft. wide. One inner anchorbeam is $18^{3}/_{4}$ in. in depth while the other inner anchorbeam is $20^{1}/_{2}$ in. in depth. Both inner anchorbeams have 2-foot scribe marks, and tenons extend 10 in. and are circular in contour. Anchorbeam-to-post union is square shouldered and triple pegged. Top of anchorbeam to floor is $12^{1}/_{2}$ ft. There are nine pairs of hewn rafters. *Verdiepingh* is 9 ft. 3 in. Purlin braces are milled. Upper transverse ties adjacent to gable walls attach just below wall plates. There are three pentice mortises at the south-gable-wall anchorbeam. H-frame braces adjacent to gable walls are much smaller than inner H-frame braces, which are about 7 x 9 in. All inner H-frame braces are chamfered, and each brace is attached at each end with one peg. All transverse ties are oak. Almost all major structural members are white pine. This barn has quite a steep roof. Circa 1795.

—G.D.H.

31. (A, F, et al.) Larger Wemp. Two hundred feet from Smaller Wemp barn.

Originally four-bay (with later two-bay addition, 24 ft. 10 in. long, to S). N-S orientation. 45 ft. 6 in. long, 50 ft. wide. Largely of white pine, but door posts, etc., of oak. $9^3/_4$- x $11^3/_4$-in. or $9^3/_4$- x 13-in. columns, spaced 27 ft. $4^1/_4$ in. transversely, face to face. 11-x 22-in. anchorbeams with 16-in. projection of neatly chamfered tongues; height from floor to anchorbeam soffits is 11 ft. $7^3/_4$ in. Longitudinal links measure $9^1/_2$ in. (vert.) x $7^1/_2$ in. (horiz.); those on E side of threshing floor are framed at 6 ft. $7^1/_2$ in. to their soffits. All but one of the four pentice mortices through the N gable-end's anchorbeam are filled with the stubs of stout oak members that are secured with long wedges bearing against the inner face of the anchorbeam. All columns have raising holes at a height of about 3 ft. down from the soffit of the purlin plate. The S pair of wagon doors has been relocated in E side wall (at southernmost of original bays). Here, and in N gable-end, all-wood hinges are still in use. Mortice holes for similar hinges remain in wagon-entrance jambs of original S gable-end. N bays of W side aisles were originally used for animal stalls, but only the rebates and notches remain in the columns there to indicate the former framing of the wooden mangers. Some unweathered portions of wide clapboarding in situ at the now-inclosed S gable-end of the original four-bay barn. Numbering of timbers progresses from N to S. Holes for eaves-trough brackets occur in wall posts opposite the columns. Unique feature: neat chamfering along edges of anchorbeam braces. Except for the irregular spacing of the wall studs, this is an exceptionally fine barn with the most careful and finished workmanship.

Axiometric drawings, Dwgs. 2 and 13; transverse sections, Dwgs. 3 and 4 at B; longitudinal section, Dwg. 5 at G; anchorbeam attachment, Dwg. 6, A and B; head-height framing, Dwg. 7 at C; rafter feet, Dwg. 10, D and H; eaves detail at A, Dwg. 18; exterior views, Plates 3, 4, and 5; interior views, Plates 27, 28, 44, and 48.

—J.F.

Extant but relocated. A museum barn. Dismantled and moved to Feura Bush in Albany County in 1990. In excellent condition although a few timbers were replaced. It is one of the best known Dutch barns, probably because of its appearance on the front cover of the first edition of this book and axiometric drawings of both the timber skeleton (Dwg. 2) and the structural core (Dwg. 13). These drawings are very useful to neophytes who are learning the basic structure and nomenclature of Dutch barns. The barn has almost all the general defining elements. I first visited here in August 1977.

It is thought that the site where Fitchen found the barn is actually its second location, as it was probably moved 100 ft. or more up from the periodically flooded Mohawk River. A few people assigned an early-eighteenth-century erection date. It has no early features, such as a very steep roof, long purlin braces attaching below anchorbeams, a short *verdiepingh*, or low side walls. Its purlin braces attach about three-fourths of the way down on the posts. It does have the date 1794 carved on a beam, which could indicate its original erection time or perhaps when it was first moved. Its roofslope does conform to barns built in the late eighteenth century. As the barn is almost all pine, it cannot be dendrodated until data for this species are established.

Fitchen cites the very neat chambering along H-frame braces as a unique trait. This characteristic has now been found on about a half dozen barns, including the smaller Wemp barn. This refinement may have been designed to prevent fire by eliminating sharp edges that would more easily ignite. Fairly steep roof. Circa 1790.

—G.D.H.

32. (B, F, and J) Wemple (Warren Taylor, p.o.), on Wemple Road, S of Rte. 7, near Becker Farm SW of Schenectady.

Four-bay. NE-SW orientation. 56 ft. 1 in. long, 47 ft. wide. Massive timbers throughout, predominantly of hard pine; all are sharp edged. $9^3/_4$- x $11^3/_4$-in. columns are spaced 26 ft. 6 in. transversely, face to face. Anchorbeams measure $11^3/_4$ x $22^1/_4$ in. in section. Tongues are full height of the anchorbeams, $3^1/_4$ in. thick, of 12 in. projection, rounded at top and bottom, and secured with two thin wedges 1 x $2^3/_4$ in.$^+/_-$ in section. Heavy wall-post studs occur at the same even spacing (56 in. center-to-center, on the average) as the rafters; thus there are three spaces per bay, with a total of thirteen pairs of rafters including those in the gables. Big sharp-edged rafters, averaging about 8 x 8 in. at their lower ends, are cut off horizontally without cogs, to rest upon the $5^3/_4$-in. (vert.) x $9^3/_4$-in. (horiz.) wall plate. At mid-length the rafters are supported on a purlin plate that is secured to each column-top with two pins. The unusually long sway braces spring from the columns at an exceptionally low level: $19^1/_4$ in. below the soffit of the anchorbeams. The anchorbeams and their 9- x $11^3/_4$-in. braces are equally wide. The latter, as usual, are steeper than 45 degrees, having coordinates of 46 in. (vert.) and $34^1/_4$ in. (horiz.). Wagon doors occur at both gable-ends, and still swing on all-wood hinges. Exceptionally, their door posts are approximately the same size as the columns, in section. There are three martin holes in the NE gable, of type C, Dwg. 17. This is a large and splendidly built barn, in excellent condition.

Transverse section, Dwg. 4 at A; longitudinal section, Dwg. 5 at A; framing of struts to column, Dwg. 7 at B; exterior views, Plates 9 and 10; original hinges, Plates 47 and 49.

—J.F.

Extant. For craftsmanship, this is the finest Dutch barn, and it has the most cathedral-like proportions. Located within a few hundred feet of the Normanskill (which connects with the Hudson River just south of Albany), it appears to be on its original site. The original two-story Dutch gambrel roofed brick house that stands 184 ft. west-southwest of the barn has characteristics that indicate a date of erection about 1760, which most likely corresponds to the erection date of the barn. Some early traits include a steep roof at a 45 degree pitch, attachment of hewn purlin braces below the anchorbeams, and rather low side walls relative to the height of the roof peak.

This four-bay barn is exclusively of pitch pine *(Pinus rigida)*, except for oak that appears in trunnels, wooden door hinges, pintles, and anchorbeam tenon wedges. The horizontal siding, original on both gable walls, is of an indeterminate type of pine. It is probable that a nearby pure grove provided the timber. An interesting study would be to ascertain the number and sizes of trees that could grow on a virgin acre of ground and then determine the number of acres required for a barn to be built with dimensions and timber sizes as found in the Wemple barn.

Inner anchorbeams are 22$^1/_2$ in. by 12 in. by 30 ft. long (including tenons), and their tenons are essentially square contoured with somewhat rounded corners. Purlin plates are single lengths of timber 56 ft. Sills are spliced under both H-frame post ranges. The *verdiepingh* is 8$^1/_2$ ft. long, and the distance from the top of the anchorbeam to the bottoms of the H-frame posts is a long 13 ft. 1 in. Side wall height is 14$^1/_2$ ft. Height of peak is about 36 ft. Each gable wall anchorbeam has three pentice mortises. The threshing floor, partially deteriorated, is made of forty-four tapered planks that are 5 to 6$^1/_2$ in. thick, up to 20 in. wide, and extend in single lengths the full width of the threshing floor, 26$^1/_2$ ft. Average plank width is 14$^1/_4$ in. The floor was originally made up of about 8,500 board feet of timber. (A board foot is 12 in. long by 1 in. wide and 1 in. thick).

The precise measurements of this barn support the notion that master builders erected barns in early America. The central aisle, at 28 ft., is exactly half the barn's length of 56 ft. The roof, at a pitch of 45 degrees, translates into an included roof peak angle of 90 degrees. The two inner bay's purlin braces form the classic 3–4–5 triangle with the plates and H-frame posts. All three inner H-frames have double raising holes per post centered with the uppers and lowers 46 in. and 73 in., respectively, below the plates. All end-bent posts maintain these numbers, except for the uppers, which appear 4 in. from the outer edge. The hewing of the timbers, especially the anchorbeams, was executed at a very high level of craftsmanship, as the beams are very sharp edged (some waney edges are present), forming near 90-degree angles between adjacent faces. Wrought nails that secure battens to front vertical boards of original side-aisle stable doors are positioned where diagonal scribe lines cross. The proportions of the various elements seem to be derived in the manner of many Gothic cathedrals that were determined by the formula "according to true measure" or the dictates of geometric principle. Consequently, we can appreciate much of the aesthetic appeal of the Wemple barn from the numbers locked into its structure.

The most interesting feature of this barn is a 3$^1/_2$-in. circular mark on the vertical face of the middle anchorbeam with two short intersecting curved lines at the top. It may be a guild mark that was positioned there by a master builder, as was done in the European tradition. Its presence in America is very rare.

The core structure and roof stand firm, as I first saw it in February 1976. Parts of the foundation wall, sill system, and floor are deteriorating, necessitating renovation work. Present owners have been making repairs to ensure its continued existence. It is unquestionably the best built Dutch barn and was one of John Fitchen's favorites.

—G.D.H.

33. (F, etc.) One mile E of Sharon on Rte. 20, N side of road.

Four-bay. N-S orientation. 40 ft. 3$^1/_2$ in. long, 45 ft. 3 in. wide. Deep anchorbeams 11$^1/_2$ in. wide span 22 ft. 6 in. transversely, face to face of 11- x 14-in. pine columns. Oak longitudinal links measure 7$^1/_2$ in. (vert.) x 6 in. (horiz.) at a height of 6 ft. 11$^1/_2$ in. from floor to soffit. Their tops are flush with transverse struts that are 11 in. (vert.) x 6$^3/_4$ in. (horiz.) in section. Anchorbeams, braces, and columns are all flush on their S faces. Easternmost of three pentice mortices through S gable-end anchorbeam retains its far-inward-jutting tenon whose long dagger-like wedge now projects some 3 or 4 in. below the soffit of the anchorbeam. The pattern of the sway-bracing is regular, but the braces themselves are unusually short and are framed at a flatter angle than 45 degrees.

Raising holes are located in all but the gable-end columns, at a height a foot or so below the point at which the braces branch from the columns. The middle column has two holes side by side; this column also has a high diagonally braced transverse tie beam that spans above the threshing floor. The rafter feet are cut with cogs that fit into transverse notches in the wall plate. One (of two?) martin holes survive in the clapboarding of the N gable peak. The roof pitches are fairly steep. This is a well-built, big-timbered barn.

Plan, Dwg. 1; transverse section, Dwg. 4 at G; longitudinal section, Dwg. 5 at B; pentice detail, Dwg. 16 at A; exterior views, Plates 1 and 2; interior views, Plates 31, 32, and 33.

—J.F.

Extant but relocated. A museum barn. Dismantled about 1970 and rebuilt at Bethpage Village on Long Island. Not open to the public. Typical of many Schoharie County barns, it is almost all pine. The barn has two odd traits: first, there is evidence that the gable-wall main wagon doors originally swung outward, in contrast to most "upcountry" barns, which had doors that swung inward; second, the H-frame braces are pitched at a steeper angle at one end of bents than at other end. The roof pitch is steep. Nave close to 24 ft. wide and *verdiepingh* about 10 ft. The barn is circa 1790.

When I visited Fitchen in Hamilton, New York, in September 1978, we were leafing through his book when he spotted the East-of-Sharon barn depicted in Plates 32 and 33, whereupon he spontaneously clenched his fist and shook it as if to say "whoever fashioned these tenons was very special, and I wish I could have been there."

—G.D.H.

34. (F) Rte. 20, E of Sharon Springs, S side of road.

Four-bay. E-W orientation. Middle bent has two anchorbeams framed into same pair of columns; the upper of these anchorbeams is of hard pine about 10 in. square in section. The chief wagon entrance is now in the N side-wall where the ground has been built up for wagons to enter at the lower scaffold level at the third bay from the E. Anchorbeam tongues have been sawed off (?) flush with the outer face of columns.

—J.F.

Extant. Original Dutch-Anglo construction. In good condition except for a poor sill system. Nave is 23 ft. wide, both side aisles are 11 ft. wide, and barn length is 50 ft. Side-wall height is almost 14 ft. The barn is composed of mostly softwood timbers, including hemlock and two very worm eaten recycled basswood (?) anchorbeams that are 19 in. in depth. Not a drive-through barn, as middle bent has low positioned anchorbeam. Eleven pairs of hewn rafters. Anchorbeam-to-post joints with three pegs. Side-aisle ties are milled. Original side-wall entrance on north wall. *Verdiepingh* $13^1/_2$ ft. Single raising holes per post. All braces are milled. Circa 1820.

—G.D.H.

35. (F) Rte. 20, 1/10-mile farther W from #34, N side of road.
A probable Dutch barn, but locked and no entry.

—J.F.

Nonextant. Original part three bays with a long added bay at west end. Original barn length $29^3/_4$ ft. and one side aisle 9 ft. 3 in. wide. Gable wall was about 40 ft. wide. There may have been an original side-wall entrance. Many softwood timbers. Two inner anchorbeams with $17^1/_2$- and $18^1/_2$-in. depth with semicircular tenons that extended 9 in. with single wedges. One gable-wall anchorbeam was 13 in. in height. One H-frame post was 11 x $8^1/_2$ in. The anchorbeam-to-post joint was square shouldered with two pegs. Inner anchorbeams were lowered on posts and were unique in that they may not have had any braces. Nave about $21^1/_2$ ft. wide. Single raising holes in posts appear several inches above purlin braces' lower end attachments, which was more than half way up the post extension. These braces were positioned flush with inner surface of post (same as barn no. 57). Many original threshing floor planks were intact, including one over 26 in. wide. Nine pairs of hewn rafters. Had "inverted" braces like the Deertz barn (barn no. 20) to the longitudinal head height ties. The barn was very ruinous with no roof in 1994. Circa 1805.

—G.D.H.

36. (F) Rte. 20, a little farther W from #35, N side of road.
Another probable Dutch barn, also locked.

—J.F.

Nonextant. Dismantled in early 1980s. One anchorbeam 18 x $9^1/_2$ in. A few photos were taken of this barn. No estimate of date.

—G.D.H.

37. (C) Van Bergen (Vedder, p.o.), on Vedder Road SW of Leeds. State marker reads "Barn built in 1680 by Marte Gerretse Van Bergen."
Five-bay. NE-SW orientation. Timbers are mainly of yellow pine. $11^3/_4$- x $19^1/_2$-in. anchorbeams are notched into $9^3/_4$- x $11^3/_4$-in. columns spaced 27 ft. 7 in. transversely, face to face. Tongues project 13 in. to 15 in. and are $2^1/_2$ in. thick. They are secured by two thin wedges approx. $^3/_4$ x 3 in. $^+/_-$. Their square ends are beveled at top and bottom corners, and they are rather coarsely chamfered. Stout braces, secured with three pins at both ends, are exceptional in that they have curving soffits. The end anchorbeams are $16^1/_2$ in. deep, and no evidence of former pentices remains above either gable-end wagon entrance. Mortices for transverse struts and longitudinal links occur in the columns at a height of 5 ft. 8 in. from the floor. There are two symmetrically spaced martin holes of type C, Dwg. 17, in SW gable. The original purlin plate survives (along with its sway-bracing), but it no longer bears the weight of the rafters. Instead, the latter are now supported higher up and closer to the middle of the building on a different purlin plate that is framed into braced and strutted members which cant inward and upward

from a sill laid across the anchorbeams where they join the columns. This newer framing has a different pattern of sway-bracing from that of the original construction; both schemes depart somewhat from the usual pattern. The rafter spacing varies from 55 in. to 58 in. on centers. Diagram of original sway-bracing shown at J, Dwg. 5.

—J.F.

Nonextant. This barn was examined by John Fitchen in June 1963, and it is likely the best known Dutch barn. The farm is in the same ownership as when Fitchen visited. It is unfortunate that only a few people examined this barn and prepared any documentation of it. The earliest known photograph of the barn was taken in 1928. Vincent Schaefer photographed it about 1940 and took some good interior shots. John Stevens, who visited the site in September 1969, in May 1972, and in June 1975, did the most extensive documentation. The barn started to deteriorate at the time of his second visit. I first visited and photographed the barn in February 1976, and then saved two anchorbeam tenons (one is partial) about 1980. They are the only known positively identified wooden remnants of the barn. At least three or four others photographed the barn, and its remnant timbers were finally discarded about 1983.

There are two nearby Van Bergen homesteads, each of which has a storied past. Much of it centers around the famous overmantel painting by John Heaten that Mabel Parker Smith is generally credited with discovering in the mid-1950s. However, it was C. G. Hine (author of *The Old Mine Road* and several other books) who, about 1906, located a painted board 7 ft. long that bore a striking resemblance to the overmantel. It now resides in Cooperstown. It depicts a wonderful circa 1735 Dutch homestead scene complete with a Dutch barn and house and two six-sided hay barracks at the Martin Van Bergen farm. However, it is the other nearby Van Bergen farm of brother Gerrit, with a dated 1729 house, that is the homestead on Vedder Road. A late seventeenth-centyury document supposedly associates the barn on Vedder Road with a construction date of about 1680. But no conclusive evidence exists that the document bears any direct relationship to the barn that came down in 1983.

A nearby historic marker states the barn was erected 1680, and many references by historians have been made to this date as the erection time. It is more likely the barn dates from the era the house was built, about 1729. Because no waney edge is present in either saved anchorbeam tenon, however, the barn can ultimately only be generally dated dendrochronologically by determining that the tree (pitch pine) the tenon came from was felled after a particular year.

Much discussion has revolved around the possible originality of the superimposed roof trusses. Rare upper purlin plates were held in place by canted timbers springing from longitudinal beams that stretched across anchorbeams just inside the H-frame posts. These canted beams were connected transversely with high ties. Vincent Schaefer proposed that original rafters were in contact with both the upper and lower purlin plates that would have effected an extremely steep roof with quite narrow side aisles. If the truss system as seen by Fitchen was original (only the upper purlins were in contact with the rafters), then the moderate to somewhat steep roof would not have been in keeping with pre-1750 steep-roofed Dutch buildings. Assuming an average side-aisle width of about 10 ft., rafters in contact with lower purlins, and an 8 ft. or 9 ft. side wall, a steep roof would have resulted that was in keeping with early Dutch roof pitches.

Analysis of differences in details such as tree species usage, wood peg diameters, type of boring tools used, scoring marks on faces of timbers, and shouldering of timbers between the timbers of the truss system and the H-frames could yield information that would further substantiate the probability of the nonoriginality of the roof.

John Stevens' documentation reveals dimensions that include a 30 ft. nave with 10 ft. side aisles. The *verdiepingh* was about 50 inches. The upper purlins were 5 ft. above the level of the lower plates, and rafters were 28 ft. long. H-frame braces, the deepest in any Dutch barn, were $14^{1}/_{2}$ in. across near their attachment to the anchorbeams. I measured the front gable wall to be about 185 ft. from the brick house across the road, dated 1729, which was originally a steep gable-roofed $1^{1}/_{2}$-story building. The house is now a full two stories with a moderate pitched gable roof.

A distinctly rural scene still dominates the area the early Van Bergen homestead occupies. Perhaps some day the land on which the barn stood will be preserved for future generations as home to a new Van Bergen barn.

—G.D.H.

Teller-Schermerhorn, Schermerhorn Road, Schenectady.

Although this is not a numbered Fitchen barn, it appears in Plate 15 and was an outstanding example of a Dutch barn. It follows the equally exceptional Van Bergen barn in this list because of its early-eighteenth-century construction date, its remarkable features, and its well-known stature.

Vincent Schaefer, who recorded and photographed local Dutch barns in Schenectady County in the 1930s and beyond, did research on the land where the barn stood and believed it could date circa 1705. That is possible. The barn may have been associated with the nearby 1730s Bradt Dutch brick house, and the barn may date from that period. It unquestionably had the steepest roof of any Dutch barn, with an included peak angle of 79 degrees. It was not thatched but had a so-called "plank" roof, a feature of many pre-1770 extant houses and barns in the upper river valleys of New York State. Adjacent boards, typically 15 to 18 in. wide, were held tight at their long edges which were widely bevelled.

The barn had very rare original-condition upper purlin plates, which helped support very long rafters. Only a few extant barns in Ulster County shared this rare trait.

Photographs taken by Schaefer in the late 1940s attest to the following traits. The barn's timbers appeared to be in good condition. Most timbers were pitch pine, and anchorbeams were close to 20 in. in depth and about 30 ft. long. H-frame braces without curved soffits were full width of posts. Long purlin braces attached somewhat above the anchorbeams. A trait seen here and in other early barns (see nos. 10 and 32) was the lack of braces in H-frames adjacent to the gable walls. A possibly original and unique feature was a lean-to type appendage to the rear at one side wall. Its function is unknown.

Schaefer bought the barn about 1933, but he dismantled it in 1947 and 1948. He said that the rafters and H-frame posts were in a fairly serious state of deterioration, and that necessitated the barn's removal.

Schaefer and famed painter of early Americana Eric Sloane knew each other, and it is the Teller-Schermerhorn barn that Sloane depicted in his well known book *An Age of Barns*. Sloane related to me that the rafters were perfectly balanced on the purlin plates. This was also one of Schaefer's favorite statements about his barn.

Two of the anchorbeams were saved and now form part of the ceiling of a room in a house near Schenectady. In late 1993 they were still sound, and they may someday be possibly dendrodated.

—G.D.H.

38. (C) Bronck. S of Coxsackie, Greene County Historical Association.

Four-bay. $10^3/_4$- x $19^1/_4$-in. anchorbeams with square-cut unchamfered tongues, each with two wedges and two additional wedge slots nearer the tongue's end. Columns measure $9^1/_2$ x $9^3/_4$ in. in section. Original transverse braces have been replaced with a pair of modern 2x8s. Two housed mortices, one above the other, occur in the lateral faces of the columns: the upper, for column ties that have been removed; the lower, doubtless for part of the former manger framing. There is a regular pattern of short, high sway braces. Raising holes are down less than a foot from the column-tops, which are gained into the purlin plate and secured to it with two pins. This barn has been somewhat altered and its original state rather poorly preserved.

—J.F.

Extant. Museum barn. One of the more important barns Fitchen examined, it occupies an extremely early Dutch settlement site where a $1^1/_2$ story stone house is thought to date from about 1665 and an adjacent steep-roofed brick house is dated 1738 (see Reynolds Plates 16 and 17). The barn, almost square at about 49 ft. on each side, is a nonoriginal one in that there was a major reshuffling of timbers from an earlier barn whose anchorbeams were incorporated into newly constructed H-frames. Anchorbeams with square tenons are of hard pine, and all H-frame posts are of oak, as are side-wall posts. Nave is $26^1/_2$ ft. wide. Distance from top of anchorbeams to floor is 12 ft. 2 in. One bent has double anchorbeams, which would preclude wagon traffic exiting out the far gable-end wall. In situ pegs for gutter brackets in posts on both side walls. The threshing floor is probably original. Barn in excellent condition, as when I first visited here in early 1980s.

The entire exterior envelope is nonoriginal, and rare tilt windows appear toward the peaks on both gable walls. Roof slope is moderate to somewhat steep. Circa 1815.

—G.D.H.

39. (C) Smaller Dewitt (Suydam, p. owner; Beatty, p. occupant). Off old Rte. 209 between Kingston and Hurley, NW side of road.

NW-SE orientation. Now reduced in width by the elimination of both side aisles. Big anchorbeams whose tongues have been sawed off. 1758 date carved on face of one anchorbeam. Carved date, Plate 52.

—J.F.

Nonextant. This barn came down because it was tilting over some time before the larger DeWitt barn (barn no. 40) burned. A short section of the dated oak timber of

1758 was saved. A circa 1900 photograph of the full three-aisle barn survives. It had classic roofline proportions with low side walls and a pentice. It probably was built in the pre-Revolutionary War Ulster County tradition. No documentation of this structure is known. A very large Dutch $1\frac{1}{2}$-story stone gable-roofed house occupies the site.

—G.D.H.

40. (C) Larger Dewitt (Suydam, p. owner; Beatty, p. occupant). Off old Rte. 209 between Kingston and Hurley, NW side of road.

NE-SW orientation. This is a huge barn, said to have been constructed from the timbers of three Dutch barns that were formerly on the same property. The anchorbeams are big, and one of them has the date 1796 carved on it. The scheme of the roof framing here is different from that of the true New World Dutch barn: for one thing, the roof is in two slightly different planes, each side of the ridge. Carved date, Dwg. 19.

—J.F.

Nonextant. It burned in April 1982. It was a very large structure with a slight kick in the roof that resulted in a gambrel outline. One interior photo exists. No documentation is known. Fitchen found a date of 1796 that may be the erection date.

—G.D.H.

41. (C) Wyncoop (Warren, p.o.). Just outside of Hurley, where Wyncoop Avenue meets Hurley Mountain Road.

Four-bay. NE-SW orientation. $11\frac{1}{2}$- x $16\frac{1}{4}$-in. and $11\frac{1}{2}$- x 18-in. anchorbeams. Tongues have two thin wedges and project 16 in. in a somewhat pointed curve. Anchorbeams are notched into columns and secured with three pins; three smaller pins secure the upper end of the transverse braces. All the columns have been spliced near their tops in order to raise the rather slender purlin plate; this has produced a steeper pitch to the roof slopes. This barn is now somewhat ruinous.

—J.F.

Nonextant. Its remnant timbers were removed about 1975. A few photos show its very ruinous condition, including the splices in the H-frame posts that Fitchen mentioned. This barn was at the site of Helen Reynolds' Plate 103, which includes a partial shot of the barn. No erection date estimate. An original Dutch stone house occupies the site.

—G.D.H.

42. (C) Garret Nieuwkirk (Kaufman, p.o.). NE of #41 on Hurley Mountain Road, right side of road.

Three-bay. E-W orientation. $9^1/_2$- x $14^1/_2$-in. pine anchorbeams; $8^1/_2$- x $11^3/_4$-in. oak columns. Tongues terminate in three sharp-angled cuts; they project $11^3/_4$ in. There are two thin, wide wedges in each tongue. The N side aisle, close to the highway, has been removed. Numbering of timbers is in oval-shaped chisel cuts. Anchorbeam tongue detail, Dwg. 6 at E.

—J.F.

Extant. In generally very good condition. Under the same ownership as when Fitchen viewed this important barn in June 1963. It is unfortunate that its many distinct features were not then noted. In September 1991, Peter Sinclair and I discovered carved letters and a date on the first inner anchorbeam that read "AHM 1766." This barn, located about 130 ft. from the gable-roofed $1^1/_2$ story Dutch stone house dated 1769, is probably on its original site. The house is discussed in Reynolds's book.

The barn's complex of traits demonstrates a tradition that apparently existed in Ulster County prior to the Revolutionary War that includes a major and minor round pole rafter system. Major hewn rafters (five pairs) are $5^1/_2$ x $8^1/_2$ in. and alternate with minor rafters (eight pairs) that are from $4^1/_2$ to $5^1/_2$ in. in diameter. All rafters are pine. Minor rafters do not meet at the peak. Six and a half feet (in the vertical) above the lower purlin plates are upper purlin plates that were originally supported by collar ties. Only the gable-wall ties are intact. Three inner ties were removed and now new vertical posts that emanate from the anchorbeams support the upper purlins. There is a remnant four-sided ridge beam. Another barn (exclusively oak and of five bays) about fifteen miles to the southeast has very similar dimensions (except that it is 60 ft. in length) and layout (but without its original roof) and has the same letters and date (see Reynolds book, Hoornbeck house, town of Rochester). The barns were most likely built by the same builder. Only two other barns in the county have this very distinctive rafter system, both of which are essentially unaltered. Seventeen other barns in Ulster County have evidence to varying degrees of this pre-war barn type.

The nave is 30 ft. wide. One intact side aisle is 10 ft. wide. Its 45-ft. length is one of the longest in any three-bay barn (surpassed by the 50-ft.-long barn at Phillipsburg Manor). Roof peak is 31 ft. high. *Verdiepingh* is 54 in. Single raising holes per post appear 22 in. from post tops. Pine anchorbeams and oak H-frame posts. Top of anchorbeam to existing floor is 11 ft. $10^1/_2$ in. Purlin plates are spliced, and the unions between these plates and H-frame posts is secured with only one peg each. Lapped half-dovetail joinery is seen in purlin braces and gable-wall bent braces. Purlin braces attach about $1^1/_2$ ft. below anchorbeams. Anchorbeam-to-post joint is secured with three pegs with sloping shoulders (diminished haunch). Anchorbeams do not have 2-foot scribe marks. Fitchen claims that "the anchorbeam's shoulders are housed in the columns (posts)" (see caption for Dwg. 6). I have not found this to be the case. Although the barn lacks one side aisle, it has classic proportions with only a 9-ft.-high side wall.

—G.D.H.

43. (C) Sagh, p.o. N of Quarryville on Rte. 32, left side of road.
N-S orientation. A rather small barn. Chief wagon-entrance is on axis at N gable-

end. Mortice holes for pentice are not cut through gable-end anchorbeam but through clapboarding just above it. Pentice detail, Dwg. 16 at E.

—J.F.

Extant but relocated. Fitchen's original name of Sagh is actually Sax. This barn stood until about 1993 when it was moved two miles away. Gable wall is 40 ft. wide and side wall is 35$^1/_2$ ft. Nave of 20 ft., side aisles of 10 ft. and 10 ft. 4 in., and a *verdiepingh* of 8$^1/_2$ ft. Single raising hole down 3$^1/_2$ ft. from tops of posts. Nine pairs of somewhat dissimilar sized hewn rafters. Purlin and H-frame braces milled. H-frame posts 9$^1/_2$ x 11 in. Fourteeninch high anchorbeams with 2-foot scribe marks with associated half circles. Moderate roof slope. Side wall height is 13$^1/_2$ ft. Circa 1810. The original 1$^1/_2$ story gable-roofed frame house at the site was torn down about 1995. It stood 217 ft. from the barn.

—G.D.H.

44. (H) Ford Slater, p.o. (Former owner: Menzo Livingston). 1.2 miles S of Sharon, on Rte. 145, W side of road.

Originally five-bay. E-W orientation. Heavy transverse sleepers supporting column sills and three additional longitudinal sills under threshing floor. Most anchorbeams have been cut out; surviving ones are terminated in semicircular tongues secured with two wedges and three pins. Sloping shoulders of anchorbeams rest on a 1-in. shelf off-center with the 12-in.-wide columns, and are therefore housed on the east side but flush with the lateral face of the column on its west side. Raising holes occur 3$^1/_2$ to 4 ft. down from the column tops. Three pentice mortices occur through E gable-end anchorbeam. Wagon doors here originally swung on all-wood hinges. This barn was ruinous when examined; it has since been destroyed. Sill details, Dwg. 11 at C and D.

—J.F.

Nonextant. No new information is available.

—G.D.H.

45. (H) A four-bay barn just S of Sharon, on Rte. 145.
One wedge in anchorbeam. Somewhat rebuilt.

—J.F.

Nonextant. A barn was seen in this area that matched Fitchen's very brief description. Four bays. Anchorbeam-to-post joint was secured with three pegs and single raising hole per post. Roof pitch moderate. Partly ruinous in 1992 and removed about two years later. Circa 1800.

—G.D.H.

46. (H) On Rte. 145 S of Sharon.

Rafters are very small in section, but notched half-way through at mid-length. High transverse ties occur at each H-frame bent. Regular pattern of sway braces. All but one anchorbeam has been cut out. This barn is much clobbered and rebuilt.

—J.F.

Extant. A barn closely resembling Fitchen's account exists in this area, but there are discrepancies between Fitchen's description and my own observations regarding the anchorbeams: I noted a small one on one bent and no others in the normal position. There are, however, two large anchorbeams positioned low on the posts (18 and 22 in. in depth) that Fitchen may not have seen. There are four bays with about a 24-ft. nave, and anchorbeam tenons extend 3 in. Single raising holes down from post tops by about $3^1/_2$ ft. In good condition and recently renovated. Fairly steep roof. Circa 1810.

—G.D.H.

47. (H) Just NW of Middleburgh traffic light, on lane to right off Rte. 30.

NW-SE orientation. Originally a three-bay barn, with three later bays added on axis to NW. About 48 ft. wide, and now 55 ft. total length. Framing of original NW gable remains intact in middle of present structure, and consists of two tiers of intermediate studs that are unsecured by pins to either anchorbeam or high transverse tie above it. Widely spaced rafters are small in section. Wood is mainly hard pine throughout; some members are sawn. There is a central floor sill to which the planking is pinned; this floor is early if not original, and is splined. The anchorbeams are 16 in. deep.

—J.F.

Nonextant but possibly saved. Route 30 is not northwest of Middleburgh but almost due north. It is possible Fitchen meant Route 145, which is northwest of Middleburgh, but a longtime nearby resident knows of no lane or barn that was ever off Route 145 in the area described. A check of the few lanes off Route 30 just outside of Middleburgh reveals no barn as described by Fitchen. No documentation or photographs are known.

—G.D.H.

48. (H) On Rte. 30, SW of Middleburgh, one mile from traffic-light intersection with Rte. 145, SE side of road.

Four-bay barn, about 45 ft. square. Very roughly hewn columns; sawn oak anchorbeam braces; white pine anchorbeams measuring $11^1/_2$ x $17^1/_2$ in. in section. Raising holes occur 27 in. above anchorbeams. Regular pattern of short sway braces. Ten pairs of rafters bear upon 9-in. (vert.) x 10-in. (horiz.) purlin plate. Exceptionally, the rafter feet are secured to the 6-in. (vert.) x 8-in. (horiz.) wall plate with vertical pins except for one where the pin is set normal to the roof slope. A hard pine addition to the NW end of the structure reveals the original gable-end clapboarding of boards that measure $^7/_8$

in. to $1\frac{1}{4}$ in. in thickness, by $11\frac{1}{2}$ in. to 12 in. in width. Columns, anchorbeams, and the latters' braces are flush on their SW faces.

—J.F.

Nonextant. There was a barn here that burned about 1990. It was not examined. Moderate roof slope. No estimate of erection date.

—G.D.H.

49. (H) 3 miles SW of Middleburgh, on Rte. 30, left-hand side of road.
A probable Dutch barn.

—J.F.

Nonextant but possibly saved. This barn was not documented. Following Fitchen's sequence of the locations of barns no. 49 to 52, the placement of no. 49 could not have been three miles southwest of Middleburgh as no. 52 farther south is about $2\frac{2}{3}$ miles from Middleburgh.

—G.D.H.

50. (H) Next to #49, same side of road.
A probable Dutch barn, but too full of hay to identify. Eight circular martin holes in three rows in gable: two close together high in the peak, over two directly above center two of the equally spaced holes in the lower row of four.

—J.F.

Nonextant but possibly saved. This barn was in good condition when I visited it in 1976, but I took no photographs, nor did I make any documentation. The barn was dismantled about 1982. No estimate on date of erection.

—G.D.H.

51. (H) Gargeo, p.o. A little way beyond barn no. 50, same side of road.
NE-SW orientation. A five-bay barn, about 42 x 54 ft. long. 9- x 18-in. anchorbeams gained rectangularly an exceptional $2\frac{1}{4}$ in. into the $9\frac{3}{4}$- x $10\frac{3}{4}$-in. columns. The transverse braces are gained almost this much into both the columns and the anchorbeams and are secured with two pins at each of their ends. Anchorbeams have their section reduced in height just before they frame into the columns, and the 3 in. projection of their tongues is rectilinear with slightly chamfered corners; two pins and no wedges secure these joints. Raising holes occur about 14 in. down from the narrow purlin plate, which is secured to each column-top with two pins. There is a regular pattern of fairly short sway braces. The head-height longitudinal struts along most of the SE side of the threshing floor reveal a row of $1\frac{1}{4}$-in. square mortices, $5\frac{1}{2}$ in. on centers and sloping upward at the angle of the oak slats that originally served the upper part of a long

manger. Two of these mortices occur on the column faces (at a somewhat lower level on account of the slope of the slats and the fact that the column face projects inward relative to the face of the struts). An off-center 2 x 3 in. mortice in the column face, some 20 in. below the soffit of the longitudinal struts, and a $1^1/_4$- x $3^1/_2$-in. notch in both of the lateral faces of the column, 25 in. lower down, are evidences of the framing of the manger that was once here. Twelve pairs of rafters are spaced 5 ft. apart, as are the wall studs. The entire NW side wall of this barn is now missing, leaving the rafters suspended from their bearing on the purlin plate. This is the only New York Dutch barn so far encountered with narrow, widely spaced roofers (a condition that suggests that the original roof may have been either of tiles or of thatch). The NE gable-end has eight circular martin holes: two close together under the peak, and two symmetrical sets of three in a triangular disposition below, to right and left. Oversailing rafters, Plate 52.

—J.F.

Nonextant but parts relocated. The name that Fitchen originally spelled "Gargeo" was actually Garger. I first visited this barn in 1976 and then photographed the barn when it came down about 1977. Some of the hemlock anchorbeams were recycled into a new nearby house and much of the original wide-pine weatherboarding (up to 16 in. wide and secured with wrought nails) was saved. This was probably a square rule era structure. When barn came down, a wagon wheel was found to support part of the sill system in lieu of the normal usage of stones. Fairly steep roof. One good black and white interior photo is shown on page 36 and 37 in Ernest Burden's book *Living Barns: How to Find and Restore a Barn of Your Own* (Boston: New York Graphic Society, 1977). Circa 1815. The original two-story gable-roofed brick house (circa 1800) still stands.

—G.D.H.

52. (H) Lacko, p.o. Beyond barn no. 51, same side of road.
SE-NW orientation. A four-bay barn, in which the entire (raised) threshing floor together with its supporting timbers including gable-end sills have been cut out and removed. Evidence remains of a manger similar to that of barn no. 51 on NE side. Column sills are rebated, providing shelf to receive ends of plank flooring, now destroyed. Anchorbeams are secured to $9^1/_2$- x $10^1/_2$-in. columns with three pins; tongues project only about 4 in. as rectangular shapes with slightly rounded corners. Raising holes occur some 18 in. down from column-tops in NE range, 6 in. or 7 in. in SW range. Ten pairs of rafters, at same wide spacing as wall studs. Stone support for column sills at F, Dwg. 11.

—J.F.

Extant. Excellent condition. In the same ownership as when Fitchen visited the site. Used for farm machinery storage. It is one of only two true form Dutch barns found along the entire stretch of Route 30 southwest of Middleburgh to Breakabeen. In 1950 there were probably at least one and a half dozen barns in this very rich alluvial flood plain, which was ideal for farming.
Nave is $27^1/_2$ ft. wide and inner anchorbeams are in the 20-in. depth range. Pine

and hemlock H-frame timbers, but two bent posts are oak as are some sills. *Verdiepingh* is 6 ft. 4 in. Several bent braces are uniquely tapered: 8 x $8^1/_2$ in. at bottom and 8 x $10^1/_2$ in. at top. Anchorbeam-to-post joint is square shouldered. All rafters are hewn. A series of empty mortises in both purlin plates indicates that they probably existed in a former barn as purlin plates. As is typical of Schoharie County barns, only one gable wall has evidence of the former existence of wagon entry doors.

Barn in same family since 1953. Roof slope is moderate to somewhat steep. Circa 1800.

—G.D.H.

53. (H) Farther along Rte. 30, beyond barn no. 52, same side of road.

A barn that is very much remodelled and added to. Gable has six martin holes, three each in a line paralleling the roof slope to right and left. Shapes are of three types: crescents, circles, and the type shown at E in Dwg. 17.

—J.F.

Nonextant but possibly saved. No documentation or photographs available.

—G.D.H.

54. (H) On Rte. 30, at turn to right to Bouck Falls.

A probable Dutch barn.

—J.F.

Nonextant but possibly saved. No photos or documentation available. A longtime local resident recalls a barn at this exact location. It was probably removed about 1975.

—G.D.H.

55. (H) On Rte. 30, half-mile beyond barn no. 54 on right side of road just before bridge.

A probable Dutch barn.

—J.F.

Nonextant. Resident at this very spot recalls a definite Dutch barn but says it was removed many years ago. A photograph survives and perhaps a part of one timber.

—G.D.H.

56. (H) Off to right from Rte. 30, beyond barn no. 55.

Originally a four-bay barn. Pegged plank floor, with flush axial beam. Wagon doors with all-wood hinges are still in use. Anchorbeams are gained into columns rectangularly and are secured by two pins. Unwedged tongues with full rounded corners project some 15 in. beyond face of column. Five martin holes in gable: one close under peak, two down the rake on each side. Upper three are in the shape shown at C in Dwg. 17.

—J.F.

Nonextant but possibly saved. This barn has never been located and no photographs or documentation are known to exist.

—G.D.H.

57. (B) Donald H. Bradt, p.o. Near Fonda, at junction of Stone Arabia and Hickory Road. (Referred to as "Larger Bradt barn").

A three-bay barn, large and well-built. E-W orientation. Anchorbeams are 12 x 23$^1/_2$ in. in section; they are gained 1 in. rectangularly into the columns and secured by two pins. Off-center tongues are semicircular in shape and neatly chamfered around the curves, with two thin wedges to each tongue. Columns are 11 x 13$^3/_4$ in. in section. Two raising holes appear in each column of the south range; upper is 1$^1/_4$ in. in diameter, lower is some 2 in. or so. Average spacing of rafters is 60 in.; they are about 8 x 9 in. at the butt and are provided with cogs that fit transversely into slots in the wall plate. A series of 2-in.-diameter holes in each wall stud (north side) start at the NE corner past 1$^3/_4$ in. below the wall plate's soffit and range in a downward slope to the west, in increments of about 1$^1/_2$ in. per stud. A unique feature of this barn is the discrepancy in the two side-aisle widths, which is not revealed in the symmetrical roof slopes of the exterior. The south side aisle is 9 ft. wide in the clear; that on the north measures 10 ft. 9 in. face to face between column and wall stud. Sway-bracing occurs only in the central bay and is not identical on the two sides, north and south. Longitudinal sections at E and F, Dwg. 5; anchorbeam framing detail at F, Dwg. 6.

—J.F.

Nonextant. This barn burned by accident in July 1989. Timbers are buried nearby. Several good exterior and interior photos were taken by a local resident.

Anchorbeam tenon wedges were almost peg-like in form. H-frame braces almost full width of posts. Middle bay had rare criss-crossed purlin braces. All purlin braces are attached so that they are flush with the inner face of posts (a rare trait). Pine anchorbeams just shy of 2-ft. depth. Nine pairs of hewn rafters. Fitchen stated this barn was unique in that it had side aisles of dissimilar width. This trait has been found in a few barns, but is most notably seen in a Greene County barn where a 5-ft. difference in widths occurs. Fairly steep roof. Circa 1790.

—G.D.H.

58. (B) Bradt, p.o. Near Fonda, on Hickory Hill Road east of Martin Road. (Referred to as "Smaller Bradt barn").

A three-bay barn, with later additions and changes. N-S orientation. The Roman numeral numbering of timbers is on south faces. Anchorbeam tongues (none of which is wedged) are shaped as pointed curves that are truncated at varying distances from the column's face; chamfering occurs along both curves and vertical ends. Rafters are large, but without cogs at their feet. Bay lengths are some 12 ft. 3 in. in the clear between lateral faces of the columns. Upper sinkage for the manger framing is a slot (sloping at 5 in 9) that is rebated across the side face of the columns just below the shoulder-height longitudinal struts. Three mortice holes for pentice support occur above the north wagon entrance.

—J.F.

Nonextant. Its gable wall faced the road. Removed about 1984. There is an excellent photo taken in 1960 that shows a fairly steep roof. No details (beyond Fitchen's account) are known of the interior of the barn. A Santa Fe artist did a painting of the barn in oils. No estimate of the date of erection.

—G.D.H.

59. (B) On Rte. 5, one mile east of Fonda, north side of road.
A three-bay barn. E-W orientation. Very much rebuilt, using timbers from a different framing, including one former column utilized as an anchorbeam. One deep anchorbeam is secured with two pins and two thin wedges. Its tongue (of some 14 in. projection) is in the shape of a wide rectangle with generously cut corners (45 degree angles) all without chamfering.

—J.F.

Extant. There is a barn at the exact spot cited by Fitchen, except the ridgeline is north-south. There is a west-side wall main opening (original?), which may account for the east-west orientation he cited. The barn has recycled anchorbeams and posts, but there is no post reused as an anchorbeam. Instead, there is a former purlin plate used as a post. Other traits are as described by Fitchen, and the barn should be considered the one Fitchen examined. Barn dimensions are 45 ft. at the gable wall and a 46-ft. length. Nave is $24^1/_2$ ft. wide. All anchorbeams at their juncture with posts are double-pegged and double-wedged. One anchorbeam is $9^1/_2$ x 21 in., and one end-wall anchorbeam has three mortises for pentice. Circa 1810.

—G.D.H.

60. (B) Bradt-Mabie, on Rte. 5S, north side of road between Amsterdam and Fort Hunter. (Candage Pony Farm, p.o.).
A large four-bay barn with big timbers throughout, about 56 ft. long by 46 ft. wide. NW-SE orientation. Very long diagonal sway braces occur in end bays only. Longitudinal section (schematic) at I, Dwg. 5.

—J.F.

Extant but in storage. In fair condition with good anchorbeams when dismantled in 1990. It was to be part of a major complex of Dutch barns to be rebuilt off Route 20. Now planned to be part of the Van-Antwerp-Mabie homestead off Route 5S (see Reynolds Plate no. 42), next door to its original location.

Dimensions, roof slope, and individual timber sizes bear a remarkable similarity to those found in the Wemple barn (no. 32) only four miles away. It is possible that both barns were built by the same master builder. Circa 1760.

—G.D.H.

61. (B) On Glen Road, south of Rte. 5S, right side of road.

Originally a three-bay barn, with one very long bay later added to SW. NE-SW orientation. 12 pairs of rafters in original portion. Regular pattern of short sway braces. Somewhat narrow five-sided anchorbeam tongues, with one wedge. Martin holes of shape indicated at B, Dwg. 17.

—J.F.

Nonextant but possibly saved. I have not been able to locate this barn. There was a barn on Codaugherty Road (no Glen Road in area) that had partly deteriorated and was removed in the early 1980s that may have been no. 61. No documentation is available.

—G.D.H.

62. (B) South of Auriesville, at NW corner of junction of Rts. 288 and 161. Abandoned farm group.

Originally a three-bay barn, with one longer bay added to north. N-S orientation. Anchorbeams framed to columns in sloping shoulders, with two pins and square-cut tongues. All upper transverse ties have been cut out.

—J.F.

Extant and in excellent condition. Nave is 24 ft. wide, with wider than normal 12-ft. side aisles. Ten pairs of hewn rafters are distinctly rectangular in cross-section. All four anchorbeams of hemlock have square tenons with about 12-in. extensions and are double wedged, and its union with posts are diminished haunch. This is a scribe rule barn, as anchorbeams have 2-foot scribe marks with half circles. Both inner anchorbeams have 22-in. depth. H-frame braces (one is $10^{1}/_{2}$ x 6 in.) are double pegged at both ends. Possible basswood H-frame posts except one that is hemlock. Top of anchorbeam to floor is 11 ft. 9 in. Short hewn purlin braces. *Verdiepingh* is $10^{1}/_{2}$ ft. Moderate to fairly steep roof. Circa 1790.

—G.D.H.

63. (B) on Logtown Road west of Glen, right side of road.

Originally a three-bay barn, with long bay subsequently added to SW. NE-SW orientation. Upper transverse ties have been cut out. Martin holes are shaped as at A, Dwg. 17.

—J.F.

Extant but 90 percent ruinous. Anchorbeam-to-post joint was square shouldered and secured with three pins. Double raising holes in H-frame posts with lower holes of greater diameter. Anchorbeams with 2-foot scribe marks are in the 14-to 15-in.-depth range, and their unwedged tenons extend 6 in. Ten pairs of hewn rafters. Many softwood timbers. Marriage marks on H-frames. Roof slope moderate to fairly steep. Circa 1800.

—G.D.H.

64. (B) On Reynolds Road off Rte. 30-A, south of Glen. Left side of road. A probable Dutch barn, with new, painted clapboards.

—J.F.

Extant but relocated. It is difficult to say that the Dutch barn that was on this road was definitely no. 64, as only one minor trait was cited by Fitchen. Clarke Blair of Fonda, who has located and studied Dutch barns of Montgomery County for many years and has known this road for forty years, says this is the only Dutch barn he was aware of.

This was an excellent barn and a very unusual one. It was dismantled in very good condition in August 1994 and re-erected in South Carolina. This four-bay barn in the heart of the Mohawk Valley, where softwood construction is the norm, was in almost unprecedented fashion made predominantly of ash. Another barn three miles away, however, has anchorbeams also of ash.

Exterior dimensions are 45 ft. long and 50 ft. wide with a 28-ft. nave and 11-ft. side aisles, and side walls are 13$\frac{1}{2}$ ft. high. Roof slope moderate to fairly steep. *Verdiepingh* 9$\frac{1}{2}$ ft. Double raising holes at every H-frame post. Uppers are down by 15 in. from post tops, and lowers are just below attachment of purlin braces. Its inner anchorbeams, 18 to 22 in. in depth with square contoured tenons, were extremely well hewn. Anchorbeam-to-post union with two pegs and diminished haunched shoulders. One H-frame post is 13$\frac{1}{2}$ x 10$\frac{1}{4}$ in. Two-foot scribe marks on anchorbeams. Top of anchorbeams to floor is 12 ft. 5 in. Hewn purlin braces. Each bay has two braces at each side wall. Wagon door posts have no slots for wooden hinges. Inner H-frame braces 10$\frac{1}{2}$ x 6$\frac{1}{2}$ in. secured at both ends with two pegs. At the bottom of the H-frame posts is evidence of former attachment of boards (manger?) received into angled notches whose top edge is 18 in. from floor. This feature, unique in New York state, appears with regularity in Monmouth County and to some degree elsewhere in central New Jersey. Both ranges of H-frame posts are supported by sills that were (at its original site) supported in turn by a perhaps unique continuous short wall of solid stone that extended from one gable wall to the other. Lower transverse side-aisle ties lie in the normal horizontal manner, whereas upper ties that appear only at end and middle bents are uniquely angled to avoid contact with anchorbeam tenons.

The roof does not have the common wide roofers or nailers but is unique in that it has hand-riven, tapered, narrow lath of oak. An entire roof constructed in this way represents a prodigious amount of labor.

Both side walls have the very unusual condition of horizontal girts that indicate the original attachment of vertical siding. Both gable walls have the normal vertical studs that allowed for placement of horizontal weatherboards. Because the roof lath was riven, it is possible that the original siding (none survived) was also riven. Since riven wood is always rare and is generally indicative of early origin, the erection date could be pre-Revolutionary. The Brandt and Johnson war raids eliminated most early barns in the Mohawk Valley, however, and the absence of early traits (except roof lath) suggests that the barn is probably circa 1785.

—G.D.H.

65. (J) On Rte. 20 west of Guilderland, at two-level railroad bridge crossings, south side of road.

Three-bay. E-W orientation. 42 ft. 1 in. long by 47 ft. wide. Long sway braces, steeper than 45 degrees, in regular pattern. 10 pairs of big rafters. Median floor sill, showing $3\frac{1}{2}$ in. flush with planking. Raising hole about 4 ft. down from purlin plate. East gable-end has small doors at both corners, and a pentice above central wagon entrance whose southern leaf is a Dutch door.

—J.F.

Extant but in storage. This barn, known as the Van Patten barn, was dismantled and was to be re-erected as part of the complex that included barn no. 60. Timbers were fairly sound as of fall of 1993. I cannot estimate an erection date because I was unable to view the barn. Photos survive.

—G.D.H.

66. (J) Palen, p.o. On Rte. 209 about 2 miles south of Hurley.

Four-bay, about 50 ft. long. N-S orientation. Wagon entrance to threshing floor occurs only at north gable-end. Unplanked floor of southernmost bay is about 5 ft. below level of threshing floor. Two anchorbeams are 10 x $14\frac{3}{4}$ in. in section. Where drop in floor level occurs, two beams, $6\frac{1}{2}$ x $8\frac{1}{2}$ in. and one above the other, serve in lieu of an anchorbeam. One alone of the anchorbeam braces is curved instead of a straight diagonal member. Anchorbeam tongues do not project. Sixteen pairs of rafters. Regular pattern of very short sway braces.

—J.F.

Extant. In fairly good condition. Parts are in need of repair. This is an excellent example of a U-barn, which occur with some regularity in Ulster County. U-barns, a term coined by Peter Sinclair, have their last bay and both side aisles in dirt to form the letter U, with only one gable-wall wagon entry resulting. This barn form may be a later adaptation to the increased needs of stabling farm animals that accompanied an early transition to dairy farming in the very late eighteenth century or early nineteenth century.

The last inner bent has uncentered opposing double doors of single height similar to the regular gable-wall threshing floor double height doors. They open to the last fully dirt floor bay.

Directional orientation is closer to northeast-southwest than to Fitchen's original citation of north-south. Nave is a very wide $30^1/_2$ ft., and the one side aisle is 10 ft. wide. Roof peak is about 34 ft. high. The floor of the southern most bay is 4 ft. below level of threshing floor, which has original pegs. Anchorbeam-to-post joint is square shouldered. *Verdiepingh* is 9 ft. 2 in. Single raising holes per post appear about 20 in. below post tops. Each bent has upper tie beam. Roof is fairly steep. Circa 1815. The original $1^1/_2$-story gable-roofed Dutch stone house stands immediately across the road.

—G.D.H.

67. (J) In village of Stone Ridge.
Both columns and anchorbeams of oak. Square tongues, wedged. Numbered mortices. Side walls only 9 ft. high. About 11 ft. to soffit of anchorbeam. This barn is in ruins.

—J.F.

Nonextant. This barn was adjacent to an extant single-aisle barn (shown at Reynolds Plate no. 104, where an image of the barn appears). No documentation is known. Steep roof. The Dutch house complex at the site is of two parts: a large 2-story gambrel-roofed stone section and an earlier attached $1^1/_2$-story gable-roofed stone section. Barn may date from 1770, as does the 2-story house section.

—G.D.H.

68. (J) South of Modena, on Rte. 32.
Four-bay. N-S orientation. $10^1/_4$- x 22-in. anchorbeams, with 10-ft.-4-in. headroom from floor to their soffit. Square-cut tongues with corners slightly cut at 45 degrees are strongly chamfered along the upright end only; they have two thin wedges. Tongues are on axis of anchorbeams, but their mortices are not centered on wide face of $8^1/_2$- x 15-in. columns. Wagon entrances originally occurred at both gable-ends; now there is but one, on east side in northern of two middle bays. Regular pattern of rather long, fairly steep-pitched sway braces. Raising holes occur 10 in. below soffit of 8-in. (vert.) x 10-in. (horiz.) purlin plate. Fifteen pairs of rather small, closely spaced rafters. 1- x 3-in. (nonoriginal?) roofers, spaced 2 in. apart. Only 5 ft. from floor to soffit of 12-in. (vert.) x 7-in. (horiz.) transverse side-aisle struts. Side walls are too low to permit any upper transverse struts.

—J.F.

Nonextant but possibly saved. No barn fitting Fitchen's description has been found.

—G.D.H.

69. (J) John Van Doren. Prof. François Bucher, p.o. North of Princeton, N.J. via Rte. 206, on Rte. 533 to Griggstown (River Road) just before Millstone, on left side of road.

Three-bay. NW-SE orientation. About 39 ft. long, $50\frac{1}{2}$ ft. wide, 30-ft. height to the ridge, some $13\frac{1}{2}$ ft. to the eaves. Fish-tailed rafters; regular pattern of short sway braces. Wall plate $5\frac{1}{2}$ in. (vert.) x $7\frac{1}{2}$ in. (horiz.) in section; purlin plate 9 in. (vert.) x $9\frac{1}{4}$ in. (horiz.). Raising holes (?) occur about 22 in. below soffit of wall plate! $11\frac{1}{2}$- x $15\frac{3}{4}$-in. oak anchorbeams have square-cut tongues that project $12\frac{1}{2}$ in. Columns are $9\frac{1}{4}$ x $13\frac{1}{4}$ in. Lower transverse side-aisle struts at $6\frac{1}{2}$-foot height; top of upper struts is $5\frac{1}{2}$ in. below soffit of wall plate. This barn appears to have been rebuilt: e.g., rafters are right-angle notched in a long sweeping cut about a foot below where they now bear upon the purlin plate; and two open slots for wedges occur near the outer end of the anchorbeam tongues, at different levels from those of the present wedges. A feature of this barn not elsewhere encountered is the original shingling of its walls. Attached near the lower edge by handmade rose-headed nails to $\frac{7}{8}$- x 3-in. or 4-in. horizontal slats spaced $6\frac{1}{2}$ in. apart, the shingles are coursed $9\frac{1}{2}$ in. to 10 in. to the weather. The old house that goes with this barn was built in 1754; local tradition asserts that the barn dates from 1720.

—J.F.

Extant and in excellent condition. This is the only New Jersey Dutch barn John Fitchen ever documented. François Bucher, a friend of Fitchen's, sold this barn to the present owner in 1971. I showed this barn to Robert Ensminger, the Pennsylvania barn authority, in August 1992. Its directional orientation is a little north of due east instead of Fitchen's citation of northwest-southeast. It is very unlikely this barn is pre-1770, as it has a nearly 10-ft. *verdiepingh* and milled purlin braces that attach to the posts over 4 ft. above the anchorbeams, which have been recycled as empty wedge slots in some of its tenons attest. It has a fairly steep roof pitch. There are short wood nailers between vertical beams on three walls, which is indicative of original attachment of wooden shakes on the exterior of the barn, a feature seen occasionally in central New Jersey barns. Oak timbering. Barn length is 40 ft. Both inner anchorbeams have 2-foot scribe marks and are 18 in. in height. Tenons extend 12 in. and are double-wedged. Square shouldered and double-pegged union of anchorbeams with posts. Threshing floor, probably original, with wooden pegs and floorboards average 8 to 12 in. wide. Nave is 26 ft. wide and side aisles are a wide 12 ft. each. Hewn H-frame braces, one of which measures 6 x 9 in. Full complement of raising holes. Fourteen pairs of hewn rafters. There are both upper and lower side-aisle ties. This is a large three-bay barn. The frame house complex of two parts stands about 245 feet north-east of circa 1790 barn.

—G.D.H.

70, 71. (J) SW of #69, same side of road (Rte. 533).
At least two other Dutch barns.

—J.F.

Possibly extant. There are now at least four other Dutch barns southwest of barn no. 69, two of which are easily seen from the road. As there may have been other barns present when Fitchen traveled here in April 1965, it is difficult to know what barns were nos. 70 and 71.

—G.D.H.

72. West of Baldwinsville on Rte. 370 near Plainville at Gates Road.
N-S orientation. Big anchorbeams with big, rounded tongues. Pentice over wagon entrance centered in north gable-end, toward road. Southern end of barn is somewhat ruinous.

—J.F.

This barn, located west of Syracuse, is far from the most western area where Dutch barns regularly occur in the Mohawk Valley. Fitchen related to me how amazed he was to realize how far a Dutch barn was removed from its normal range. No documentation or photographs are known. Fitchen apparently did not visit this barn, as no letter (A to J) corresponding to the map in Appendix B appears next to the no. 72.

—G.D.H.

73, 74. Two "Schoharie barns" north of the St. Lawrence River, in Upper Canada Village.
These barns presently house the early agricultural exhibits in this extensive assemblage of authentic old-time structures. They have been removed from their original sites and rebuilt. They are open to the public.

—J.F.

Extant. Can be seen in Upper Canada Village.

—G.D.H.

75. Sleepy Hollow Restorations, north of Tarrytown on the Hudson River.
A reconstructed Dutch barn removed from Hurley, New York.

—J.F.

Nonextant. The barn was moved to the Sleepy Hollow Restorations site in the late 1940s, and the well-known Ulster County architect Myron Teller was involved in the project. My visit to the barn in 1977 showed that it was not a good example of a Dutch barn. It burned about 1980. An excellent barn near Guilderland in Albany County was relocated to Sleepy Hollow and replaced the burned Hurley barn in 1982.

—G.D.H.

76. The New Windsor Cantonment, National Temple Hill Association at Vails Gate, New York.
A disassembled Dutch barn is soon to be reassembled here.

—J.F.

A Dutch barn that faced imminent destruction about 1965 because of Route 84 construction in the Fishkill area of Dutchess County was taken down and its timbers were moved here. Photos exist of timbers being carried over the Hudson River by ferry. A foundation was constructed but the barn was never erected. The timbers were covered for a number of years and were then left out in the open.

—G.D.H.

Appendix D

Huber's Responses to Fitchen's Text

The first edition of John Fitchen's *New World Dutch Barn* was presented in three major sections: descriptions of barns, structural considerations, and conjectural procedures of erection. In this appendix, I will comment on each section of Fitchen's original text (pages 13 to 64), focusing on the findings of research conducted since the first edition was published in 1968. I encourage readers to review Fitchen's work in conjunction with this new information so that Fitchen's statements can be compared to more recent findings. The page numbers that follow subsection headings in this appendix refer the reader to the relevant portions of Fitchen's text. In some cases, new research has corroborated Fitchen's claims; in such sections I do not provide comment. In other cases, I introduce new areas of research topics that were not addressed in Fitchen's original work.

DESCRIPTION (PAGES 13 TO 32)

Characteristics (pages 13 to 15)

The following numbered topics correspond to the original numbered discussions of aspects and attributes of Dutch barns presented by Fitchen.

One. Barns vary in original plan from nearly square to distinctly rectangular, depending in general on the number of bays. A study of the last remaining twenty-seven (original condition) classic Dutch barns in Somerset County, New Jersey, found that the total average width (gable wall) was 47 ft. $^2/_3$ in. and the total average length (side wall) was 38 ft. 4 in.[1] The four four-bay barns averaged 48 ft. 3 in. wide by 47 ft. 4 in. long. The twenty-three three-bay barns averaged 47 ft. 1 in. wide by 36 ft. 5$^1/_2$ in. long. Thus, the study shows that the width of three-bay barns is about 11 ft. greater than their length, whereas four-bay barns are nearly square. Additionally, two original-condition side-wall entrance barns of three bays with much widened middle bays were found to have an average width of 41 ft. 2$^1/_2$ in. and a length of 42 ft. 1 in.

In the fall of 1991, I studied the last of five original-condition classic barns in

---

1. Ursula Brecknell and Greg Huber, *Farmstead Siting of Dutch Barns: A Study of Somerset County (N.J.) Original Barns* (Trenton: New Jersey Historical Commission, 1991).

Bergen County, New Jersey, and found the total average width to be 42½ ft. and total average length to be 37 ft. The single four-bay barn was 53 ft. wide by 49 ft. long. The four three-bay barns averaged 40 ft. wide by 36 ft. long. Here, all barns were found to be shorter in length than width by 4 ft. In addition, I measured two of the three surviving original Dutch barns on Long Island, all at its western end. These two three-bay structures had widths of 42 ft. and 41 ft. and lengths of 40 ft. and 34 ft., respectively. The relative proportions of width versus length in three- and four-bay barns of New York State reflect in general the conditions seen in Bergen and Somerset counties. One clear exception is the four-bay Wemple barn in Schenectady (Appendix C, barn no. 32), where the length exceeds the width by 9 ft. Another four-bay barn in Fulton County is 15 ft. longer than it is wide. Five- and six-bay barns appear only in New York state. Some five-bay barns are close to square, whereas some are distinctly rectangular with the length being the greater dimension. Only about six six-bay barns are known, and all are definitely longer than they are wide. The length of the unique seven-bay Wagner barn in Rensselaer County was 8½ ft. greater than its width.

It is important to know that these bay numbers include only those bays in the original barn plan. Many barns, especially in the upcountry, have added on bays and do not figure into the numbers just reviewed.

Two. About two to three dozen barns have been found with original condition side-wall wagon entrances. Several barns have original basements under the threshing floor and side-aisles, ostensibly for general storage, and later ones (post-1820) occasionally have sections for stabling.

Three. Perhaps up to two dozen barns in both New York and New Jersey have original vertical siding. A few barns have horizontal siding on gable walls but vertical siding on side walls.

Four. A Bergen County, New Jersey, barn has 6-ft.-high side walls, and there are other barns with heights of less than 10 ft. Several barns, mostly of late vintage, have heights of up to 18 ft.

Five. At least two barns, both in Rensselaer County, New York, each have an original elevated area (like much enlarged house shed dormers) on one roof slope for accommodating loaded hay wagons to enter through the side wall.

Six. One New Jersey barn in Bergen County has both side walls of stone, while another barn in Hunterdon County has at least one partial stone gable wall. A number of barns in the lower Hudson Valley and throughout New Jersey have original wagon entrances with metal hinges.

Seven. Most barns have three aisles, but several, as mentioned above, have a one-aisle format. An original condition barn (circa 1820) in Dutchess County, New York, is unique in that it has an original but partial fourth aisle that is adjacent to the side of one of the regular side aisles.

Eight. Many middle aisles or naves are much more than twice the width of each of the side aisles. Several barns have a ratio of nave width to side-aisle width close to 3 to 1. Naves normally vary from about 16 to 32 ft. wide. The majority of barns have nave widths of 22 to 26 ft. Only a very few measure over 30 ft. At the other extreme, one late barn (with recycled timbers) in Columbia County has a 12-ft. nave. Naves are measured from the outer edges of the H-frame posts. Fitchen measured from the inner edges.

Nine. A number of barns have their anchorbeams attached to their posts at variable positions above their midpoints. A consistent feature (80 to 90 percent of the time) is the distance from the top of the anchorbeam to the threshing floor, which is approximately 12 ft. (plus or minus 6 in.).

Ten. Braces do not always secure gable wall anchorbeams to their posts such as in some pre-Revolutionary barns in the upper river valleys of New York. The circa 1790 museum barn at the Stone Fort in Schoharie County has this feature as does the Wemple barn (Appendix C, barn no. 32).

Eleven. About thirty to forty five-bay, six six-bay, and six two-bay barns occur in New York state. One two-bay barn (nonextant) supposedly appeared in New Jersey. One unique seven-bay barn (nonextant) was discovered in Rensselaer County, New York. Bay widths normally vary from 9 to 14 ft. Most are from 10 to 12 ft. They are often evenly spaced in a given barn. Several barns, especially those built after 1800, have much longer end bays—16 to 20 ft. long.

Thirteen. Bays in individual barns can vary considerably in disposition of purlin braces. Bays can have either one or two purlin braces per side, and rarely will two braces criss-cross. One Montgomery County barn is unique in that it has side-by-side parallel braces in two bays, and these braces are necessarily of unequal length. Some bays in five-bay barns do not have any braces. Some barns have bays where braces extend below anchorbeams and other bays where braces attach above anchorbeams. Some three-bay and four-bay barns have single, long braces per bay per side. One four-bay barn in Schoharie County uniquely has long hewn braces in its end bays and short milled braces in the middle two bays. There are other variations of purlin plate arrangement.

Fourteen. Collar ties occasionally occur that link rafter pairs. The Wemple Barn (Appendix C, barn no. 32) has them only at the gable walls. An Ulster County pre-Revolutionary War building tradition includes lapped half-dovetail joinery in collar ties at every other rafter pair. The Wortendyke barn in Park Ridge, New Jersey, has collar ties at every other rafter pair. A few single-aisle barns have collar ties.

Contrast with Old World Examples (pages 15 to 16)

A few numbered items in this section contain information that has been corrected in the foregoing "characteristic" section. Only new information is included here.

Seven. The Ulster County pre-Revolutionary War tradition typically includes four-sided hewn ridge beams. One barn in southern Dutchess County has a unique five-sided ridge beam, but its roof is structured in the normal manner.

Eight. One or two Bergen County, New Jersey, barns may have had their rafters spliced at the purlin plates. In addition, pre-Revolutionary War era barns in Ulster County have major hewn rafters that run only from the roof peak to the lower purlin plates. They are spliced onto minor round pole rafters that then run down to the wall plates.

Nine. In the Ulster County pre-Revolutionary War era tradition, upper and lower purlin plates are present. Double level plates also occurred in the Teller-Schermerhorn barn[2] (shown in Plate 15). The upper plates in the Van Bergen barn (Appendix C, barn no. 37) were probably not original.

---

2. This information was taken from a photograph shown to me and taken by Vincent Schaefer.

Ten. Several New Jersey barns, especially in the west central part of the state, have original diagonal windbracing.

Eleven. Many anchorbeams in many barns are thickest at their midpoints and taper by 2 to 4 in. as they drop toward their attachment to the posts. Some purlin plates display a natural taper, probably due to the natural taper of the trees they came from.

Twelve. At least two barns with thatch appear in early-twentieth-century photographs. One was in Montgomery in Orange County, New York, and the other in Bergen County, New Jersey.

Sixteen. Seventeenth-century Dutch American contracts indicate separate sections in at least six buildings that included both house and barn.[3] This condition is widely found in the Netherlands, although no such buildings remain in America. How common this practice was is not known. It is possible that it extended into the eighteenth century. It should be noted that many houses built during the seventeenth century in America were separate from the barn.

Specific Description (pages 21 to 31)

No extensive data for orientation of barns is available, except for two counties in New Jersey and one in New York state. In Bergen County all twenty-five barns face or just miss the southeast quadrant, except two—one that faces due east and one that faces southwest. Of twenty-nine three-aisle barns in Somerset County, eighteen face the southeast quadrant and an additional six barns just miss, for a total of about 80 percent. In addition, eleven barns in Rockland County, New York, face or just miss the southeast quadrant, except one that faces south-southwest.[4]

In central New Jersey, several barns have been found with shake siding, some of which is original with rose-headed nails. Several barns originally had vertical siding, and a few had a combination of horizontal gable-wall siding and vertical siding on the side walls. The Bull barn in Orange County has this trait, as does barn no. 64 in Appendix C. A few Dutchess County barns have vertical siding.

One true form nonextant four-bay barn (circa 1790) in Monmouth County almost uniquely appeared to have had its original roof shakes intact with wrought nails (under a later covering of asphalt shingles). Shakes were 31 to 33 in. long, $6^{1}/_{2}$ to $7^{1}/_{2}$ in. wide, and $^{3}/_{8}$ in. thick, with 8 to $9^{1}/_{2}$ in. exposed to the weather. They were nailed in three rows of two nails each, which is indicative of placement of narrow roofers below.

Original board siding on New Jersey barns is quite rare, and only three barns have martin holes. In one barn they appear to take the form of bells.

Pentices appear on some New Jersey barns, but none is original. One barn in southern Somerset County appears to have notches in one gable-wall anchorbeam that may have been for an original pentice. Two barns in Ulster County have their original hewn pentice arms, which stretched from the first inner anchorbeam over the gable-wall anchorbeam and terminated about 4 to 5 ft. beyond the outside wall. Three or four other New York barns have original remnants of pentice arms. The typical upcountry

---

3. McMahon, "Achter Col Colony."

4. Greg Huber, "Dutch Barns in the Stony Lands of Rockland County," *South of the Mountains* 43, no. 4 (Oct.-Dec. 1999): 3–19.

anchorbeam pentice mortises do not appear in the southern Hudson River Valley or in any part of New Jersey.

Original gable-wall wagon doors with wooden hinges, most often of oak, are extant on perhaps fifteen to twenty barns, all in New York state. In two cases, the hinges extend about one-half the width of each door. Wooden hinged wagon doors originally appeared throughout most of New York, except in most of Dutchess County and perhaps some of southern Ulster County. The Bull barn in Orange may have had framed threshing floor doors as does barn no. 21 (See Appendix C).

Main wagon doors originally opened outward throughout New Jersey and occasionally in southern New York, probably because of lesser amounts of seasonal snow buildup in those areas.

The tops of anchorbeams are most often within 2 to 6 in. of 12 ft. from the threshing floor. A few barns, especially in Bergen County, have those numbers reduced by 6 to 10 in. All these measurements reflect accommodations that permitted loaded hay wagons to enter the barns and proceed under the anchorbeams with some small clearance.

Fitchen said the depth-to-thickness ratio of anchorbeams is unprecedented. This is often true in many barn types in the Northeast, but there is at least one clear exception: the swing beams in the so-called swing beam barns have ratios that are very similar to those of anchorbeams. These barns are often found in the upcountry (post-1810), in west central New Jersey (often 1770–1820), and sporadically elsewhere. They are original-condition, side-entrance barns, and the single swing beam (per barn) spans the entire barn width and therefore has no extended tenons. One swing beam in a barn in Hunterdon County, New Jersey, has a ratio of nearly 3 to 1, and another has a ratio of $2^1/_2$ to 1. Such ratios are never found in anchorbeams.

One nonextant barn (circa 1815) south of New Paltz in Ulster County was exceptional in that it had oak siding secured with cut nails that appeared to be original.

Fitchen used the word *strut* to denote the link between Dutch barn H-frame posts longitudinally and to side wall posts transversely. The term *strut*, however, is normally used to indicate supports found in the roof structures of various traditional buildings in Britain.[5] The appropriate word would be *tie*.

There are at least three barns that did not have transverse side-aisle (in at least the non-gable-wall bent) ties: the Skinkle barn (Appendix C, barn no. 10), an early extant barn near Catskill, New York, and the Schaeffer-Ingold museum barn in Schoharie County. One barn in central New Jersey has three side-aisle ties per bent per side. Many barns in the upcountry have two or three evenly spaced side-aisle ties that join to longitudinal ties between adjacent H-frame posts. These ties supported planks above for crop storage. It is very unusual to find transverse ties that are braced, such as those in the Westbrook barn in Sussex County, New Jersey. Fitchen did not stipulate in his depiction of transverse sections (see Dwg. 4) whether they were of gable-wall framing or interior framing schemes as certain upcountry barns can apparently have gable-wall frames that have upper transverse ties, whereas interior frames have no upper ties. The original word for side aisles in both barns and houses in seventeenth-century Dutch American contracts was *uytlaeten*, which literally meant *outlets*.[6]

5. Richard Harris, *Discovering Timber Framed Buildings* (Buckinghamshire, Eng.: Shire Publications Ltd., 1978), 63, 85, 96.

6. New York Historical Manuscripts (Baltimore: 1974) Vol. 1 p. 378.

Longitudinal ties very often appear at different heights at each H-frame post range in a given barn. They vary anywhere from about 6 to 15 in. For a theoretical example, all ties at one post range may appear 8 in. higher from the threshing floor than do the ties at the opposite post range. The ostensible purpose of this disparity was to accommodate taller stabled horses at one side and shorter cattle at the opposite side.

Several barns in central New Jersey have high upper longitudinal ties and are often braced. The ties were included for greater longitudinal stability and appear only a few feet below purlin plates.

A few barns have spliced purlin plates (Appendix C barns no. 10, 23, and 42). This was apparently because of a lack of sufficiently long timbers, or perhaps because some builders utilized remaining lengths of trees that were used initially for other beams. Some purlin plates (of single length timbers) are up to 60 ft. long.

Sway is the original word used by Fitchen for the bracing between H-frame posts and purlin plates. Any brace is supposed to prevent swaying owing to wind action and other forces. *Purlin brace* is a more accurate term, and it exactly indicates the location of the brace in question. The inverted "sway" bracing in the Deertz barn (Appendix C, barn no. 20) cited by Fitchen is not unique but is found in a few other barns, including barn no. 35 and the Westbrook barn in Sussex County, New Jersey, near the Delaware River.

Four barns have been discovered to date that have the aforementioned major and minor rafter system. The first barn (Appendix C, barn no. 42) was found by Fitchen in 1963, but the structural layout of the roof and most other attendant traits went undetected. I discovered the second and third barns in Ulster County in 1993 and 1994, respectively. The three barn roofs are very similarly constructed except that there are pairs of minor rafters between adjacent major rafters in the first barn, whereas in the other two barns only single pairs appear between adjacent majors. The fourth is the Westbrook barn, which has been known for many years because it is in the Delaware Water Gap National Recreation Area, and it is significantly different from the other three. Double minor rafter pairs appear between adjacent majors. The majors extend as single lengths of timber from peak to wall plates. There is no ridgebeam, no upper purlin plates, and no collar ties, and lapped joinery is present only in upper H-frame braces.

There are two cases of extant Dutch barns that have oversailing rafters and therefore had projecting eaves. One such barn is in Somerset County, and the other is near Pine Plains in Dutchess County, New York.

A number of barns have positive attachment of their rafters at the wall plates, usually by means of long iron spikes.

STRUCTURAL CONSIDERATIONS (PAGES 33 TO 49)

Provisions for Meeting Tensile Stresses (pages 34 to 35)

Fitchen suggested that lengthening the anchorbeam tenon "provides a very much increased area of resistance to longitudinal shear, making it unlikely that the pin or wedge will rip its way out through the end of the tenon." Although this assertion is technically true, it should be remembered that many barns, mostly in the upcountry, have extended anchorbeam tenons with no wedges at all. In addition, anchorbeam tenons were extended to varying degrees from 1 or 2 in. to as much as 2 ft. An average range is about 6 to 10 in. The reason why ancient builders in continental Europe, from whence the tradition came, extended and wedged anchorbeam tenons in traditional barns is lost to obscurity. Seemingly, these tenons were extended and often wedged to secure the anchorbeam and post joint rigidly. This may have been particularly significant in the tilting up process in erecting the H-frames where the posts were somewhat weakened by mortises that were made for anchorbeam insertion.

This particular reasoning may be difficult to understand but builders here in America may have extended anchorbeam tenons because "that's the way it was done." This lack of conscious choice may explain in part why tenons were extended to variable degrees. It appears that some building traditions continued on without builders being fully aware of why they were using certain practices. This is not at all to imply that they did not have well thought-out plans for why and how they built the way they did. But one of the most palpable features of most Dutch barns—the extension of its anchorbeam tenons—may lend significant insight into the fact that builders were tradition bound in certain ways that even they may not have been aware of.

Conjectural Procedures of Erection (pages 51 to 64)

H-frames (page 53)

Fitchen was mistaken when he suggested that the H-frames were not reared up from a horizontal to a vertical position because of the supposed vulnerable stub tenons at the bottom of the posts. Barn renovators today report that they most definitely tilt up the H-frames to their erect vertical position because the tenon is only about 3 in. long and it is not in danger of breaking off.

It is interesting to note that Fitchen did not suggest that the raising holes in the posts, a feature he introduced, served in any capacity in erecting the bents. Timber framers probably inserted wooden pegs into these holes (see Illus. 16) and attached ropes to them, which in turn were connected to gin poles with block and tackle. Other methods may have been used. The bents were then raised from a horizontal to vertical position. This technique is why Fitchen never found "any of the tell-tale scars on the smooth faces of columns (posts) or anchorbeams that would indicate the use of pike poles in their erection." His idea about the use of lifting slings is appealing but is not supported by available evidence. Indeed, a number of raising holes have in situ peg remnants that were probably original, which reinforces the idea about the use of gin poles or other hoisting mechanisms postulated above.

It will be seen that virtually all Dutch barns have their inner H-frames with frame elements (anchorbeams, posts, and braces) all flush on one side. This flush condition, called the layout or reference face, was not a random choice by builders but rather facilitated the assembly of bents. In addition, all inner bents in a given barn have their flush sides face the same direction for ease of rearing to a vertical position. Another reason for the flush arrangement of elements may have been for uniformity of appearance. A rare exception to this orientation rule is found in Appendix C, barn no. 10.

Finally, a number of barns, especially in the upcountry, have H-frame posts with double raising holes. At least two barns in Somerset County have three holes per post. The extra holes may also have been used to help raise the bents. Other barns have no raising holes at all.

Illus. 16. Barn near Hillsborough in Somerset County, New Jersey. Rare peg extending out of H-frame post raising hole just below purlin plate that probably assisted in raising bent.

Sway Bracing and Purlin Plate (page 56)

The scenario offered by Fitchen about the manner in which the purlin plates were raised and positioned to their final resting spots seems very unlikely (see Dwg. 14). It is difficult to imagine that many men positioned high up on the posts would have been capable of shouldering very heavy plates (35 to 60 ft. long) and still able to delicately insert all the many tenons of braces and posts exactly into place without becoming totally fatigued. Here again, the gin pole (or an equivalent) was used, the plate was correctly positioned, and all the braces were secured and pegged.

Side Walls (page 61)

Fitchen was correct when he proposed "that it is just possible" that the sill was first put in place and then the entire side wall frame was reared into position and then secured. But then, he thought, the whole assemblage would be "too rickety." He may not have allowed for the fact that wood is a forgiving medium and quite capable of a certain amount of "abuse." Fitchen then asserted that "the side-wall members were raised and secured one at a time." But this would have been an immense and unnecessary expenditure of time and labor. His first guess—that the sill was placed first and the side-wall frame then raised as one unit—was correct, and it is this procedure that is reported today by barn renovators.

Roof (page 62)

Many renovators say they simply slide individual rafters up and over the purlin plates on each side and then connect them in pairs at the top. The chevron method that Fitchen advanced appears to be possible but probably did not normally occur.

It was Fitchen's belief that the roof construction of Dutch barns was, like the anchorbeams, a unique structural characteristic of Dutch barns. The swing beam barns of the Mohawk and Schoharie River Valleys have virtually the same roof structure. Here, however, the purlin plates are supported by queen posts. The dynamics behind the existence of the unique major and minor rafter system in Ulster County is a mystery but likely represented a closely knit group or family of local builders who, in turn, may have been strongly influenced by certain European building traditions. The use of hewn major and minor round pole rafters is known in the Netherlands.[7]

7. Berends, *Historische Houtconstructies*.

Glossary

aisle: three barn length longitudinal areas in classic Dutch barns, each of which is located between posts in a range in H-frames or side walls. Middle aisle is area between H-frame posts in a range at each side. Two side aisles may appear at each side of nave.

anchorbeam: large horizontal member of H-frame, most often with salient extended tenons. H-frames stretch across nave.

ankerbalk (ankerbalkgebint): Dutch word from which the term *anchorbeam* was directly derived. Prototype of Dutch American anchorbeam.

bay: area between adjacent H-frames and continuous with area at side aisles.

bent: main framing unit or H-frame consisting of anchorbeam and two posts and braces at each end. Also refers to the framing unit at each side wall erected as a unit (except sill).

cantilever: rare in Dutch barns, the projecting area above the main threshing-floor doors on gable walls, which probably functioned for ventilation to barn interior.

classic (Dutch barn): barn with original three-aisle format with original wagon entry either at one or two gable wall(s). Also known as true-form barn.

collar tie: horizontal beam that stretches between two rafters (at about their midpoints) in a rafter pair, most often united with lapped half-dovetail joinery.

cup marks: unique oval-shaped marriage marks often found in major—and minor-rafter-type barns in Ulster County, New York.

dekbalk (dekbalkgebint): timber framing type, found in the Netherlands, in which the tie beam ends are mortised to receive the tenons of end posts. There is no extension of post above the tie. One unique nonextant example found in Bergen County, New Jersey.

dendrochronology: method of tree-ring dating that compares patterns of rings found in timber beam of a particular structure to a standard that can date a building if certain criteria are met.

diminished haunch: normal reference to tapered cut found where anchorbeam enters into post that is cut with identical taper. Most often found on pre-1790 barns.

domain: main area of Dutch barn-building tradition, consisting of about eighteen counties in the eastern river valleys of New York state and eight counties in the northern half of New Jersey.

Dutch-Anglo barn: a barn that is one of two main types: (1) an original one-, two-(rare), or three-aisled structure with H-frames and original side wall main wagon door entry; (2) an altered classic original barn with an introduced main wagon-door entrance at side wall(s), and reoriented roof, often built during 1830–70.

English barn: agricultural building, decidedly smaller than Dutch barns, whose main wagon entry is originally on side wall. Most often of three-bay arrangement. Main roof support derived from side-wall posts.

first effective settlement: principle stating that the pioneering culture in a particular area established the building style that subsequent cultures would emulate.

Fort Orange: fort built by Dutch during the summer of 1624 in what is now Albany, New York.

Frisian farm building: aisled form found in the Netherlands with *dekbalk* construction and high central nave for crop storage from floor to roof peak. Cattle kept in one side aisle. Not a precursor of the Dutch-American barn.

gable: normally that part of the end wall of a rectangular building above the eave level that forms the triangular part (with one roof slope per side) that extends to roof peak.

granary: partitioned area against one gable or end wall in a side aisle in one bay for storage of grain, particularly wheat in early Dutch days.

gunstock post: post that has a flared or enlarged part toward its top for the reception of a plate and tie beam. Several barns in central New Jersey have them.

hallehuis: building form in the Netherlands that most closely resembles the Dutch American barn, and from which the latter probably originated.

hay barracks: accessory storage buildings with adjustable roofs and usually four posted. Used on Dutch homesteads since the 1630s. Their timbers were occasionally recycled into barns, especially in Ulster and Albany Counties.

hewn: timbers whose surfaces are hand-cut, most often with a broadax.

H-frame: sometimes referred to as H-bent, consists of usually heavy anchorbeam and two end posts, braced. Dutch barn is the only major early or pre-1830 barn style of the Northeast to have this construction.

joinery: method of uniting timbers.

kopbalk (kopbalkgebint): timber framing type found in the Netherlands where the tie beam's end is trenched and received into post that is slotted at its top end. There is no post extension above tie. No examples have been found in New York or New Jersey as main bent tie beam. Found in some Pennsylvania forebay barns.

layout face: also known as the reference face, this is a condition, for example, where all members in an H-frame are flush at one side for ease of assembly.

loft beam: term found in some seventeenth-century contracts to denote anchorbeam.

longitudinal ties: called longitudinal head height struts in original Fitchen text, these ties are found at about head height stretching from one H-frame post to an adjacent H-frame post in one post range.

major and minor rafter system: unique roof system peculiar to pre-Revolutionary War barns in Ulster County, New York, that features upper purlin plates, a ridge beam, and collar ties. Also attendant are short *verdiepingh*s, cup marks (often), and half-lapped dovetail joinery found in varying degrees in H-frame braces and purlin braces. This system may have existed in Bergen and Rockland Counties.

Manhattan: very early settlement of Dutch in 1625.

martin holes: decorative holes found most often on original exterior weatherboarding on gable walls, ostensibly to allow certain birds access to interior of barns to check vermin population. Probably little function in ventilation.

milled: timbers and boards that are sawn at a mill. May have either up or down parallel marks or circular marks.

mortise: pocket or chiseled-out area in beam for reception of tenon of articulating beam.

nave: central aisle in classic three-aisle barns for threshing and possibly winnowing that normally varies in width from 16 to 32 ft.

New England barn: agricultural building (post-1825) of three-aisle format found in New England whose main entry is on gable wall. Apparently not derived from Dutch traditions. Middle aisle is not a threshing floor but only for wagon drive-through.

Palatine German: ethnic stock from Germany in the Palatinate who came to America in early 1700s and apparently erected Dutch barns.

Pennsylvania forebay barn: barn style originating in Pennsylvania in which the second floor cantilevers over the basement stable wall.

pentice: exterior hood-like projection of 4 or 5 ft. over the gable wall threshing floor doors in New York Dutch barns. Very little evidence of original pentices exists in New Jersey barns.

pintles: elements of wood or iron set into or onto door frames that allow doors to pivot.

plates: Longitudinal timbers that connect posts either at one H-frame range or at a side wall.

posts: vertical beams either in H-frames (called columns by Fitchen) or in side walls found opposite the H-frame posts.

purlin plates: in Dutch barns, longitudinal beams that connect H-frame posts at their tops at one side of nave in a range. Most often of single lengths of timber but sometimes spliced with scarf joinery.

queen post: vertical beams emanating from upper tie beams that support the longitudinal purlin plates that are frequently found in Pennsylvania and English barns. Also often found in nonoriginal Dutch-Anglo barns.

raising holes: transverse holes in H-frame posts that appear on average $1^1/_2$ to $3^1/_2$ ft. below purlin plate where wooden pins were inserted to assist in raising bents from a horizontal to vertical position. Several dozen barns, mostly in the upcountry and occasionally in northern Ulster County and sporadically elsewhere, have posts with double raising holes.

regionalism: a particular characteristic seen to varying degrees in barns extending over variable geographic areas.

remnant barns: barns that have had a variable amount of their original structure removed over time.

Rensselaerswyck: only longtime successful patroonship or manor system that was established in Albany area in 1630.

ridge beam: beam at ridge line.

ridge line: line at roof peak at points where rafters meet in a pair.

roof rotation: barns, mostly in New Jersey, whose original roof disposition was reoriented 90 degrees so that new ridge line is perpendicular to original ridge line.

sapling poles: thin round trees that were placed over anchorbeams to support crops.

scarf: joinery type—splicing two timbers together often with no true mortise and tenon.

scribe rule: early (pre-1815) system of uniting timbers in which, for example, corresponding members of H-frames in a given barn are not interchangeable.

side wall: wall that extends between gable walls at each side of a rectangular building.

sills: system of beams that support superstructure of barn. Appears under threshing floor in middle aisle and along outer periphery of barn at side aisles.

square rule: later (post-1815) system of uniting timbers in which, for example, corresponding members of H-frames in a given barn are interchangeable.

square shouldering: shoulder or shelf cut on post that supports tie beam (anchorbeam) that forms square outline at its top and bottom.

strut: Fitchen's term for longitudinal and transverse ties. The term is normally assigned to certain supporting elements of roof structures in buildings in England.

tenon: thin tongue of wood of one timber that is inserted into mortise of other articulating timber.

threshing: process of separating seed from chaff. Performed on nave.

tie beam: normally large horizontal beam that joins two posts at each end to form a bent.

transverse side-aisle tie: beam that stretches over side aisle between H-frame post and side-wall post.

true form: classic Dutch barn of three-aisle arrangement with main threshing doors at one or most often two gable wall(s).

tussenbalk (tussenbalkgebint): same as *ankerbalk* (prototype of Dutch American anchorbeam) but without extended tenons.

2-foot scribe marks: scribe lines found on lay-out face of anchorbeam 2 ft. from lateral face of H-frame post used by timber framers in uniting structural members.

U-barn: barn form occasionally found in Ulster County the entire last bay of which has a dirt floor probably for stabling of farm animals and forms the letter U in concert with dirt side aisles.

upcountry: Schoharie and Mohawk River valleys and west side of upper Hudson River valley.

uytlaeten: term for side aisles mentioned in some seventeenth-century Dutch American contracts.

verdiepingh: extension of H-frame post above anchorbeam that is mentioned in some seventeenth-century contracts. Also modern Dutch word for story or floor.

waney: last annual tree ring that is still intact on timber; appeared just under the bark of the tree. The last ring allows for dendrochronological dating to be done. Many barn timbers do not have waney edges intact.

wedged half-dovetail joinery: very rare type of joinery in Dutch barns where tenon of a tie beam (or tie) is half dovetailed and locked into position by wedge.

Zeeland barn: farm structure found in the Netherlands with three threshing floors.

Index

Italic page numbers denote illustrations.
Parentheses denote Fitchen's barn numbering system.

hay barracks, lix–lx, 9
hayfork track, 48–49
hayloft. *See* loft
Heaten, John, 185
Herkimer County, New York, xxxiii
H-frame braces, xxiii–xxiv, xxv,
    xlvi–xlvii; H-frames: anchorbeam
    compared to, xxv; anchorbeam joined
    to, xlvi, *100–101, 135, 136, 142–45,*
    205–6; classic *vs.* true hybrid barns,
    xxvii–xxix; as defining element,
    xxiii–xxv; description of, 14, 37;
    erection of, 53–56, 210; weight of, 55
Hine, C. G., 185
hinges: all-wood, 18, 25, *153, 154;*
    installation of, 64; for wagon doors,
    208; wrought-iron, 18, 25, *154*
Historic American Buildings Survey, 73
    n3
Holland. *See* Netherlands
horizontal struts, 29, *148*
house, separation from barn, 4–9
house-barn, xliii–xliv, 3–4, 16, 66, 207
Huguenot Historical Society, lxiii
Hunterdon County, New Jersey, xxxiii,
    xxxiv
Hurley, south of, barn (24), *117, 150,*
    155, 176

Indian Castle, east of, barn (26), *97,*
    108–9, 177
Indian Castle barn (25), 26, 43, 45, 46,
    57, *97, 100–101, 104, 116, 135,*
    176–77
Industrial Revolution, xxiii
interior characteristics, 14–15, 65–67,
    205–6
internalized post. *See* H-frames
In the Catskills (Burroughs), 71–72 n2,
    80 n6

joinery, xli–xliii, 103, 206
joints: diagonal braces, 36; pegging of,
    37–39, *102–3, 104, 105, 108–9;* scribe
    rule method and, xlv–l; square rule
    method and, l–lii; variations in, 44,
    100–101, 102–3

Kalm, Peter, 76–78 n3, 81–82 n9, 90–91
    n3
Kaufman barn, 27, 43, 45, *100–101*

Kinderhook barn, 29, 43, *98–99. See also*
    Van Alstyne barn (11)
Kings County, New York, xxxiii
kopbalk (kopbalkgebint), xxxiv–xxxv,
    xxxvii–xxxviii
kopbalk (kopbalkgebint) variation, xxxvii
    n19

Lacko barn (52), *106–7,* 164, 193–94
Lape, Forrest, barn (18), 86 n15,
    *104,*173
Larger Bradt barn. *See* Bradt barn,
    larger (57)
Larger Wemp barn. *See* Wemp barn,
    larger (31)
layout face, 210
Lewandoski, Jan, xlii n30
lifting procedure, 54–55
literature on barns: in America, xix–xxi,
    69–72 n2; in England, 74 n4; in
    Germany and Holland, 72–73 n3
livestock. *See* animals
living quarters, 16
location of barns, 90 n3
loft, 9–10, 30–31, 48–49
loft beam, xxxvi–xxxvii
Logtown Road barn (63), 197–98
Long Island, New York, lxii
longitudinal sections, 98–99
longitudinal shear, resistance to, 33–34
longitudinal ties, 209
Lower Post Road barn (9), 48, 169

manger, 64, *148*
marriage marks, xlvi, li
martin holes, 23, 65, *116*
master builder, 182
mechanization, l–li, 54–55
Mercer County, Kentucky, xxxiv
Mercer County, New Jersey, xxxiii
Michigan, xxxiv
Middleburg, southwest of, barn (48),
    22, 191–92
Middleburg, west of, barn (47), 191
Middleburg area, New York, 32, 86
    n15, 88 n3, *116*
Middlesex County, New Jersey, xxxiii
modifications: add-ons, 47–48; to
    anchorbeam, 31; to classic barns,
    xxvii; disassembly of structure, lix;
    extensions, 32, 47; hay barracks,